"Michael Jinkins has the rare gift of making complex theological doctrines accessible to lay people and beginning theological students without 'dumbing down.' In this book he interprets Christian doctrine with the cheerful and joyful good humor that is appropriate for a theology that has to do with the good news of God in Jesus Christ. An especially helpful feature of the book is the way it encourages teachers and students to learn together to relate the implications of the Christian faith to everyday life."

SHIRLEY GUTHRIE JR., *Emeritus Professor of Systematic Theology, Columbia Theological Seminary*

"Jinkins here invites us to participate in both the joys and the challenges of the theological task. With the expectancy of a colleague proposing a new approach to an old question, he draws us into conversation with the figures, themes and problematics of the Christian tradition. With the guiding hand of a good teacher he reminds us that the work of theology should not be undertaken lightly. Students and laypeople new to the discipline will especially benefit from Jinkins's creative balance of 'lectures' and 'homework assignments,' all geared to train us to be theologians—to better know and bear witness to the character of God."

CYNTHIA L. RIGBY, *Associate Professor of Systematic Theology, Austin Presbyterian Theological Seminary*

"I'm glad that I accepted Michael Jinkins's invitation to study theology with him. Jinkins makes good on his promise that theological study will come alive when it helps us to see our world—and our own lives in that world—through the reality of the living Christ."

RICHARD J. MOUW, President and Professor of Christian Philosophy, Fuller Theological Seminary

"Michael Jinkins has provided us with an accessible and readable theological primer. His lively introduction to the central doctrines of the Christian faith is borne of a conviction that theology matters deeply not merely for a small professional group but for the whole people of God. This book is likely to be used and valued by many, particularly within the Reformed tradition."

DAVID FERGUSSON, *Professor of Divinity, New College, University of Edinburgh*

"Michael Jinkins's invitation to theology is lively, fresh and reader friendly. Centered on the trinitarian love of God as source of new life in communion with God and others, Jinkins's book ties together Christian doctrine, worship and service, and helpfully exposes the destructiveness of modern individualism in both church and society. An excellent choice for a first course in theology."

DANIEL L. MIGLIORE, *Charles Hodge Professor of Systematic Theology, Princeton Theological Seminary*

"Michael Jinkins is offering much more than a basic theological text book on the Creed; he is presenting an approach to theology and theological learning which comes out of his experience as a teacher of adults in seminary and Sunday school. I warmly commend this exciting resource for group learning and agree with Jinkins's conviction that doing theology is a community activity with a practical end. Those who immerse themselves in this course, in the conversations with great thinkers of the past, and in the creative thinking and exploration that is encouraged can hardly fail to have a clearer understanding of the fundamentals of their faith. As the course is designed to be done as a community activity, the hope and expectation is that with a renewed grasp of the gospel, there will be a fruitful renewal of the life of the church. Read as a text by individuals, the attractive prose and clarity of presentation should inspire group use and collaborative learning. Dr. Jinkins's book deserves to be widely read and used."

THE REV. CANON DR. VINCENT STRUDWICK, *Director of Theology Programmes, Department for Continuing Education, University of Oxford, and Fellow of Kellogg College*

"I heartily endorse Michael Jinkins's *Invitation to Theology.* Eminently readable, Jinkins provides a fresh, even elegant, articulation of core doctrines of the faith in a lively and engaging style. His imaginative analogies and helpful penchant for interrelating doctrines breathe an energizing vitality into theological reflection. Jinkins portrays doctrinal issues in ways both savvy to historical context and also engaging of readers where they live. Most attractive to me is the trinitarian/christological lens through which all key doctrines are viewed. At last we have a survey that regards the Trinity not merely as an addendum or a part of the chapter on the doctrine of God but as integrally woven into the whole fabric of the theological tapestry giving refreshing cohesion to every doctrine. I have long awaited such an unapologetically trinitarian-angled book for use as a text in my Christian doctrine classes."

JEANNINE MICHELE GRAHAM, *Assistant Professor of Religion, Whitworth College*

Invitation to
Theology

MICHAEL JINKINS
Foreword by Alan Torrance

InterVarsity Press
Downers Grove, Illinois

InterVarsity Press
P.O. Box 1400, Downers Grove, IL 60515-1426
World Wide Web: www.ivpress.com
E-mail: mail@ivpress.com

InterVarsity Press® is the book-publishing division of InterVarsity Christian Fellowship/USA®, a student movement active on campus at hundreds of universities, colleges and schools of nursing in the United States of America, and a member movement of the International Fellowship of Evangelical Students. For information about local and regional activities, write Public Relations Dept., InterVarsity Christian Fellowship/USA, 6400 Schroeder Rd., P.O. Box 7895, Madison, WI 53707-7895.

Cover illustration: Sally Gall/Swan Stock/Image Bank

ISBN 0-8308-1562-7

Printed in the United States of America ∞

Library of Congress Cataloging-in-Publication Data

Jinkins, Michael, 1953-
    Invitation to theology: a guide to study, conversation, and practice / Michael Jinkins;
foreword by Alan Torrance.
    p. cm.
    Includes bibliographical references and indexes.
    ISBN 0-8308-1562-7 (pbk.: alk. paper)
    1. Theology, Doctrinal—Study and teaching. I. Title.
BT77.3 .J56 2001
230'.071 21   00-47169

25 24 23 22 21 20 19 18 17 16 15 14 13 12 11 10 9 8 7 6 5 4 3 2 1
22 21 20 19 18 17 16 15 14 13 12 11 10 09 08 07 06 05 04 03 02 01

In grateful memory of
Alan E. Lewis

Contents

Foreword

Some years ago I witnessed a lively debate between a good friend, who was carrying out research in marine biology, and his father, who was a well-known professor of theology. During the argument the son, who was enthusiastic about his research into the feeding habits of fish, expressed some doubts as to whether theological research aspired to a similar level of practical significance. In a gracious but devastating riposte his father quietly pointed out that it was the world of ideas that had shaped the history of Western thought and civilization, indeed, the whole structure of the world in which we live—and probably not studies into the dietary preferences of sticklebacks!

Within the church and even, dare I say, theological education it has been widely believed that in order to be relevant one has to be concerned with practice. And to be concerned with practice is to be concerned with practice in purely applied ways. As a result, we have tended to overlook, first, the extent to which Christian thought has shaped the history of Western culture and, second, how much a faithful and clear-headed grasp of the gospel has to offer our Western culture—so very much more indeed than Western culture could ever offer itself! The practical benefits of a clear-headed and faithful grasp of the gospel are, quite simply, beyond quantification.

The other side of the coin is at least as relevant to assessing the significance of a book of this kind. Few would disagree that no single activity in the history of the human race has caused more war, bloodshed, marginalization, oppression and general human misery than "God talk." This can be illustrated in the history of the Crusades, the Third Reich and the "German Christians," the justifications of the apartheid regime by Afrikaner theologians, or the androcentrism (and Eurocentrism) of so much Western civil religion. In short, one finds oneself obliged to ask a simple question: Has any single factor had more tragic consequences in the recent history of the West than the simple failure to understand the theological significance of the incarnation—the perception that in Christ we have the fullness of God dwelling with us as One in whom there is neither Jew nor Gentile, male nor female, black nor white, Serb nor Croat?

Positively, however, the implications for social, personal and cultural healing of a proper reorientation of our thinking in the light of who God is toward us in Christ are beyond measure. The contributions of Catherine Mowry LaCugna, Jürgen Moltmann, Miroslav Volf and so many more illustrate graphically that when our underlying theology is true to God's inclusive embrace of humanity in Christ, our whole understanding of ourselves and, indeed, the other—not least the "radical other," the enemy—is transformed. We are liberated to become what we were created to be, namely, liberating, inclusive and reconciling agents who "image" or correspond to God's embrace of the "radical other" (even us) in an unanticipatable and otherwise inconceivable act of identification, acceptance, forgiveness and affirmation.

In the first instance, therefore, theology does not concern abstract speculation or the appropriation of impersonal systems of dogma; it concerns serious and hard-nosed consideration of what it means to be the church, to be a Christian, to be a participant in God's mission to a lost and alienated humanity. It is concerned with the dynamics of grace, of worship, and Christian practice as these are grounded in the dynamics of God's engagement with humanity. It concerns what it is to be, what it is to be in truth. As such, the opportunity on the part of human creatures to engage in theology is a profound privilege to be engaged in energetically and enthusiastically.

Unfortunately the teaching of theology has too often failed to serve these ends. It has convinced students of its own apparent irrelevance—either by being identified with abstract, dogmatic systems or abstruse "second order" debates about questions of method. The failure here is the inability to communicate the essential relatedness between who God is and who we are. When this is grasped and understood, theology stands to become the most exciting and relevant discipline in which one could conceivably engage.

What is so impressive about this book by Michael Jinkins is that it is an easily readable introductory course that is not merely academically perceptive and historically informed but theological in the profoundest and most relevant sense of that term. It is a fluent and lucid exploration of the gospel and its significance. Far from being a traditional didactic course of the kind one mindlessly swats up with exams in view, it is an account that will excite students theologically and challenge them to reconsider creatively their perspectives on the very heart of the faith and its implications. At the same time, it will establish the foundations on which further and deeper theological reflection can build.

As such this book is relevant, practical and potentially transformative—in precisely the sense understood by the professor to whom I referred in my opening paragraph. Like the theology of the one to whom the book is dedicated, Dr. Jinkins articulates the kind of trinitarian theology that not only stems from and inspires Christian worship on the one hand but encourages the most relevant and constructive social analysis and critique on the other.

If, of course, you want to study something more practical and down to earth, then there is the feeding habits of sticklebacks!

Alan J. Torrance, Chair of Systematic Theology, University of St Andrews, Scotland

Introduction

The Vitality of Christian Community

Theological reflection on the practices and beliefs of the church ranks among the most crucial tasks of our common life as Christians. The theological integrity of the church is grounded in this task of disciplined critical examination of the meaning of our discipleship. When we do this work well, it illuminates everything else we do. When we neglect this essential task, we risk losing our integrity, our vision, our identity as people of God—perhaps even the very reason for our existence as Christian communities of faith.

There is always a danger in the church that we may forget our essential theological task while attending to other important, even pressing though penultimate, matters. And yet as I have spoken to various groups of students, laypeople and ministers over the past several years in North America and in Britain, I have found enormous interest in theology. Christians are eager to think about their Christian faith, to *examine* what they believe and why they believe it, and to reflect on what it means to follow Jesus Christ in the world today. Indeed there is evidence on every hand that the church continues to recognize the truth of what G. L. Prestige said many years ago: "A thinking Church, a Church that professes to love God with all its mind as well as with all its heart, cannot be content to lie for ever in an intellectual fallow."[1]

The problem is we don't always know how to go about this process of

---

[1] G. L. Prestige, *Fathers and Heretics: Six Studies in Dogmatic Faith*, The Bampton Lectures for 1940 (London: SPCK, 1940), p. 3.

thinking theologically. We need resources and leadership to help us learn the ABCs of theological reflection.

This book addresses itself to this elementary need by introducing us to Christian thinkers from every age in the history of the church and by providing a framework to assist us as we attempt to understand the faith we have received. I'm not interested in providing an academic treatise, plowing new ground, impressing peers or amazing critics. What you have before you is a basic guidebook, a primer for thinking through our Christian faith. It contains discussions of some basic areas of Christian belief following the general outline of the Apostles' Creed in the time-honored fashion. This ancient creed, the origins of which lie in the worship life of the early church (the form of the creed we know gradually became established between the second and the ninth centuries) is used because it is the single most familiar confessional statement in the Western church.[2] As Jack Rogers observes, "Most Christian people have memorized the Apostles' Creed along with the Lord's Prayer. It is used in worship more often than any other creedal formula."[3] The creed properly belongs at the heart of Christian worship, as a summary of our beliefs and as a kind of pledge of allegiance. Because of the approach we shall take in this study—understanding theology as an act of faith and worship—it is altogether appropriate that we should follow the outline of this great statement of faith.

This book also provides a variety of exercises to facilitate reflection and discussion. In part the book could be seen as a sort of collection of classroom presentations (lectures if you will), though every attempt will be made to keep it as far as possible from dry and pedantic dogmatics. But even more this book is intended to serve as a signpost along the way of our Christian pilgrimage, to point out where we can go to find the most stimulating teachers, witnesses and conversations, so that we can personally engage in the best Christian thinking of all time. This resource

---

[2] Alister E. McGrath writes that the word *creed* refers specifically to those statements of faith that summarize "the main points of Christian belief . . . common to all Christians." The "term 'creed' is never applied to statements of faith associated with specific denominations." Such statements of faith are called, instead, "confessions." "A 'creed' has come to be recognized as a concise, formal, and universally accepted and authorized statement of the main points of Christian faith." *Christian Theology: An Introduction* (Oxford: Blackwell, 1994), p. 17.
[3] Jack Rogers, *Presbyterian Creeds: A Guide to the Book of Confessions* (Philadelphia: Westminster Press, 1985), p. 57.

attempts, in fact, to be something more than a book. It seeks to serve its readers as a blueprint for personal study and dialogue, practice and activity. To put it in slightly different terms, the book is meant to be an introductory course in Christian theology, written especially for laypersons and beginning students in theology, though it might also serve as a refresher course for pastors.

Undergirding this whole course of study is an assumption that I have found repeatedly affirmed from fathers of the ancient church like Athanasius and Augustine to modern Christian thinkers like Dietrich Bonhoeffer and Karl Barth, from Lady Julian of Norwich and John Calvin to Gustavo Gutiérrez and Catherine Mowry LaCugna: Knowledge and comprehension of God are grounded in our common life before God, and the purpose of our study of God is nothing less than the transformation of our lives "by the renewing of our minds." You will notice this affirmation surfacing over and again in the class lectures and in the reflection exercises.

Theology is our critical (that is, analytical) and prayerful reflection on the totality of life. It is not an isolated, abstract, intellectualist affair; it is not the reserve of aesthetic dilettantes or of ideological systematicians. Theology involves and engages all we are and all we do, and demands our attentiveness to everything around us. *Theology is the essential business of faithful reflection on human life lived consciously in the presence of God.* We all do theology on a regular basis, whether or not we are aware of the fact. This course is designed to help us do it better.

When I began to organize this study, drawing on courses I've taught over the past several years in seminary and in adult Sunday school classes, at first I nearly despaired. How in the world can you put into a book the kind of theological processes you do ordinarily with groups of people conversing with one another? How can you encourage the sense of discovery to challenge others to ask difficult questions if you can't talk to them in person? How can you support and critique, argue and laugh together, when you can't see each other eye to eye?

To put it bluntly, *you can't.*

A book of mere statements can never do what persons ordinarily do in conversation. I am reminded of the quandary the philosopher Ludwig Wittgenstein found himself in as a young man because of the frustration he felt with Bertrand Russell. Russell, the famous mathematician, philosopher and popular speaker, did not hesitate to write about his religious views, often reducing complex issues for the sake of rhetorical style and popular consumption. Theology, according to Wittgenstein, was too subtle, rich, complex and precious to risk reducing in the act of writing down. The most important things in life, as Wittgenstein understood, can only be approximated, hinted at, *shown,* not *said.* Our most precious beliefs and hopes and values are so hard to express. They have the consistency of onionskin writing paper that has been burnt. The ash may hold together—that is, until you try to handle it. There may have been words written on the paper before it was burnt. You may just be able to discern that there is writing on the burnt pages. You may want to read what is written there. But the moment you pick it up, it falls apart. Even a puff of wind can make it fly helter skelter.

The study of theology in a classroom is exciting and fragile, like handling ashes in the wind. The teacher may lecture, lead formal discussions, schedule times for students informally to raise troubling questions and propose answers and ask still more questions. Everyone—students and teachers—becomes learners together, gaining new understandings, testing hallowed views in light of critical reflections, reading and talking and listening and worshiping. A course in Christian theology is a matter of faith development and formation and reformation, personal, communal, dynamic and immediate, in continuity with the faith development we experienced as members of the congregations that taught us the Word of God and formed us in the power of the Spirit. All of this is relatively easy to communicate in a theology classroom.

But in a book we so easily reinforce the most common misconceptions of theology: that theology is a private and individual endeavor; that theology is a work performed in the head not in the heart; that theology, if it is to have academic integrity, must be undertaken high in an ivory tower far from the madding (and even maddening!) crowd of humanity; that theology is a matter of dispassionate thinking, removed from emotions, affections and actions; that theology is a subject that one studies "objectively," *the theologian* removed from *the theology,* like a laboratory technician observing a rat in a maze. These misconceptions can be overcome by a good teacher in a classroom or church fellowship hall where theology is seen clearly as a community endeavor, actively engaged in, often on the run between other responsibilities, constantly under scrutiny, passionate, even (dare we say) fun, but these misconceptions are more difficult to overcome in printed form. Thus so many look at the fat, hardbound volumes on their pastor's or their professor's shelves, whose spines bear ominous words like *prolegomena* and *dogmatics* and *systematic theology,* and it is no wonder they imagine the worst, that theological studies bear all the charms of handling a cadaver. But nothing could be further from the truth, as anyone knows who has enjoyed the vigor and energy and wonder of studying the mysteries of God and the joys of Christian life with good friends and a capable teacher.

What I have attempted to do, therefore, is to develop a theology course between book covers. The writing style is more informal and immediate than what one usually finds in theological textbooks. The sessions, if you will, are not chapters; they are meant to resonate as classroom presentations (based on oral presentations spoken in academic classrooms and fellowship halls). They begin with prayer and end with homework, discussions, assignments, reflection activities. They are written to convey a sense of the *spoken* and *heard* word.

The entire study presented in these pages is designed to be used in groups of Christians actively seeking to grow in their faith in Jesus Christ. That is the primary focus of the study. This book is really designed primarily to facilitate a course of study among groups of people, to provide opportunities for active reflection, conversation and a deeper understanding of the practices of Christian faith. What you have before you then is an invitation to theology, an invitation to a never-ending voyage of exploration and discovery.

The Theme of Our Course

Before diving off into the deep end I think it will help for you to get a sense of the theological theme of the course. It is this:

> The meaning and shape of our life together
> as a community of persons
> is grounded in the inner life of God, the Trinity,
> and has been revealed to us
> in the life, death and resurrection of Jesus Christ.

This is the unifying theme of our entire study, which emerged gradually during the process of developing the presentations on which the substantive sections of this book are based. I had been teaching this subject in congregations and even in seminary in various forms for years before the theme clearly emerged. I didn't actually begin with the intention of developing the theme; in other words it just bubbled to the surface over the months and years of reading, reflecting, lecturing and conversing with all sorts and conditions of people. This book is the product of a living experiment in theology.

The students (both theology students and laypersons) who have participated in the various classes I have taught over the past twenty years or so helped shape this study. And it is our common work that appears in these pages. During our work together we critically reflected on the biblical sources and various confessional standards of the church, and we brought our study under the glare of personal experience in the life of the Christian congregations to which we have belonged. We prayed together for needs in our communities. We sang. We laughed. And we wept. It is difficult, reading the printed page, to hear the singing, the laughter and the sorrow that forms the essential backdrop to this study. But *it is the essential backdrop of the study.*[4]

The combined voices of the community of students and the congregations with whom I have ministered and learned echo through these pages. Again, I did not write this book alone. No theology that aspires to be Christian theology can pretend to be written by anyone alone. Christian theology is the product of Christian communities. And as this study in particular has unfolded, I have become more and more convinced of the theological insight that is at its heart: *The life we share together as people of God is a reflection of the inner life of God, the Trinity.*

This insight has the extraordinary effect of giving wholeness to an often-paranoid discipline. The word *paranoid,* in its most basic sense, speaks of a condition in which there are other minds separate from and alongside one another. It is from this condition that the fear, one might say the *panic,* of so much contemporary theology results. We have become accustomed to isolating our theological disciplines from our social and political and ethical spheres of influence, so that theologians can rather

---

[4]Ellis Nelson has said that the life of the congregation is the primary curriculum of Christian faith. It is, he writes, "the normal and natural way for faith and belief to be communicated." This is certainly true of this study in theology that affirms that the triune God who has his very being in communion is unknowable in isolation, indeed that this God only reveals himself in Jesus Christ through the life of his Spirit in human community. C. Ellis Nelson, "Toward Accountable Selfhood," in *Modern Masters of Religious Education,* ed. Marlene Mayr (Birmingham, Ala.: Religious Education Press, 1983), p. 165.

easily become metaphysical specialists who speak only of social, political and ethical involvement as an addendum to theological reflection. This model tends to the paranoia of splitting apart the mind—the reflective consciousness—of the theologian so that the theological project is first one thing and then another.

One finds a fear or a chronic anxiety (the other and more common meaning of paranoia) evident wherever this fragmentation of the reflective consciousness occurs. For example, evangelical theologians sometimes fear the thought of liberation, feminist and womanist theologians. And some liberation, feminist and womanist theologians may fear the work of certain evangelical theologians. The paranoia is unfortunate in large part because of what it does to theological community, undercutting the possibility for trust, for mutual respect and for encouragement, each of which is necessary for the integrity of our theological work.

I present here a modest alternative to theological paranoia, a way to understand our social, political and ethical life as grounded in the inner life of God, the holy Trinity—a life revealed in the person of Jesus of Nazareth whom we believe to be the Christ of God, a particular person on the margins of human society who, through the power of God's Spirit, creates new society from the shambles he finds. Our theological reflection works just like the rest of our life works—living with others, working, dreaming, hoping and being disappointed, loving and being loved, wishing we were loved, loving badly and loving well, being rejected, trying to make sense of our days, testing new possibilities, examining ideas, regretting what we have done and trying to do better, wondering what it all means, why we are here and what we should do about being here. And as theologians we reflect on all of this common stuff of life in light of who God is shown to be in our Lord Jesus Christ.

Protestant Reformer John Calvin's familiar saying provides a helpful point of reference for us. Calvin said that *in all of life we have our dealings with God (in tota vita negotium cum deo).*[5] This, I believe, is the key to healing the paranoia of theology in our time to recapture a vision of the essential wholeness of life and life's essential connectedness in the loving heart of God. All of the relationships of ordinary life are shot through with

---

[5]John Calvin, *On God and Political Duty*, ed. John T. McNeill, 2d ed. (New York: Bobbs-Merrill, 1956), p. vii.

eternal significance, and theology is the discipline through which we attempt to discern and map this reality.

Christology and Chronology

One of the most obvious features of the way we'll go about this theological project is the centrality of the person of Jesus Christ. This may be a little puzzling, at least at first.

How is it, for instance, that we begin by talking about our personal experience and faith, about God, the almighty Creator and Father, but then find ourselves almost immediately talking about Jesus of Nazareth, a man who lived in a backward province of the Roman Empire two thousand years ago, a long time removed from our contemporary experience of faith and by all accounts a very long time after the creation of the universe? Perhaps the best way to explain this puzzling aspect of Christian theology is to tell you a story from my own experience of faith.

My theology has gone through enormous changes over the years. Brought up in a very conservative Christian home, in a church with revivalist roots, I went to a small denominational liberal arts college where I took a degree in biblical studies and New Testament Greek; then I went on to a denominational seminary where I concentrated in theology. Like most of my friends and colleagues during those years, I held to the theology that I had inherited and was only slowly beginning to subject that theology to careful scrutiny. While in seminary, following a considerable struggle of conscience, I made the decision to depart from the faith traditions of my family. During this time of change, and even some rebellion, I was guilty on occasion of throwing out the proverbial baby with the bath. However, it wasn't until I was studying for my Ph.D. in theology at the University of Aberdeen under the supervision of James Torrance that I came to this awareness. Like many others before me, the pendulum of my religious experience had swung from evangelicalism to skepticism. I found myself in the midst of what the medieval mystic St. John of the Cross calls the "dark night of the soul," a time when God's hand was on me (I now see), though at that time I felt lost and utterly forsaken by God, intellectually confused and spiritually bankrupt. I feared that I had actually lost my faith in a quest for critical and academic sophistication.

One day I was visiting with a friend who was also in the Ph.D. program. I told him that I just couldn't understand anymore why the church says that

Jesus is God. The whole gospel seemed to me riddled with philosophical holes. Without being aware of the philosophical rut I was in, I had become mired in the rather abstract mode of thinking in which theological positions are seen almost as mathematical equations that one must construct, one theorem connecting to another.

"It just doesn't add up!" I said. "Professor Torrance talks about the reality and necessity of Christ's full divinity, how crucial it is to see Christ at the very center of our theological work. But I don't see Christ's divinity as real and necessary at all. It seems to me that his teachings are the only things that are more (or less) important. Jesus could just as easily be one of many inspired teachers, and his way of life, which leads ultimately to the cross, could be understood as a powerful example of how evil can be over-whelmed by the goodness and sacrifice of an authentic human life. But his being God just doesn't make sense to me, and his resurrection seems alto-gether nonsense and wishful thinking. I just don't see it."

Gary Deddo, the friend with whom I was talking, very patiently asked me to try to look at this whole issue from a completely different angle. Instead of trying to add things up in a philosophical equation or to develop an argument of one premise following another, he asked me simply to try this: "Look at your life," Gary told me, "as though the gospel of Jesus Christ is true. Just suspend your disbelief for a while and ask yourself this ques-tion: Does life as a whole make more sense in light of the gospel than it does without the gospel?"

As I tried Gary's experiment, it occurred to me that this was a really sig-nificant exercise, and it has become one that I have recommended to oth-ers struggling with their Christian faith. I tell them, "Imagine that Jesus Christ—fully God and fully human, God in the flesh, alive, dead, buried and risen—is a sort of lens, such as a pair of eyeglasses. Put these glasses on, look at the world around you, your own experience and the whole tra-jectory of human history. Then take off the glasses. Try it again: glasses on, then glasses off. Ask yourself now, *Which way does it all come into focus better, glasses on or glasses off?*"

What I have found through this experiment is something the church has maintained for two thousand years: *Everything comes more clearly into focus by looking at life through Jesus Christ. Christ makes sense of the world we live in. Christ makes sense of our humanity and our human history.*

When I take this insight into the heart of Christian theology, I find that as

I look at each teaching of the church through Jesus Christ, it comes more clearly into focus. In fact, I have found that it is only by reading the Bible, Old Testament and New, through the eyeglasses of Christ that the Bible comes into focus. Jesus Christ himself is the single most important element in biblical interpretation.

We'll see the significance of this insight throughout our theological approach, and for this I am grateful to Gary for his experiment and to James Torrance for his insistence that the only way we can really comprehend Scripture, Christian faith and our whole human experience is christologically, not chronologically. Which brings us to a final feature of this theological project.

A Subversive Theology

The substantive sections of this book, as I mentioned earlier, came together first as lectures and oral presentations delivered to theological students and laypersons in local congregations. The students were first-year seminarians for whom this course was their very first introduction to the whole field of theological endeavor. In a sense, then, though they were theology students engaged in a master of divinity program, they were actually laypeople too, and laypeople, incidentally, from a dizzying variety of backgrounds and perspectives.

Among the seminarians were people who had been trained in engineering, education, law, nursing, sales and counseling. There were Presbyterians, Methodists, Baptists, nondenominational charismatic Christians, a Jewish woman recently converted to Christianity and a Unitarian Universalist. There were people whose church experience was shaped by "old-line, mainline orthodoxy," revivalism, fundamentalism, evangelicalism and the classical liberalism that flowed originally from Northern European sources as well as by streams of feminist and liberationist thought. There were the usual young male faces fresh from college, as was the rule in Protestant theological education for most of the twentieth century, but they were outnumbered by second-career students and many women students. There were African American students from several church traditions and Korean students from the burgeoning Korean Presbyterian Church, all of whom brought exciting new perspectives and new questions to our study of theology.

It became apparent from the very beginning that if I wanted to communicate effectively with this divergent group the material would have to be clear, well-focused, interesting and as nontechnical as possible. I would also need to find ways to help the students integrate this whole new world of theological reflection into their own immediate experience, and in order to do this effectively I would have to avoid binding myself to any denominational affiliation, though I would also need to be up-front about my own theological perspective, shaped as it is by the Reformed traditions. What I had to pursue was a theological study of what C. S. Lewis once called "mere Christianity."

I was deliberately subversive in my approach. As I told the students, my first goal in the class was to harrow their fields, to turn over and break up the topsoil with a sharp plow so that they could plant a new crop of Christian theological thought. The planting would be mostly their work, the plowing mostly mine. The lectures were a little unsettling to some, terrifying to others. But this was one of the lectures' purposes, to challenge comfortable assumptions and to help us refocus and rethink the faith we hold and frequently take too much for granted.

One week I asked the students to answer a kind of riddle for me. I played a live recording of the blues singer B. B. King, and then I asked them, "What do B. B. King and the doctrine of *perichoresis* have in common?"

This was only the second class meeting, and I think it is safe to say that none of the students had even heard mention of the doctrine of *perichoresis* before in their lives (they were still finding out what the words *doctrine* and *dogma* mean). But I let the question hang there, undefined and unexplained, and I resisted answering it for them. The next morning, before the class small group seminars began, a student met me in the hall. She said she had spent most of the previous night in the library, reading everything she could find on *perichoresis* (the doctrine in higher trinitarian thought that says the three persons of the Trinity interpenetrate one another and co-inhere with one another in the eternal act of mutual love, emptying each one into the other in the supreme act of divine self-giving that is fully revealed in Jesus Christ). The student had become so excited about her discovery she had hardly slept a wink. In fact, she spent most of the night writing a reflection paper that connected the doctrine of *perichoresis* to work she had previously done in analyzing Impressionist art.

A year or two later another student, this time a layperson I had taught in an academy for Presbyterian lay preachers, called asking me if I could tutor him through a project he was undertaking in a hospital chaplaincy. He was working with AIDS patients, and he wanted to utilize the same trinitarian doctrine of *perichoresis* to assist AIDS patients to deal with life qualitatively instead of quantitatively.

What both of these students grasped is the profound relationship of theology to life, specifically the connection between the inner life of the triune God revealed in Jesus Christ and our life together in the image of this God. Gaining a personal understanding of this relationship is the purpose (the "chief end") of our course in theology.

Not only did those who participated in these courses listen to B. B. King and Miles Davis (and other "classical" artists), not only did we sing a hymn each week at the opening of the class (something you may want to try while reading this book, unless you are reading it in a library), we also did what we called "mapping exercises" (we'll discuss "mapping" in our homework assignments). It was my wife, Deborah, a professor in education, who suggested we try this. By mapping our theological reflections we were able (literally) to draw our ideas so we could see the interconnectedness and interrelatedness of the theological reflections we were working out and the lives we were living. In yet another way we were reminded that theology is never an end in itself. The goal of theology is always the deepening of our lives in relationship to God our Creator and Redeemer.

Acknowledgments

Finally, before we launch into our course, I must extend my appreciation to several people. First, I want to thank the leadership of Austin Presbyterian Theological Seminary in 1991-1992, Jack Stotts, the president (now retired), and Robert Shelton, the academic dean (now president), at whose invitation I originally taught the course in modern theology and the introductory course in systematic theology and with whom I have had the privilege of serving on the Austin Seminary faculty since 1993 in the church's ministry department. I also want to thank Alison Riemersma, Hilda Harnden and Martin Loberg, whose tireless efforts helped bring this manuscript together, David Gambrell for his help in producing the graphic aspects of the project and Mrs. Loretta Hodde, the secretary of the Brenham Presbyterian Church, whose editorial assistance was so crucial early in the development of this book. I especially appreciate the efforts of Terry Muck, professor of religion at Austin Seminary and formerly executive editor of *Christianity Today,* who read the manuscript with his keen editorial eye and made valuable suggestions throughout.

I have been blessed with exceptional teachers who taught me to love theology: James Shields, Bert Dominy and James B. Torrance in particular. Indeed, the influence of my mentor and friend James Torrance, professor emeritus of systematic theology at Aberdeen University, runs throughout this study, and to him I am most grateful for counsel and support. I want to thank the forty-three students of TH. 104: Introduction to Christian Theology for allowing me to serve as their teacher, to Robert L. (Doug) Dalglish and Edward Heunemann who assisted me with this class and led small group seminars. Aspects of many of the lectures of the basic course in theology made their way into this study. I am also grateful to the pastors, sessions and members of churches (especially University Presbyterian Church, Westminster Presbyterian Church and Westlake Presbyterian Church of Austin) who over the past several years have invited me to teach courses of study in Christian theology and the history of Christian thought for their adult classes. These engagements with local congregations contributed much to the final shape of this book.

I want to express my most profound gratitude to my colleagues at Austin Presbyterian Theological Seminary, whose friendship underlies and informs virtually every aspect of my work. I will always remain grateful for the opportunity to know and to call friend the late Alan E. Lewis, to whose memory this book is dedicated. I am also deeply grateful to Cynthia Rigby, Stanley Robertson Hall, Scott Black Johnston, Stephen Breck Reid, Bill Greenway, Lewis Donelson, Ralph Underwood, Laura Lewis, Ellis Nelson, Andy Dearman and Timothy Lincoln for their collegiality and fellowship, and the rich climate of mutual support, admonition and correction that we share. Finally, I want to thank Gary Deddo, my editor at InterVarsity Press, for his insights and encouragement, and Alan Torrance, formerly senior lecturer at King's College, University of London, and now professor of theology at St. Andrew's University, for his very kind foreword to this volume.

Class 1

What's the Use of Theology?

THE GERMAN LANGUAGE HAS A WORD THAT DESCRIBES THE MOOD OR ATTI-tude of an age—a *Zeitgeist.*[1] Literally translated "time-ghost," we usually render it "spirit of the age" and assume that every age has its own. Our age certainly is no exception to the rule. But our *Zeitgeist* unhappily appears to be a bit more noisy than some others have been, a sort of *Polterzietgeist,* a pot-clanging "spirit of the time," a spirit that feeds on the fairly common view that the most important things in the world are the things that can be handled, grasped, bought, sold and used to make more things to be han-dled, grasped, bought and sold. In fact, if our *Zeitgeist* got a lead in a hor-ror movie, the movie might be titled *The Revenge of the Empirical Vampires.*

This is probably the most striking feature of the world of higher education

---

[1]This chapter is an extended version of an article previously published by *The* (London) *Times*: Michael Jinkins, "What's the Use of Divinity: An Apologia for the Study of Theology in the University," *The Times Higher Education Supplement,* June 2, 1989, pp. 13-15.

in the contemporary era; theology, as an area of academic study, is constantly trying to come to terms with the fact that it has the hots for questions that leave most of the academic community stone cold. When theology is considered at all in the general academic community, it is more likely than not considered impractical and out of touch and vaguely superstitious. The question often asked is this: "What is the *use* of theology?" But the question itself, however conscientiously it is raised, betrays some tricky assumptions in the minds of those who ask it. In order to address ourselves to the question of the value and importance of the study of theology, we must seriously look into the environment in which we study theology today.

Karl Barth once said that *we* (specifically we who do theology—and that includes all of us who have ever tried to talk about God) "always seem to be handling an intractable object with inadequate means."[2] This statement may be a good deal less lofty sounding than St. Anselm's motto that "faith seeks understanding," but it's basically on the same track. As Daniel Migliore explains, theology can be "defined broadly as thinking about important issues from the perspective of Christian faith."[3]

Theology, then, is fundamentally an attempt to make positive and constructive statements about *who* God is—and *who* we are in light of who God is. Theology is concerned with the ultimate questions. Or to put it more personally, as Shirley Guthrie observes, theology deals with the questions that are really the most interesting questions of life: sex, politics and God (though not necessarily in that order).[4] Theology, in other words, concerns itself with all of life and with death and with love as "strong as death" (Song 8:6). Theology deals with a quality of trust that makes life endurable and with a hope that burdens us even as it also stretches the horizon of our human vision beyond all that can be dreamed or imagined. Theology seeks to understand reality, our limitations and our possibilities. It is the most important area of study in the world. And as such it continually makes tremendous demands on our feeble resources.

(Ah, but I've just tried to slip one past you, haven't I? I zipped right past

---

[2]Karl Barth, *Church Dogmatics* I/1, ed. G. W. Bromiley and T. F. Torrance, trans. G. W. Bromiley (Edinburgh: T & T Clark, 1936), p. 23.

[3]Daniel L. Migliore's introduction to Christian theology takes as its title St. Anselm's dictum: *Faith Seeking Understanding* (Grand Rapids, Mich.: Eerdmans, 1991), p. 1.

[4]Shirley Guthrie Jr., *Christian Doctrine,* rev. ed. (Louisville, Ky.: Westminster John Knox, 1994), p. 1.

it so quickly that maybe no one noticed the huge assumption I just made, so maybe I should just shut up.) Theology is the most important area of study in the world *if* and *only if* we understand all of life as a spiritual issue, only if we believe that ordinary life, ordinary relationships, ordinary give and take, the day-to-day bumps and bruises of life, are shot through with eternal significance. We believe that theology is the most important discipline in the world *only if* we believe, to borrow John Calvin's phrase, that it is with God we are dealing in all of life. If we don't believe this, indeed, if we believe that "what you see is all you get," then theology may appear the silliest, most unnecessary, awkward and meaningless area of study imaginable. And there are certainly lots of folks around today who would see theology in just that way.

At one time theology was considered the "queen of the sciences," a title it held without much serious competition for a very long time. A couple of years ago on a visit to Oxford University's Bodleian Library, as I wandered through one of the oldest sections of the university, the divinity hall, I was struck by the way the university was once grounded in the divine sciences. The queen of the sciences ruled benevolently from the divinity school at the very heart of the university.

Even today the study of theology includes a vast kingdom of disciplines: constructive theology (a.k.a. dogmatic, confessional or systematic theology), historical theology, biblical and philosophical and pastoral theology, liturgical theology (the study of worship), Christian ethics, biblical studies, biblical languages, church history, evangelism, homiletics (the study of preaching), religious studies, philosophy of religion and comparative religion. And yet, while once this grand collection of disciplines was considered the queen, today it must satisfy itself with a much humbler station in life. To most people in our society, theology is (at best) a sort of a metaphysical housekeeper. In the upstairs-downstairs society of academics, theology has been forced to move into the smaller rooms in the attic, leaving the spacious ground-floor apartments (complete with their own in-suite bathrooms and fireplaces) to the modern sciences and technologies.

The shift in theology's accommodations parallels a shift in social attitudes. Theology clings to the idea that the most important things in life cannot be measured or merely put to use and that even the most ordinary activities are fraught with eternal meaning. These are not popular ideas in a society where the most valued academic disciplines are those that produce and analyze quantifiable and marketable stuff. Theology is, for this reason (among others), often pictured as the discipline of dusty tomes (if not dusty tombs), the angels-dancing-on-pinheads school, the divine comedy of unscientific science.

And we must admit there's a lot to be said for the disciplines of "stuff": medicine, engineering, chemistry, physics, biology, economics, sociology, psychology, computer sciences and so forth. These sciences (sciences both soft and hard) are of great value to contemporary society. However, theology stands among these other sciences to say clearly and with certainty that there is more to our humanity than the skull beneath the skin. There is more to life than the accumulation and protection of the things that give us a measure of control over this often-chaotic world. Theology, at its best, attempts to guard against our falling into the intellectual traps that abound in our world today. Theology has to be all the more vigilant because the traps of contemporary culture are such attractive traps that they hardly seem like traps at all.

There are two basic traps into which we are likely to fall. The first is of very old construction. We fall into it when we judge the value of something by determining if it is sensible, material, quantifiable stuff. The second trap is like the first: we fall into it by judging the value of something on the basis of whether or not we find the thing useful. What I'd like for us to do for just a few moments is to reflect on both of these value tests to understand something about the value of Christian theology.

The Trap of Measurability

Once upon a time, long, long ago, in a land far, far away—though perhaps not so very far away as the philosophical crow flies—Greek thinkers made a rather far-reaching assumption that many people to this very day continue to make as though it expressed the most fundamental and obvious fact of common wisdom.

The assumption went like this: *There is an unbreachable boundary between the world of matter, the existential and "sensible" world (the world we can all see and touch and know through our senses), and the world of ideas, that is, the "intelligible" world.* This assumption drove a sharp wedge between the concrete and mutable (changeable) world and the absolute, perfect and immutable (unchanging) world of ideals. This split resulted eventually in an absolute dichotomy. It assumed that between these separate worlds was an enmity, a deadly opposition, a holy war, if you will. The world of spirit was seen to be opposed to the world of matter, the sensible world was understood as opposed to the intelligible world.

This philosophical assumption underlies many of the earliest and most threatening heresies in the early Christian church. But it also underlies the systematic statements of many of our most respected orthodox theologians. For example, the fourth-century heretic Arius (who taught that Jesus Christ is a creature and not of the same essential being as God) is widely interpreted as a sort of misguided protector of monotheism (the worship of one God). But that wasn't really his primary concern. Arius wasn't tying to guard the traditional monotheistic understanding of God from polytheism. He was trying to guard the concept of God from *mutability* (change). He believed that if we say that Jesus Christ is God and that Jesus Christ (as God) assumed human flesh and so crossed the boundary between the eternal realm of being and the realm of matter, then we must attribute to God the quality of changeability. And this, he maintained, is unthinkable. God is pure actuality *(actus purus),* in whom there is no shadow of change or possibility. Thus, according to Arius, God could not have become a creature. Jesus Christ, said Arius, was the highest of created beings. But Jesus Christ could not be God. His prior assumptions prohibit this possibility.

The thing that Athanasius, the champion of fourth-century orthodoxy and Arius's archenemy, understood was what the Arian view of God did to the biblical message, the message contained in the Gospels, the message that had within it the power to transform human creatures into children of God. Athanasius saw clearly that Arius's theology drove a wedge between the eternal realm (of God) and the mutable realm of matter (inhabited by humanity) and, in turn, claimed that God's being is unknown and unknowable to us, that God does not reveal his essential being in the person of Jesus Christ (in what theologians frequently call "the economy of salvation"). Arius, in his allegiance to Greek philosophy, threw out the biblical affirmation and the experience of early Christian communities that confessed: *When we have seen Jesus Christ, by the power of the Holy Spirit, we have looked into the very heart of God.* Arius would have Christian faith dissolve into a pious agnosticism in which we never have any genuine knowledge of *who God is.* And of course, that is the point of the split between the eternal and the material worlds. Athanasius took seriously God's intimacy with God's creation, the way God works through history, the way God assumed our humanity in all its contingency and frailty so that humanity might be healed from its sickness unto death.

There were also some important orthodox thinkers who bought into the radical split between the eternal and the material. We certainly see this tendency in Justin Martyr (the first apologist or philosophical defender of the Christian faith)[5] and in Augustine (the greatest theologian of the early church).[6] This split was also woven into the piety of the church in the Middle Ages by mystical writers, from the author we know as Pseudo-Dionysius onward. It is arguable that this split (variously labeled Platonic or Neo-Platonic) has proven to be the most potent and tenacious philosophical assumption ever.

The idea comes into the contemporary era because it received a new breath of life in the age of rationalism. Many, if not most, philosophers in the age of reason took up the ancient idea that the eternal realm is split apart from the material. Some in time went even a bit further than the ancients, saying that because we cannot see the invisible realm of eternal ideals, we can reasonably talk about only the visible world. In other words, the age of reason tended to enshrine and build on the implications of a view of knowledge similar to the one that Arius assumed: the eternal is separate from and unknowable to the material.

Other philosophers went even further to conclude that the invisible world, which (according to their assumptions) could not be spoken of rationally, is not very important anyway, and so we might as well get on with the really significant stuff of life (which "we can all see"). As Lesslie Newbigin and others have noted in recent years, this provided the necessary framework within which theology and morality were cordoned off into a sort of private ghetto of opinion, while leaving the so-called scientific disciplines to work in the world of empirical knowl-

---

[5]See Gerald Bray, "Explaining Christianity to Pagans: The Second-Century Apologists," in *The Trinity in a Pluralistic Age: Theological Essays on Culture and Religion*, ed. Kevin J. Vanhoozer (Grand Rapids, Mich.: Eerdmans, 1997), pp. 9-25.
[6]See, for example, Garry Wills, *Saint Augustine* (New York: Penguin Books, 1999), an excellent and very accessible biography of Augustine in the Penguin Lives series; and Saint Augustine, *Confessions*, a new translation by Henry Chadwick (Oxford: Oxford University Press, 1991).

edge.[7] Theologians and other Christians, in this intellectual environment, can offer their private opinions about the eternal realm. But theology cannot deal in *real* knowledge, it is reasoned, because nothing can be known about the eternal. Anyone's guess about theological matters is as good as anyone else's. Only the disciplines that deal with quantifiable material are entitled to the name "science." The scientific disciplines deal in provable facts, in public knowledge, not in private opinion or beliefs. So eventually the rather benign dichotomy between the visible and the invisible, the sensible and the intelligible, grew up into the beautiful blue-eyed seductress "Materialism" who charms so many people into believing that she is the only girl in town.

Determining the value of something on the basis of whether or not it can be seen, touched, felt and, most important, measured is an intellectual trap of the first order. We are forced to decide—before we ever encounter an object or an event—whether or not we will allow that object or event a place in our system of knowledge. And so many will say, even before beginning the voyage of discovery, that they will not recognize as real those things so radically new or otherwise unique as to call into question their framework of assumptions about the way reality functions. This sort of (what is often called) an *a priori defining of the frame of knowledge* may make one comfortable with his or her preconceptions, but it guarantees— by definition—that one will never meet reality in any terms that are genuinely new or unique. These prior assumptions bar the gate to any possibilities that are outside the boundaries of what we have already conceived. In other words, this aspect of Enlightenment thinking becomes an extraordinarily close-minded and unscientific way in which to do any kind of inquiry.[8]

It is this trap that theology guards against in its dogged determination to remain open-ended to existence, to the reality that demands to be met on its own terms. Christian theology shapes its discipline around the possibility that *something new* has happened in the midst of the old, and this *some-*

---

[7]Lesslie Newbigin, *Foolishness to the Greeks: The Gospel and Western Culture* (London: SPCK, 1986), pp. 1-19.

[8]See T. F. Torrance, *Transformation and Convergence in the Frame of Knowledge* (Grand Rapids, Mich.: Eerdmans, 1984). Also see Colin Gunton, *Enlightenment & Alienation: An Essay Towards a Trinitarian Theology* (Basingstoke, U.K.: Marshall Morgan & Scott, 1985); and John Polkinghorne, *Science and Theology: An Introduction* (London: SPCK, 1998).

thing new demands of us *new ways of thinking* because it refuses to be captured within our prior categories.

This is why Arius, the archconservative theologian of the fourth century, represented such a deadly threat to orthodox Christian faith. He demanded that the new wine of the gospel be poured in an old wineskin (a Hellenistic wineskin, in this case). But Athanasius, the radical theologian, led the vanguard of orthodoxy. God became human, he said; therefore we need a new way of thinking about God and humanity, Creator and creature, to take into account the possibilities this new understanding of reality raises.

To return to Karl Barth's comment that "we always seem to be handling an intractable object with inadequate means," we can see that the intractable object we are trying to handle (knowledge of God) is always forcing us to find more adequate means, means that are better fit to understand who God is. Or, to refurbish Anselm's motto, our *faith is forcing us to reshape our understanding*.

The Trap of Utility

The second trap into which we can so easily fall is a relatively new one. This is the trap of setting up "utility" as the ultimate criteria by which we judge the value of something. If we can "use" something in our present experience—especially if we can use it for economic gain—then we say that the thing is valuable. If the thing cannot be put to practical use, then we say it has no real value. "Practical use," in this way of speaking, can imply a social, industrial, business, management or military application among others. *Real* should be translated as "material," "visible" or "economically profitable." And so we see how closely the two traps coincide.

This trap of use is more subtle than in the previous trap because often the test is very, well, "useful." Practical utility is a reliable criterion for determining the value of so many things.

Take an automobile, for instance. If I design an automobile that is beautiful but will not start up when the key is turned and move when put into gear, it is of no practical value. An automobile's value is determined, first and foremost, by its function. A motor vehicle is made to carry persons and goods from point A to point B. All the other reasons for buying a car (as demonstrations of our affluence, our taste, our sexuality and so forth) are secondary to the primary function. An automobile that does not fulfill the primary function of transportation is practically useless and practically valueless, despite its appearance.

Another example: suppose someone devises a fascinating new economic theory, a sort of grand unified theory of economics, that would suddenly transform the entire monetary landscape. But if the theory proves unreliable when it is put to the practical test, then it is useless. It is of no practical value despite how fascinating it is, how aesthetically pleasing it is or how many copies of the book announcing the new theory the author has sold. (By the way, the first time I used this example of how a grand unified theory of economics is useless unless it works, I received a letter from a furious lecturer in economics in England. She said that she *knew* I was referring to her theory and that she'd finally worked out all the bugs, and the theory did work now. I never did rally the courage to inform her that I had never heard of her or her theory before!)

The test of utility is often useful. However, there's a vast world of reality that does not submit itself to this test. There are situations in which the test of utility proves useless for assessing value. The problem, however, is not so much the *use* of the test of utility, but the *indiscriminate and universal use* of a test which has specific and limited application.

For instance, it is useless to ask what is the use of Monet's "Water Lilies." When one encounters it for the first time, perhaps dashing into the museum where this panoramic painting is housed in Paris to escape a sudden rain shower, shaking off the water in the foyer, waiting in a line, not knowing what to expect, then stepping expectantly into the presence of the artist's vision with an audible gasp—the question of the "practical utility" of the painting is rendered meaningless.

Or take another example: love. Love calls the criterion of utility into question at the deepest level. In order for love to be love it must be, much of the time, useless in any terms that can be practically defined. The greatest love does not answer a craving need. It flows out without thought of being received. The love that is unconditional in its acceptance of us is by definition useless because it comes from One (God) who has no need of us at all and yet who (out of an overflowing bounty of self-giving love) created us for life and for relationship. We may or may not make use of the life that God has given us. We may or may not become all we are meant to become in gratitude to God and in joyful response to God's grace. But our use of the gift does not determine the value of the love that gives the gift or the love that characterizes the Giver.

In specific cases, in rather limited kinds of situations, the test of utility is appropriate and may prove very helpful. But when it comes to evaluating and understanding many things, including some of the most important things in life, like love and beauty, the test is useless.

The Value of Theology

So just to recap: In testing the value of things, the test of measurability fails at the point of its fundamental assumption about the nature of reality, splitting apart into opposing spheres the realm of intelligible eternity and the realm of sensible matter, the private realm of opinion and values, and the public realm of knowable facts. And the test of utility fails at the point of its universal application. There are some things that transcend the merely useful. Both tests become traps into which we can easily fall. And Christian theology obviously can and does at times fall into these traps. Nevertheless, theology can also serve to provide a reasonable alternative to these rather limited viewpoints.

Theology can do this by remaining true to its proper subject: God. To be more precise, God as God is known to the faith of the human community as Father, Son and Holy Spirit. The God who is ineffable in mystery, transcendent and hidden, beyond every and all efforts of finding out is found out in the divine humanity of Jesus Christ without ceasing to be the divine mystery. The triune God, who created all things seen and unseen in unconditional love and who sustains all things now by unbounded creative will, graciously is bringing all things to completion and reconciliation in Jesus Christ. God is *known by faith*. God is *really known and believingly known* as God's Spirit engages us to worship and enjoy and adore this infinitely adorable God, to reflect on his Word and to live in his radiance.

Now, everything I have just said involves an explicit rejection of any idea that spirit and matter can be split apart into two discrete and opposing realms. Everything I have just said also involves the rather disturbing idea that genuinely new, even unique, possibilities surround us and that these new and unique possibilities present themselves to us in ways that demand new and unique ways of thinking and speaking.

As Christians we believe that theology is the church's work of critical reflection performed in the afterglow of a new and unique encounter with God, an encounter that forces us to redefine what we mean by knowledge and reality. Rather than forcing on this encounter with God a grid of prior assumptions about God, creation and humanity, according to which we are forced to categorize the divine-human encounter in ways we have previously defined as valid and possible, we choose instead to come to this encounter asking God to be God according to God's own criteria, allowing our walls of perceptual alienation to be broken down.

The value of Christian theology lies in the ways it challenges the mythologies of every age and the manner in which it literally turns upside down the whole question of usefulness. Christian theology, inasmuch as it remains true to the God it attempts to speak of, mirrors the altogether strange ideas of utility God has (described in what Jesus called the "kingdom of God" or the "reign of God"): putting the last people first and the first people last, binding up the broken, feeding the hungry, setting prisoners free, showing gratuitous generosity to underachievers, throwing banquets for hookers and layabouts, welcoming prodigals home in the most absurd festival of impracticality the world has ever seen.

Summary. The value of theology is not determined by how well it reflects the values of a particular age or even the theology's practical and economic application. The value of theology is determined by how faithfully it bears witness to the voice and the character of its subject: God.

As we begin our exploration of Christian theology, we are going to do so in a way that tries to avoid the two traps of measurability and utility. We'll hear about possibilities that are genuinely new, so new they force us to redefine what is possible. We'll hear about values that go deeper than usefulness, *values of the greatest value.* And we'll discover these new possibilities and deeper values revealed to humanity in the life, death and resurrection of Jesus of Nazareth, whom we Christians believe to be the Christ, the Son of God. We'll discover how this affects our theological reflections as we consider theology both as an act of faith and as a science. But we'll leave that till our next class.

Homework Assignments

Like any course worth its salt, this one has homework. If you are reading this book by yourself, you may want to write out your homework assignments as a way of making yourself accountable to yourself. Be sure to have your homework in on time! If you are studying this book with a group, you'll find these assignments a lot more fun as group projects. To start out, today's homework will focus on basic comprehension.

1. Go back through the first class lecture. Make sure you understand every word, every technical term and phrase that is used. Many of the words that we toss around glibly may need more careful definition. For instance, here's a few relatively common but tricky words:

orthodox
heretic
polytheism
Enlightenment (as in Age of)
reason
agnosticism
Hellenism
materialism
utilitarianism

It would probably be a good practice to underscore or highlight every unfamiliar or technical word you come to in the course. Then go back through with a good dictionary (*Oxford English Dictionary*, for example), and make sure you understand how the word is being used in this context. Some of the more specifically theological words may not be defined too well in standard dictionaries, so let me suggest that you take a look at *The Pocket Dictionary of Theology Terms*, ed. Stanley J. Grenz, David Gruetzki, Cherith Fee Nording (Downers Grove, Ill.: InterVarsity Press, 1999), *The Oxford Dictionary of the Christian Church*, ed. F. L. Cross and E. A. Livingstone, 3d ed. (Oxford: Oxford University Press, 1997), or *The Westminster Dictionary of Christian Theology*, ed. Alan Richardson and John Bowden (Philadelphia: Westminster Press, 1983). When it is time to start writing your term paper (Yes, a term paper is required in this course), you may also want to turn to these dictionaries to get your bearings on your subject.

2. Let's think about "measurability" and the dangers of materialism. The following observation is made in the lecture: "The trap of determining the value of something on the basis of whether or not it can be seen, touched, felt and, most important, measured is an intellectual trap of the first order. It forces us to decide—before we ever encounter the knowable object or event—whether or not we will allow that object a place in our system of knowledge." Is that on target or off the mark? Why do you think so?

(If you have access to a library, examine a similar line of thought developed by Lesslie Newbigin in his book *Foolishness to the Greeks: The Gospel and Western Culture* [London: SPCK, 1986]. Newbigin's manner of expressing some of these ideas is quite different from mine because his work grew up in rather different cultural settings, but there are interesting parallels.)

Let's think about what I call "the trap of utility." When is the test of usefulness useful? When isn't it?

3. When I speak of genuinely "new" possibilities that surround us, what do you think I mean? What does it mean for the Christian faith to speak of possibilities that are genuinely new? Does the Christian faith bear witness to possibilities that many people would consider impossible? Why might people consider these things impossible? What tests might they use to determine possibility?

This first session ends with some reflections on "the value of Christian theology." What is Christian theology? What is the value of Christian theology, in your own view? Is Christian theology valuable for your study? Will it make a difference in the way you live? pray? worship? act in relationship to others?

Class 2

Methods
in the Madness

*"I beseech thee, good Jesus, that to whom thou hast graciously granted
sweetly to partake of the words of thy wisdom and knowledge,
thou wilt also vouchsafe that he may some time or other come to thee,
the fountain of all wisdom, and always appear before thy face,
who livest and reignest world without end. Amen."*

THE VENERABLE BEDE (C. 673-735)

I'VE BEEN READING *ALICE'S ADVENTURES IN WONDERLAND* LATELY. IT'S A VERY theological book. One of the most helpful theological insights I've come across is a piece of advice offered by the King of Hearts at the trial of the Knave.

If you remember the story, the Knave was on trial for stealing the tarts. The trial got off to a rather bumpy start when the King ordered the jury to render their verdict before they had heard the evidence. Then there was some controversy over the nature of the evidence itself. The King of Hearts was not the cleverest person God ever put on this green earth. As a matter of fact, just about the only clever thing he says in the whole story is his advice to the White Rabbit. And when he says this clever thing, you sort of get the feeling that it's only by accident that he has gotten this right.

The White Rabbit, acting for the prosecution, brings in what is understood to be a piece of particularly incriminating evidence, a letter allegedly written by the Knave. The King orders that the evidence be presented. The Rabbit asks the question, "Where shall I begin, please your Majesty?" And the King replies: "Begin at the beginning . . . and go on till you come to the end: then stop."

The single greatest challenge in theology is *finding the right place to start*. Our starting point shapes the form, the method and ultimately the content and outcome of theology. Or to put it another way, *the questions we raise and the way we go about asking these questions largely determine the answers we get*.

That's why Karl Barth, arguably the greatest theologian of the twentieth century, kept starting over and over again and again throughout his long career. Barth understood, as he said, that "theological work is distinguished from other kinds of work by the fact that anyone who desires to do it . . . [must] every day, in fact every hour begin anew at the beginning."[1]

Early in his career as a student and then as a young pastor, Barth took as his starting point the subjectivity of persons (in the spirit of Friedrich Schleiermacher) and the usefulness of religion for the ends of human society (in the spirit of classical liberal Christianity, following Albrecht Ritschl). But at the dawning of the First World War he found that this starting point brought him to a dead end. Theology had become merely a reflection on our various religious attitudes and values and feelings, often little more than a rubber stamp of approval on our already firmly entrenched cultural, racial and nationalistic assumptions, with little critical judgment regarding whether these attitudes are true or false. So Barth started over again, this time with a radical sense of God's otherness, God's transcendence, God's separation from history, God's standing over against human culture (this time in the spirit of the Danish existentialist philosopher Søren Kierkegaard).

This theology of crisis, as the approach of Barth and others came to be called, began at a starting point that led Barth to be more critical of every theological assumption, of every human word uttered constructively and positively about God. Barth discovered in these early days of his work the truth Blaise Pascal articulated so beautifully in the seventeenth century: "Any religion that does not say that God is hidden is not true." But even this starting point ultimately led only to another dead end, a kind of Christian agnosticism that kept

---

[1]Eberhard Jüngel, *Karl Barth: A Theological Legacy,* trans. Garrett E. Paul (Philadelphia: Westminster Press, 1986), pp. 18-19. Also see Thomas F. Torrance, *Karl Barth: Biblical and Evangelical Theologian* (Edinburgh: T & T Clark, 1990), pp. 1-2; and Eberhard Busch, *Karl Barth: His Life from Letters and Autobiographical Texts,* trans. John Bowden (Philadelphia: Fortress, 1976), pp. 33-209.

its adherents on guard against the idolatrous tendency to make for themselves false gods that cater to their fears while leaving them also theologically tongue-tied, speechless in the elusive presence of the "wholly other" God.

Thus as a young professor of theology, throughout the 1920s Barth struggled to find yet another starting place, a starting point that would allow him to speak faithfully and constructively of God, to avoid the presumption of saying more than we know and the agnosticism of saying less than we are compelled to say by the mystery of God's revelation in Christ.[2] It wasn't until around 1930 that he found what he had longed for, a starting place for theology that takes seriously the "infinite qualitative difference" between God and humanity, and yet affirms the possibility for genuine knowledge of God as God's gift to humanity in Jesus Christ. For the remainder of his life Barth was determined to begin all over again, day after day, hour after hour, the work of theology from, as he says, the beginning point that has a name: Jesus Christ. For the remainder of his long and distinguished career as a theologian, each day Barth would place every teaching of the Christian church under the light of this name, asking repeatedly, what does it mean to confess this, to pray or sing or preach that, if we believe God has been revealed in Jesus Christ.

As we ask the question "Who is God?" (arguably the most important question in Christian theology), we also begin at this starting point, which is not primarily a dogmatic assertion or even a confessional affirmation but is first and foremost simply our bearing witness to a particular person: Jesus of Nazareth whom we believe to be the Christ. In a sense, Christian theology is that exercise of heart and mind, that rush to bring our critical and constructive powers of reflection to bear on a relationship with a person who challenges us to redefine what we mean by so many of the words we commonly use, words like *God* and *humanity*, *Creator* and *creation*, *Word* and *world*, *Spirit* and *spirituality*. Theology

---

[2]The mystery of the God who is hidden in his revelation and hiddenly revealed runs throughout Karl Barth's theology. Stephen H. Daniel writes, "When Barth comments that God 'cannot be unveiled,' he does not mean that God is somehow intelligible behind his revelation and it just happens to be inaccessible to us. Rather, he means that God's intelligibility is inherent in his revelation: there is no other, more substantial text than the veil of revelation." See Daniel's perceptive essay, "Postmodern Concepts of God and Edwards's Trinitarian Ontology," in *Edwards in Our Time: Jonathan Edwards and the Shaping of American Religion,* ed. Sang Hyun Lee and Allen C. Guelzo (Grand Rapids, Mich.: Eerdmans, 1999), p. 60.

is an attempt to account for this relationship with Jesus Christ that turns life and death upside down and never stops turning us upside down until we draw our last breath. Theology is what we try to do to make sense of who Jesus, this other person (this wholly Other person) is who has met us and who continues to meet us, and who has established with us a new matrix of particular relationships that call into question all our relationships with others.

Our way of thinking and talking in Christian theology is defined and shaped by who this person, Jesus Christ, is. The uniqueness of this starting point demands of us two things—at least to begin with:

☐ that we approach theology as an expression of faith in the God who reveals himself in Jesus of Nazareth by the power of the Holy Spirit

☐ that we approach theology as a discipline with its own special critical methods, methods that are appropriate to understanding the God who is known in relation to humanity in Jesus of Nazareth

So, first we'll consider theology as an act of faith (a matter of trust), and then we'll consider theology as a kind of science (i.e., a disciplined endeavor to know and understand).

Theology as an Act of Faith

Theology, as an act of faith, can be defined as relational reflection. Theology is a careful and ordered reflection on the relationality or communion within the very being of God the Father, Son and Holy Spirit, and also between God and creation, and among God's creatures.

☐ The God who has his being in the communion of Father, Son and Holy Spirit has made himself known to humanity in the person of Jesus, who lived in utter dependence on the Father through the power of the Holy Spirit.[3]

☐ Confronted as we are by Jesus Christ, through the power of the Spirit, we are given access to the Father on whom Christ depended. The nature and quality of our theological reflection, therefore, are grounded in our

---

[3]I want to mention a few resources that are very interesting and enlightening on the subject of God's own communion as Father, Son and Spirit. First, a very popular treatment of the subject: G. K. Chesterton, *The Everlasting Man* (London: Hodder & Stoughton, 1925), in which Chesterton speaks of the Trinity as "holy family" (p. 262); John D. Zizioulas, *Being as Communion* (Crestwood, N.Y.: St. Vladimir's Seminary Press, 1985); Alan J. Torrance, *Persons In Communion: Trinitarian Description and Human Participation* (Edinburgh: T & T Clark, 1996), an excellent and constructive survey of current contemporary trinitarian thinking; and Hans Urs von Balthasar, *Prayer,* trans. Graham Harrison (San Francisco: Ignatius Press, 1986).

perception of these intertwined relationships.[4]

Our theological reflection is, therefore, an expression of our personal faith in God, but even more, it is a reflection on the faithfulness of God expressed toward us in Jesus Christ and made necessary by God's self-expression. Theologically we bear grateful witness to the character of the God made known to us in Christ.

As T. F. Torrance has said:

> God is utterly ineffable and incomprehensible to us, for his sublime greatness and majesty infinitely exceed the capacity of human beings to know and describe him as he is in his own nature. However, while retaining inviolate the mystery of his own being, God has chosen to make himself known to us through a movement of love and infinite condescension in which he has drawn near to us by becoming incarnate in Jesus Christ, thereby bringing himself within the range of human knowing. Jesus Christ thus constitutes the bridge between God and man, between the invisible and the visible, the incomprehensible and the comprehensible, the immeasurable and the measurable. It is, then, in Jesus Christ, through "union and communion" with him in love, and through sharing in the love of God incarnate in him, that we are enabled to know God in such a way that our knowledge of God is firm and sure, for it is anchored in the ultimate reality of God's own supreme being. That would not be possible without the aid of the Spirit of God. But in and through the Lord Jesus Christ God has accustomed his Holy Spirit to dwell in human nature and at the same time has adapted human nature to receive the Holy Spirit, which enables us through the gift of the Holy Spirit to share in the relation of mutual knowing between the Father and the Son and thus in God's knowledge of himself.[5]

God does not simply stand over against us or outside our horizon of understanding as an object inaccessible but daring us to be investigated, explored, found out. God, in Christ, has entered into our humanity and has created a capacity within our humanity for knowing God through his Word and Spirit. God draws us into authentic, participatory knowledge of himself as the Spirit leads us through the Word into that same trustful reliance on the Father that we see in Jesus Christ. Our theological work is nothing less than reflection on this dynamic primary relationship in the inner life of

---

[4]T. F. Torrance. See *The Mediation of Christ,* rev. ed. (Colorado Springs, Colo: Helmers & Howard, 1992).
[5]T. F. Torrance, *The Trinitarian Faith* (Edinburgh: T & T Clark, 1988), p. 32.

God, this reality of God's character, shared with us in our own flesh and blood.

You may know the name Olive Wyon. Olive translated much of Emil Brunner's work from German into English. James Torrance tells the story of how Olive, when she was translating Brunner's magisterial study of the atonement of Christ, *The Mediator,* sitting there at her typewriter, repeatedly would feel compelled to stop working, to kneel and pray right where she was translating, not because the German was too much for her but because as she read Brunner's reflections on the atonement, she was overwhelmed with gratitude, confronted with the reality of God in Christ, the Mediator.[6] In a manner of speaking, *all of theology is a work of prayer.* As William Perkins, the great sixteenth-century theologian said, "Theology is the science of living blessedly for ever."[7] Theology, in other words, is more than a head-trip, more than an intellectual parlor game. Theology is an essential expression of our living the implications of that life God shares with us.

Certainly this was John Calvin's understanding. You may already know the opening lines of the *Institutes of the Christian Religion,* where Calvin says:

> Nearly all wisdom we possess, that is to say, true and sound wisdom, consists of two parts: the knowledge of God and of ourselves. . . . In the first place, no one can look upon himself without immediately turning his thoughts to the contemplation of God, in whom he "lives and moves." For, quite clearly, the mighty gifts with which we are endowed are hardly from ourselves; indeed, our very being is nothing but subsistence in the one God.[8]

Calvin understood theological knowledge as bound up with an awareness of our "subsistence in God." As he carefully leads the reader through the labyrinths of his logic, he helps us to see that even knowledge of ourselves derives from knowledge of God. "It is certain," he says, that a person "never achieves a clear knowledge of himself unless he has first looked on

---

[6]Emil Brunner, *The Mediator: A Study of the Central Doctrine of the Christian Faith,* trans. Olive Wyon (London: Lutterworth, 1934).

[7]William Perkins, *The Work of William Perkins,* ed. Ian Breward (Appleford, U.K.: Sutton Courtenay, 1970), p. 177.

[8]John Calvin *Institutes of the Christian Religion* 1.1.1, ed. John T. McNeill, trans. Ford Lewis Battles (Philadelphia: Westminster Press, 1960).

God's face, and then descends from contemplating him [God] to scrutinize himself."[9]

This is a theme that Calvin elaborates throughout his work. We cannot even understand ourselves unless we find ourselves in Jesus Christ. And how do we go about knowing God, so that we can (in turn) know ourselves?

We know God by loving and worshiping, glorifying and enjoying God. Calvin goes so far as to say that God is not known outside of this relationship of love and adoration because knowledge of God involves trust and reverence.[10] To put it another way, our knowledge *about* God follows our knowledge *of* God. Or, as Anselm put it, as we have already noted, theology is faith in search of understanding.[11]

Theology is, to borrow John Leith's phrase, "the life of the mind as a service of God."[12] Theology is, you might say, an act of worship, in which we *stand under* (thus, understand) and *in relationship to* the Word of God *through the power of the Holy Spirit.* We say our word about God in response to the living Word of God who knows us and invites us to know him.

Without believing (that is, outside the boundaries of this relationship of love and trust with God) *we cannot know God* because the God we want to know makes himself known only through a particular relationship of love and trust.[13] To turn this around positively, the God who is in his innermost being Divine Love is known to us as we share in his life of love, as we are drawn to return the love of this God in adoration and to extend the love of this God to our neighbors. Not only the goal but also the source of this knowledge is adoration, love, piety, a quality of the spirit.[14]

---

[9]Ibid., 1.1.1-3.

[10]Ibid., 1.2.1-2.

[11]Anselm of Canterbury, "Proslogian," in *A Scholastic Miscellany: Anselm to Ockham,* ed. Eugene R. Fairweather (Philadelphia: Westminster Press, 1956). Also Anselm's letter to Pope Urban II on the subject of the incarnation, in same edition.

[12]John H. Leith, *The Reformed Imperative: What the Church Has to Say that No One Else Can Say* (Philadelphia: Westminster Press, 1988), p. 14.

[13]The greatest theologian of the ancient church, Augustine, elaborates on this theme in his *Confessions,* trans. Henry Chadwick (Oxford: Oxford University Press, 1991), see books 1, 5, 6 and 8, for instance.

[14]James Torrance expresses this beautifully in his monograph on Duns Scotus. Christ "is the one in whose person there is revealed the Triune purpose of God, that we were created to be co-lovers, *condiligentes Deo.*" James B. Torrance and Roland C. Walls, *John Duns Scotus* (Edinburgh: Handsel, 1992), p. 10.

Theology as Science

Theology is not only an expression of our faith in God, theology is also a "scientific discipline."

But what does this mean?

In contemporary culture a science is generally thought of as a study of physical phenomena by means of controlled experiments, the findings of which must be verified independently by others who repeat the methods and test the results of the previous experiments. Defined in this way it is patent nonsense to speak of theology as a science.

The subject matter of theology is God. And the existence of God cannot be demonstrated according to laboratory methods. The Christian faith is grounded in the belief that God became flesh, that the incarnate God lived and died and was raised from the dead. The whole message of the Christian faith assumes that something utterly and completely unique to creaturely experience has happened in Jesus Christ, something possible only for God, something that we cannot duplicate in scientific laboratories.

How then can we speak of theology as a science?

In fact, the word *science* has been placed in a methodological straightjacket by many of its modern practitioners, a straightjacket that has proven too constrictive even for some of the best physical scientists of our time. Certainly in the popular mind science and theology are often thought of as mutually exclusive, so much so that the idea of "scientific theology" would appear to many people to be an oxymoron. But this situation is the result of a basic misunderstanding of what a science is.

The term *science* carries in it a history of usage far broader than the narrow current usage of the word conveys. When a fourteenth-century writer said, "God of sciens is lord," and Sir Thomas More in 1532 paraphrased the apostle Paul's exclamation, "O the heyght and depense of the ryches of the wysedome and syence of god," they were using the word *science* in its basic sense: "The state or fact of knowing: knowledge or cognizance of something specified or implied; also, with wider reference, knowledge (more or less extensive) as a personal attribute."[15]

---

[15] *The Compact Oxford English Dictionary,* 2d ed. (Oxford: Clarendon, 1991), p. 1674.

The word *science,* even in its more technical usage, actually describes a rational process of critical and analytical study. The method of any science must be appropriate to the particular subject that is being studied, as T. F. Torrance observes in his landmark study *Theological Science:*

> It is because things are amenable to rational treatment that we can apprehend them at all; we understand them, or get light upon them, in so far as we can penetrate into their rationality and develop our grasp of it. Scientific knowledge is that in which we bring the inherent rationality of things to light and expression, as we let the realities we investigate disclose themselves to us under our questioning and we on our part submit our minds to their intrinsic connections and order. . . . It is always the nature of things that must prescribe for us the specific mode of rationality that we must adopt toward them, and prescribe also the form of verification apposite to them, and therefore it is a major part of all scientific activity to reach clear convictions as to the distinctive nature of what we are seeking to know in order that we may develop and operate with the distinctive categories demanded of us.[16]

Thus Karl Barth appropriately described theology as a science in his lectures to students in the post-World War II ruins of the University of Bonn: "I propose that by science we understand an attempt at comprehension and exposition, at investigation and instruction, which is related to a definite object and sphere of activity."[17] Theology is a science in that theology is a critical and analytical attempt to study a subject, an attempt (and always just an attempt) carried on with methods appropriate to its subject matter.

And what, we may well ask, is the subject matter of theology? Ultimately theology is a *word* about God. The term *theology* derives from the Greek: a *logos* about *Theos.* That's just what the word *theology* means. But how can we speak a meaningful word about God? How can we enter into a critical analysis of the God who is divinely hidden, eternally inaccessible to mortals?

We can only do theology because God has entered into our history (into our very humanity) and made the life and knowledge of God accessible to us. God entered into and is present in our human history as Creator and Sustainer of creation, and particularly through the history of

---

[16]T. F. Torrance, *Theological Science* (Oxford: Oxford University Press, 1969), pp. vii-viii.
[17]Karl Barth, *Dogmatics in Outline,* trans. G. T. Thomson (New York: Harper & Row, Harper Torchbook, 1959), p. 9.

his covenantal dealings with the nation of Israel, a covenantal relationship Christians believe culminates in the life, death and resurrection of Jesus Christ. In a very real sense the focus for our critical analysis (that is, the field of our study) is the history of the dealings of God with humanity and humanity with God. Theology is, then, the scientific (i.e., the careful, disciplined, critical and analytical) study of the relationship between God and his creation, particularly as that relationship is expressed in the history of Israel, a history, according to Christian thought, altogether embodied in Jesus Christ. This certainly doesn't sound like the kind of science we are accustomed to in the chemistry lab across the street with its test tubes, petri dishes, Bunsen burners and periodic table. And it isn't. But theology is a science appropriate to investigating the subject of God: the immortal, invisible God whom we worship and adore, serve and enjoy.

Our approach to doing this study—including the method, grammar and logic—are all determined by who God is and what God has done in his entering into our humanity and human history, and making himself available to us in and through human history. The science of theology is, therefore, *the critical expression of our faith, using analytical methods that are appropriate for reflection on the knowledge of the God in whom we trust in Jesus Christ.*

Some Methods in the Madness

Robert Farrar Capon, in his funny and insightful book *Hunting the Divine Fox,* says that "Theology . . . is a hunt for the Mystery—and the theologian is primarily a sportsman."[18]

Theology is, indeed, a quest into mystery, a search for understanding. As such, it must be joyful and even playful, but it is never merely a parlor game. We are seeking to understand the meaning of ultimate reality. As incredible and audacious, as presumptuous and even arrogant as this search may seem, we believe we are compelled to do it.[19]

At its best the whole history of orthodoxy (which means literally the

---

[18]Robert Farrar Capon, *Hunting the Divine Fox* (New York: Seabury, 1974), pp. 81-82.

[19]Look, for example, at Eberhard Jüngel's extended discussion of this issue in his book *God as the Mystery of the World: On the Foundation of the Theology of the Crucified One in the Dispute Between Theism and Atheism,* trans. Darrell L. Guder (Grand Rapids, Mich.: Eerdmans, 1983), pp. 3-42.

"right teaching" of the Christian faith)[20] has been an endeavor to promote this search for understanding by preserving those images, metaphors and ideas that others have found most helpful in tracking the "divine fox" (as Capon calls God). To put it a little differently, the Christian faith (at its best) has been most concerned with delivering to us through the centuries those *questions* that help us most in this quest.

The purpose of the great creeds and confessions of the church has been to preserve the questions that point toward the mystery of God. The creeds and confessions do not reduce God to a simplistic formula. That is specifically what they are resisting; they are saying No! to the attempts by what we call heretics to reduce the mystery of God's being and action to a simplistic definition. And so we have the often mind-boggling paradoxes and logical tensions of the great confessions, preserving the questions that we must go on asking.[21]

And this is where we get to a really sticky point. Not all questions are created equal. And the questions we ask largely determine the answers we will get. Like the old bad joke: Suppose someone asks you, "Answer yes or no. Have you stopped beating your dog?" There's just no good answer to that question given the question's framework. The question doesn't allow the one answering to say, "I have never mistreated my pet!" So Christian theology has always been a battleground over which questions we will ask and how we will go about asking these questions.

A theologian who understood this whole business of asking questions, maybe better than anyone in recent memory, was Dietrich Bonhoeffer.

---

[20]John Webster, in his inaugural lecture in the Lady Margaret Chair of Divinity, writes, "Christian theology's culture is that of Christian faith—its store of memories, its lexical stock, its ideas, its institutions and roles, its habits of prayer and service and witness, the whole conglomeration of activities through which it offers a 'reading' of reality. That culture precedes and encloses reflective theological enquiry, and it is within, not in isolation from, that sphere that Christian language and concepts acquire their intelligibility. This is why the supposed polarity of enquiry and orthodoxy is specious. For it is only a debased form of orthodoxy which is dominated by the compulsive dynamics of repetition, sameness and closure. Praciced well, orthodoxy is not about domination but about what my predecessor . . . has called 'shared attention.' Orthodoxy is participation in a tradition which directs itself to a source of convertedness. It involves a setting of the self—including the knowing self—within patterns of common action and contemplation, of speech and hearing." John Webster, *Theological Theology: An Inaugural Lecture Delivered Before the University of Oxford on 27 October 1997* (Oxford: Clarendon, 1998), pp. 22-23.

[21]Robert R. Hardy, ed., *Christology of the Later Fathers* (Philadelphia: Westminster Press, 1954), pp. 37-38.

Most of us remember Bonhoeffer as a Christian martyr, a person who paid with his own life the "cost of discipleship." But Bonhoeffer was also a brilliant scholar. One of his finest books is a book he never wrote. His students assembled it from the notes they took as they listened to his lectures on Christology, which is the doctrine that attempts to describe who Jesus Christ is. In this slim volume we find Bonhoeffer saying that the primary question we must answer in Christian theology is not the abstract and impersonal question *How is this possible?* (whatever "this" refers to). Rather, the primary question we must answer is the question Jesus Christ puts to each of us personally: *Who do you say that I am?*[22]

Every other question is secondary. And every secondary question relating to *how, what, where* and *when* must be answered in light of the prior question of *who*. Even such a simple question as the one we have been examining—What is theology?—can be answered only in light of the prior question, *Who?*

Who is theology?

Theology, in the first instance, is the Word who is God. The normative *logos* of God is God's own self-expression. "God is his own interpreter," as the eighteenth-century hymnist William Cowper wrote. We can see this clearly when we trace the origins of the word *theologian*. The origins of that term are directly related to the question "Who is theology?"

Only two people were granted the title "theologian" in the ancient church: St. John the Evangelist (or to be more exact, the author of the Fourth Gospel) and St. Gregory of Nazianzus (one of the so-called Cappadocian Fathers, a group of three early Christian leaders, including also Gregory of Nyssa and Basil of Caesarea, who contributed enormously to the theological understanding of the church in the fourth century).[23] John and Gregory received the title theologian because for them *Christ became the lens through which everything in life is brought into focus.* Christian theology, if we can take our cue from our first two theologians, affirms that *the Word who is God* is the source and the standard for evaluating every other

---

[22]Dietrich Bonhoeffer, *Christ the Center* (New York: Harper & Row, 1960), p. 17. I owe the special development of "the who question" to James B. Torrance who (in response to Bonhoeffer's Christology) has made this question the focal point of his entire theological program.

[23]For a fuller and very readable account of these three theologians, see Anthony Meredith, *The Cappadocians* (Crestwood, N.Y.: St. Vladimir's Seminary Press, 1995).

word we wish to utter about God. *The Word who is God* encounters us personally. Thus our own most crucial theological question is also a personal question addressed to God: *Who are you, Lord?*

Applying the "Who" Question

The question of "who" can be used by us as we attempt to understand and to evaluate the variety of theological methods around us. We shall see that some theologians have started with different questions. Quickly let's race through a few of the questions with which various theologians began their work to see how varying the question can radically alter the outcome. We will get a little ahead of ourselves, but I think this exercise illustrates the value of starting with the right questions.

The question of divine purpose. Looking at the giant of medieval theology, Thomas Aquinas, and the question of purpose that guided his theological discipline, we see that Aquinas's theology was teleologically rich where theological thought in our own society is so often teleologically impoverished. That is, Aquinas understood the whole of creation as having meaning because God, the eternal Designer and Author, made all things for his own purpose. Everything that exists, exists precisely as it is because of God's purpose for it. Thus Aquinas's theology conveys a powerful sense of divine providence. All of life has meaning because God created it for a purpose. Few theological methods can compete with Aquinas's in the area of divine purpose. However, Aquinas seems to have begun his theology not with the question *Who is this God for whose purposes all is created?* but with the rather more abstract question *How is there a divine cause?* (to be more exact, *whether* there is a "God." How can we prove or rationally demonstrate the existence of the Uncaused Cause?). From the basis of that question (the *how* question) Aquinas worked toward the question of *who*.[24]

Aquinas's starting point, despite the tremendous contributions he made, leads to so many problems. He established first a conception of an essential, underived divine cause on the basis of natural reason. Only later did he attempt to weld on to this view of God the information about

---

[24]Thomas Aquinas *Summa Contra Gentiles* I.Q.q., trans. Anton C. Pegis (Notre Dame, Ind.: University of Notre Dame Press, 1975), 1.13., and *Summa Theologiae*, trans. Fathers of the English Dominican Province (New York: Benziger, 1948), pp. 2-48.

God that he said we derive from revelation.

Of course, this scenario plays into the supposed split between God in God's own being (or God *in essentia*) and God in relation to humanity (as revealed in the *economy of salvation*). The alternative to this method would be to start with Jesus Christ as the one in whom we have seen the very heart of God, *the very Who of God.* Unfortunately Aquinas's starting point was adopted by a multitude of theologians, including virtually the entire Protestant scholastic movement of the seventeenth and eighteenth centuries.

The question of human effect. Looking at Friedrich Schleiermacher, whose brilliant theological work established him as the greatest Reformed theologian between John Calvin and Karl Barth, we discover that for Schleiermacher the primary theological question was the question of religious feeling (or intuition or immediate self-consciousness) of our dependence on God. He asked, What is the character of my feeling of absolute dependence?[25]

Schleiermacher wanted to establish a more reliable method for pointing toward the divine Whence, as he referred to God, the Origin. And so he largely abandoned the idea that religion is bound either to authentic knowledge of God or to morality, and he sought to establish theology as a kind of reflection on the intuition of absolute dependence on God. He provided a helpful critique of purely intellectualist theological approaches to asking the theological questions. And he rescued the Christian faith from the reductionist religion of mere moral responsibility, following Immanuel Kant. But, for all his brilliance, Schleiermacher leads us into the blind alley of subjectivism and the eventual individualization and privatization of Christian faith that has been criticized so perceptively in recent years by Robert Bellah and Stephen Carter.[26]

The question of obedience. We would do better to hear, in our own time, the voice of Gustavo Gutiérrez and others within the movement of liberation theology who have challenged us to answer Christ's question "Who do you

---

[25]Friedrich Schleiermacher, *The Christian Faith*, ed. H. R. Mackintosh, trans. J. S. Stewart (Edinburgh: T & T Clark, 1926), pp. 3-31.

[26]Robert N. Bellah et al., *Habits of the Heart: Individualism and Commitment in American Life* (Berkeley: University of California Press, 1985); also see Robert N. Bellah et al., "Individualism and the Crisis of Civic Membership: Ten Years After *Habits of the Heart*," *The Christian Century* 113, no. 16 (1996): 510-11. Stephen L. Carter, *The Culture of Disbelief: How American Law and Politics Trivialize Religious Devotion* (New York: BasicBooks, 1993).

say that I am?" by *doing* something. Theology properly understood, Gutiérrez tells us, is critical reflection on praxis, that is, practice, actions. We know God by doing justice. And our theological reflection must take seriously this active center of faith. The question of *Who* becomes a normative standard by which we evaluate our theological efforts. The way in which this question is heard and responded to personally by those who do liberation theology is a powerful corrective to so much contemporary theology that asks questions far removed from life.[27] Indeed liberation theology reflects or, perhaps, echoes an understanding of theology expressed by John Calvin when he said, "True knowledge of God is born out of obedience."[28]

But this starting point may prove less than adequate when we tie the question Who is God? uncritically to our own particular vision of justice, thus attributing to God's eternal being those characteristics derived from our cultural and political assumptions about right and wrong. This is a tricky area, but I believe liberation theology benefits us enormously when it is brought into conversation with what has been known as "the theology of the cross."

The question of the cross. The theologians who have made the cross of Jesus the central motif for their theological reflection have allowed their work to be shaped by this question of Who is God? at the most fundamental level. Take, for instance, Lady Julian of Norwich, the fourteenth-century English anchorite whose whole attention was so fixed on the cross of Jesus Christ that everything else was seen in light of this single event. Even Julian's understanding of the Trinity rests in her contemplation of the crucified Christ.[29]

This theology of the cross has been championed by Protestant Reformers Martin Luther and John Calvin, by the great Scottish theologian John McLeod Campbell during the nineteenth century, by P. T. Forsyth, and today by Jürgen Moltmann and Eberhard Jüngel.[30] In each case the theolo-

---

[27]Gustavo Gutiérrez, *A Theology of Liberation* (Maryknoll, N.Y.: Orbis, 1973), pp. 3-15, 189-208.

[28]This passage from Calvin is cited by Karl Barth in his *Evangelical Theology*, trans. Grover Foley (Garden City, N.Y.: Anchor, 1964), p. 14.

[29]Julian of Norwich, *Revelations of Divine Love*, trans. Clifton Wolters (London: Penguin, 1966), pp. 64-67, 94-98.

[30]Martin Luther, *Commentary on Galatians* (1891; reprint, Grand Rapids, Mich.: Baker, 1970); John McLeod Campbell, with an introduction by James B. Torrance, *The Nature of the Atonement* (Grand Rapids, Mich.: Eerdmans, 1996); Michael Jinkins, *John McLeod Campbell: Love is of the Essence* (Edinburgh: St. Andrew Press, 1993); P. T. Forsyth, *The Person and Place of Jesus Christ* (London: Independent Press, 1909); P. T. Forsyth, *The Work of Christ* (London: Independent Press, 1910); Jürgen Moltmann, *The Crucified God*, trans. R. A. Wilson and John Bowden (New York: Harper & Row, 1974).

gian's concern is faithfully to respond to the God who confronts us in the suffering humanity of Jesus Christ and the crucified God who confronts us with this question: "Who do you say that I am?" As in the case of liberation theology, the theology of the cross leaves some key secondary questions unanswered or sometimes inadequately answered, but the central question of Who is God? is responded to with clarity and force. We know who God is because of what God has done in Jesus Christ as we follow Christ in the way of his cross.

The central question that confronts each of us, then, as we begin this study of theology is the same question that confronts each of us in life, the question that confronts us in the waters of baptism and at the Lord's Table. *Who do you say that I am?* It is this question that must be answered faithfully with our lives. It is this question on which we must reflect critically and carefully at every step along the way. We must understand the business we are about. This is the most important question any of us will ever answer. And to answer this question we must, as Luther observed, begin where Christ is. We must meet Christ where Christ meets humanity, in the manger and in the marketplaces of this world. And we must follow him where his path inexorably leads, to the cross where he suffered and died, and to the tomb where he was buried, and where on the third day he was raised from the dead, so that we can see clearly the love of God that is stronger than death.

Summary. Christian theology is an attempt to reflect on the meaning of all reality from the perspective of the God who is revealed in Jesus of Nazareth. As such, theology is both an act of faith (adoration and worship) and a technical discipline (a science). Our primary concern as theologians is to hear God's Word to us through God's Spirit. God addresses each of us with the personal question, "Who do you say that I am?" We must answer with our lives.

Homework Assignments

1. One of the most familiar passages in the Bible is where Jesus tells us that "the first and greatest commandment" is "You shall love the Lord your God with all your heart, and with all your soul, and with all your mind" (Mt 22:37-38). Jesus is quoting a passage that every devout Jew would have known by heart: Deuteronomy 6:4-5, the *Shema:* "Hear O Israel: The LORD is our God, the LORD alone. You shall love the LORD your

God with all your heart, and with all your soul, and with all your might."
The question I want you to answer is this: How does Christian theology, as
both an act of faith and a science, relate to the greatest commandment?

2. Today the following statement was made: "The questions we raise
and the way we go about asking these questions largely determine the
answers we will get." Where do we as Christians go to get the sorts of
questions that will help us in our theological task?

The long quote from Thomas F. Torrance indicates that the theological
task must be conceived of as a particular sort of relationship. Go through
Professor Torrance's statement sentence by sentence, paraphrasing his
ideas in a way that is clear and in your own terms. What exactly is he telling us?

What do you think John Calvin means when he says that "all wisdom . . .
consists of two parts: the knowledge of God and of ourselves"?

3. We don't usually think of theology as a science at all. Yet traditionally
this is exactly how it has considered itself. The German word we normally
translate "science" is the word *Wissenschaft*. It conveys better than does
our English word *science* the fullness of the idea this lecture is getting at
because it has always been broader and more flexible. *Wissenschaft*
denotes learning, knowledge and scholarship. It is used as the root word to
which other words are attached to speak of physical sciences, medical sciences or philosophical sciences, and sciences that reflect on arts and
humanities. In our culture, what do you think happened to lead us to
develop a relatively narrow conception of "science"?

Obviously it is possible to deal with the Christian faith without dealing
with it in a critically reflective manner. What are the positive points of not
reflecting critically and methodically on the content of the teachings of
Christianity? What are the costs or the negative points of failing to deal with
our faith (at least sometimes) in a "scientific" or critical manner?

The lecture encourages us to reflect on a number of theological perspectives in light of the primary question we must ask in theology: "Who do
you say that I am?"

Read through this section, then choose one of the theologians mentioned that you personally want to become acquainted with during this
course of study.

Dietrich Bonhoeffer is mentioned. You may want to read Eberhard
Bethge's excellent biography of Bonhoeffer and Bonhoeffer's own power-

ful and beautiful writings *Discipleship* or *Life Together* or *Ethics* or *Christ the Center.*

Thomas Aquinas is mentioned. You may want to read G. K. Chesterton's delightful biography *Saint Thomas Aquinas: The Dumb Ox.* That will whet your appetite if anything will! Then you can move on to read a good modern interpreter of Aquinas, Etienne Gilson, and some of Aquinas's own works, perhaps selections from *Summa Theologica* or *Summa Contra Gentiles* (available in good English translations). You will find Thomas much easier to read than you may anticipate.

Friedrich Schleiermacher is mentioned. You may want to dip into his *Speeches on Religion* and *The Christian Faith.*

Then there are the theologians of liberation. Let me recommend that you look at Robert McAfee Brown's excellent introduction to the subject: *Unexpected News: Reading the Bible with Third World Eyes* (Philadelphia: Westminster Press, 1984). I would suggest you not neglect Gustavo Gutiérrez, *A Theology of Liberation* (Maryknoll, N.Y.: Orbis, 1973), arguably the most important and influential resource in liberation thought.

Finally, the theologians of the cross, and my favorite mystical writer, Lady Julian of Norwich. Reflection on her *Revelations* can be richly rewarding. The lectures also have suggested readings in Luther, Calvin, Campbell, Forsyth and Moltmann. Each would be worth a semester of intense study. All would be valuable.

Choose one to start with, then come back for more!

Class 3

I Believe in God

"Teach me, O God, not to torture myself,
not to make a martyr out of myself through stifling reflection,
but rather teach me to breathe deeply in faith."

SØREN KIERKEGAARD (1813-1855)

*T*HE EARLIEST FORMS OF THE APOSTLES' CREED DATE FROM THE FOURTH CEN-
tury. They are called the Old Roman and the African forms of the creed
because of where they were first used. The Old Roman form of the creed
was in use among Christians in Rome from before A.D. 341. The African
form was employed in African Churches by at least A.D. 400. The creed,
in what scholars call the *forma recepta* (the "received form," in other
words, looking pretty much as we have it today) dates from the sixth
century or perhaps a little later.

The Apostles' Creed began simply as a baptismal formula, a short
confession of faith spoken at services of baptism. The creed evolved
slowly as it was used in worship. As the creed came into use in various
churches throughout the western regions of the Roman Empire, it was
altered slightly here and amended there, so local versions varied in certain details. But as we begin our exploration into Christian theology,
following the contours of the Apostles' Creed, there's something we
should note. All the various forms of the creed begin alike, with these
words:

Credo in Deum (in Latin)
Pisteúō eis Theon (in Greek)
I believe in God.[1]

To understand the significance of what the Apostles' Creed is saying in its opening phrase, and (maybe even more important) how it says this, we're *not* going to focus first on the early church where the creed began. Rather, we're going to look at a rather depressive Danish writer from the nineteenth century because he understood so well what it means to say "I believe in God." We'll start our investigation into the basic teachings of the Christian faith by looking at one aspect of the thought of Søren Kierkegaard.

The Truth Will Set You Free

One day I overheard some of our more philosophically minded students dancing around the pinhead of subjectivity and objectivity. The idea came up after class and in one of the afternoon discussion groups, and it deserves some closer examination. Karl Barth, in his *Dogmatics in Outline,* gets into a discussion about what he calls the "subjective fact of faith" in contrast to "the objective Creed." He says, rather cryptically, "Whoso means to rescue and preserve the subjective element shall lose it; but whoso gives it up for the sake of the objective shall save it."[2]

Not that his paradoxical statement was really just loads of help or anything. But at least Barth's statement forces us to look seriously at what it means *subjectively* to confess our *faith* in God and what it means *objectively* to confess our *beliefs* about God. I'd like now for us to go one step beyond where Barth leaves us with his statement because I think it will help clarify the whole discussion and, incidentally, what Barth is getting at. And we're going to take this step with the help of Kierkegaard.

One of the guiding ideas of Kierkegaard's religious thought is that truth is subjective. But when most of us hear this, what do we hear him saying?

Most of us hear him saying that truth is relative. We hear him saying something like this: "I have a view of truth that is private to me; you have a view of truth private to you. Truth is a matter of personal or individual taste." Most of us hear an expression of the fairly common notion that truth

[1]Philip Schaff, ed., *The Creeds of Christendom, with a History and Critical Notes: The Greek and Latin Creeds,* ed. David Schaff, rev. ed., (Grand Rapids, Mich.: Baker, 1983), 2:45ff.
[2]Karl Barth, *Dogmatics in Outline,* trans. G. T. Thomson (New York: Harper & Row, Harper Torchbook, 1959), p. 16.

is a matter of opinion, of individual, private judgment, and that my opinion is just as valid as yours. Some modern philosophers of the existentialist movement (a philosophical approach that often claims Kierkegaard as its parent) would go so far as to say that all meaning must be created by the individual in his or her own subjective experience, implying that there is no such thing as objective meaning or objective truth or objective values at all. "Truth, like beauty, is in the eye of the beholder," they might say.

In fact, this is not even remotely what Kierkegaard meant when he said that truth is subjective. And it is exactly here that he provides so much help for us as we try to understand what it means to say, *I believe in God.*

Kierkegaard says that truth cannot be engaged in from a posture of disinterested neutrality. Truth does not yield to passivity. Truth yields to passion. Truth can only be known through decisive involvement, through commitment, through a passionate and personal giving of ourselves to the truth that "is real, objective and demanding." Truth demands that we surrender ourselves (our values, our self-understanding, our past and future, our concerns and our aspirations) not merely to a statement or a philosophical position that we hold as true but to the God who is himself true. To put this in perhaps a more consciously biblical frame: The truth does set us free, but only in as much as we give ourselves to it.[3]

Now, let's turn Kierkegaard's insight loose on the creed.

The creed begins with the words "I believe in," that is, "I place my trust in" or "I give myself to" God. But not simply to just any old thing that goes under the generic term *God.* The creed says, in effect, that I trust *this* God, this *particular* God, and not some other god. Once I've made the personal confession *(I place my trust in God)* I spend the rest of the creed making clear *which* God it is I trust.

The first concern of the creed then is radically subjective: *I* trust. But the God in whom I trust is not determined by my trust. In fact, quite the contrary. The very nature of my trust is shaped and given a specific content by the God in whom I trust. And while my perception of God may vary from someone else's perception of God, nevertheless *God is who God is* regard-

---

[3]Søren Kierkegaard, *Concluding Unscientific Postscript,* trans. David Swenson, with introduction and notes by Walter Lowrie (Princeton, N.J.: Princeton University Press, 1941), pp. 520-44; also Kierkegaard, *Training in Christianity,* trans. with introduction and notes by Walter Lowrie (Princeton, N.J.: Princeton University Press, 1941), pp. 26-39.

less of our partial and fragmentary perception and our individual and eccentric experiences. Or to say it another way, the creed is, from one perspective, radically *subjective* (in the sense in which Kierkegaard uses the word subjective). It is a statement of *my* passion, *my* surrender of myself to the Other. And yet the creed is just as radically an *objective* statement concerned with the character of the God to whom I have surrendered myself completely, an attempt to describe *who* this God is. So rather than inquiring into the nature of my belief, the creed is completely preoccupied with the identity of the God in whom I trust. And by being preoccupied with the identity of the God I trust, the character of my belief is clarified. Thus the point of Barth's maxim: "Whoso means to rescue and preserve the subjective element shall lose it; but whoso gives it up for the sake of the objective shall save it."

We have returned then, by a different route, to the primary question of Christian theology, the question with which we must begin over and over again: the question of *Who*.

I believe. That is, I give myself away, not to my beliefs but to this God. And this God is not captive to my ideas about God. Indeed, this God is a very real threat to my ideas about God, even my most treasured ideas about God.

The radical subjectivity of the Christian faith means that I surrender myself (the believing, thinking, feeling subject, *I*) to the object of faith (God, the Other, the wholly Other). The creed attempts, in a provisional way, to identify this God in whom I trust. The creed is a collection of statements describing the God in whom I have faith.

In light of this insight, there's another question that you may already be anticipating: *How do statements of faith develop?*

After all, the business of theology is to investigate faith statements. That's what Barth's comments on dogma and dogmatics are all about. Dogmatics is, he says, the "most thankful and *happy* science" wherein we study dogma, the confessions and preaching of the Christian church.[4]

To put it in slightly more familiar terms: Theology is the study of our faith statements. Theology is a study undertaken from the perspective of Scripture, tradition (including a variety of creeds and the various witnesses of the "doctors" and "saints" of the church, that multitude of elevated and common

---

[4]Karl Barth, *Evangelical Theology*, trans. Grover Foley (Garden City, N.Y.: Anchor, 1964), p. 10.

voices emerging from communities of faith that frequently have virtually nothing in common but the Christ they worship) and in light of our own personal experiences in the context of our contemporary faith communities.

So the first thing we have to recognize is that faith statements develop naturally from active, reflective Christian life and practice, faith and worship. As we entrust our lives to God and grow as persons in relationship with other persons in light of our knowledge of God, as we worship God and serve in God's world, we are compelled (at some level, to various degrees of sophistication) to reflect on the God we adore, trust, worship and serve.

A helpful way to think about this process is described by what is called the hermeneutical circle. The version of the hermeneutical circle that I will use (and expand on a bit) is found in Robert McAfee Brown's excellent book *Unexpected News: Reading The Bible with Third World Eyes*[5] (see figure 3.1).

Our understanding of faith begins in our practice and language, in concrete and specific action and speech. We believe and think and speak in particular ways. (It is almost as though we have our own faith idioms peculiar to the dialects we speak and the various cultures in which we live.) And we have these peculiar faith idioms because of all sorts of very specific social, racial, political and cultural factors. In other words: *we start where we start, in the concrete actuality of our own lives, doing these things and not doing other things, believing this and not that, speaking about God and the world in these ways, instead of those ways.*

As we believe, talk, live and act, our understanding is (from time to time) challenged, questioned, perhaps even shattered, by new perceptions and new ideas, and by practices that are out of our ordinary. In specifically theological language we might say that sometimes God breaks through the conventional boundaries of our lives and speaks to us, though it is often difficult to explain what this means.

□ It may mean that we find ourselves confronted by a radically new vision of who God is and who we are meant to be in reading and studying the

---

[5]R. M. Brown, *Unexpected News: Reading the Bible with Third World Eyes* (Philadelphia: Westminster Press, 1984), pp. 30-31. An excellent, though more technical treatment of hermeneutics is found in Anthony C. Thiselton, *The Two Horizons: New Testament Hermeneutics and Philosophical Descriptions with special reference to Heidegger, Bultmann, Gadamer and Wittgenstein* (Exeter: Paternoster, 1980).

5. The scope of the action widens

1. Action in the world leads
to a jarring experience

4. This leads to a new level
of action

2. Our overall understandings
are shattered, and we reflect on the
need for new ones

3. We turn to the Scriptures
with new questions

Figure 3.1. The hermeneutical circle

Bible with other Christians. And so we might say that the Spirit of God has spoken to us as the Word of God through the words of Scripture.

□ Or it may be that we are shaken in a way fundamental to our reading of the Bible by something unexpected in life. And so the Word speaks in ways that go against our prior understanding of Scripture.

□ It may be that we find ourselves suddenly cast as a minority of one, in opposition to our traditions and faith communities, yet convinced that the Word of God has spoken to us through our personal experience.

□ Or it may be that we have become stuck in a solitary, insular faith, isolated from the voices of our traditions and our faith communities, only suddenly to find ourselves "spoken to" by the voices of brothers and sisters in Christ (perhaps, by "saints" from across the ages). So we abandon our isolation and become more open to learn from the larger Christian communities.

At any rate, in the midst of our lives, at significant moments, we find the adequacy of our actions, understandings and faith languages challenged. The Word and the Spirit break through among us, leading us toward, as Brown says, "a new level of action." We may also be led to new levels of understanding, speech and worship, of course, because of our actions. Our faith is widened and we move on and on and on. Remember! This is a circle. This happens and will happen over and over again as we grow in Christian faith.

There's a natural rhythm to faith. And our theological reflection follows this rhythm. We move from action and worship and understanding through the various crises of life and faith when the Word of God speaks through or in confirmation of, or in spite of our traditions and our communities, to new dimensions of action, worship and understanding. If we take seriously the idea that theology describes a living reality, then we can see that the phrase *I believe in God* brings together the radical, subjective commitment of our selves with the radical objectivity of this God to whom we are giving ourselves.

Theological Omelets and the Strange Brew of Authority

Making theological omelets requires a lot of broken eggs. It's a messy business. And one of the messiest parts of the whole business has to do with what we call authority. We've been leading in this direction from the beginning of today's class, and now we have to deal with it.

On what basis or for what reason do we believe in *this* God and not some other gods? What leads us to this belief? Why do we believe God is like *this* and *not* like something else? When we read a confession of faith and it describes God, why do we believe it? When we read a confession that describes God in a way we aren't comfortable with, how do we evaluate it? Authority is the key question for everyone who is seeking to understand the character of the God to whom we are giving ourselves.

One of my favorite stories is told by Alf Wight, a.k.a. James Herriot, the Yorkshire veterinarian. He starts his first book, *All Creatures Great and Small,* by telling of how he stripped to the waist one night in a cold barn in the middle of a North Yorkshire winter and laid on his back in cow dung and mud, straining to pull a new calf from its mother. And the whole time he was struggling in the muck and the mud he was cursing under his breath the lovely picture of birth he had been shown in textbooks at veterinary college in Glasgow. The photos in the textbooks were of vets dressed in white lab coats, standing in a clean concrete holding stall, delivering a calf without a drop of blood or muck around.

Okay, now this is absolutely insane. But I'm going to tell you the truth about authority. It doesn't really work like the textbooks say. The textbooks aren't lying. They're just not telling you how it really happens where we actually live. Most issues relating to authority happen when we're waist deep in muck and mud, shivering and straining at the back end of a cow.

Authority's a messy business in reality.

The conventional wisdom (the textbook model) says that the Bible has the highest authority, then tradition (that is the traditions and teachings of the churches), then our individual experiences. That makes sense. And it is true. *Sort of.* We should indeed submit whatever we believe first to the Bible, then to tradition, then to our own individual experiences.

If we diagramed this textbook model, it might look something like this:

The testimony of the Scriptures

_____ *has priority over* _____

tradition

(including the confessions and

creeds, the teachings of the church in

various ages, and the thought of "doctors" and "saints")

_____ *has priority over* _____

our own individual faith experience

(within our particular and contemporary faith communities).

Any particular belief that is under scrutiny would need to be run through these various filters or be seen in light of these various authoritiesin order to discern whether or not we will accept it as trustworthy. For instance, someone says that she believes that God is absolutely powerful. So she goes to the Bible to see whether her idea of God's absolute power is consistent with what the Scriptures say; then she examines her idea of God's power in light of the great confessions of faith and the teachings of the church's greatest teachers like Augustine, Aquinas, Luther and so forth. Then she asks around the church she attends to find out what others think. And finally she looks deep into her own experience of life. At every step along the way she weighs her understanding against these tests of authority. And this is great!

Except this isn't really how life works, is it? Life is a lot messier than this. We've got cold and sharp wind, mud and muck to contend with.

We don't start out in life by writing theological textbooks in sterile settings. We start out by living. And living as we do, we have a bundle of beliefs, mostly passed on to us by parents and family and friends and church. And with this bundle of frequently unexamined beliefs, we do what we do, we talk as we talk and we live as we live. And every once in a while we hit a bump of some sort, and we have to reflect on this belief or that one. Then we say, Wow! Why do I believe that? It doesn't fit what I've experienced or what Jim says or what Christians in Latin America are saying in that interview I saw last night on channel four.

So we stop and think and question or even change that belief or a part of that belief, and we go along until we rethink and then maybe we discover that there is an idea, handed down from traditions previously unknown to us, that makes sense of what we had originally been told, and it doesn't contradict our experiences. Then maybe, later on, we discover that our individual experiences weren't really all that hot. And then there's the whole question of the Bible, because sometimes the Word of God breaks through the written words of Scripture, and by the mysterious and totally unpredictable power of the Holy Spirit we find our experiences and everything we've been told called into question. Or maybe we find our experiences just as unexpectedly confirmed.

What we are searching for (and what we are sometimes running from) is truth. If we believe that truth is not simply a proposition or a set of statements but a person (the Truth, as in "I am the Way, and *the Truth,* and the Life," Jn 14:6), then what we are trying to understand isn't some*thing* but some*one*, and that gets messier by the minute and a lot more interesting and a great deal more open-ended. So we see that the way we come to evaluate what we believe, and whether it is believable, is closely related to the entire development of our faith, which is tied to the whole business of living life from birth to death, as we saw described simply and schematically in the hermeneutical circle.

Several years ago a young woman in a theology course came by to talk to me about why she believed what she believed. She's from a Unitarian Universalist background. The Unitarian Universalist faith originated as a branch of Christianity (though not all Unitarians today would call themselves Christians) that saw in Jesus of Nazareth a charismatic figure whose example is important but who is not God. They thus reject the doctrine of the Trinity, and so their name, Unitarian. Early in the development of this tradition their teachings generally were based on scriptural authority, but in time, reason and the individual conscience replaced the Bible as primary sources of authority.

My student, a bright and extremely creative person, wanted to delve more deeply into these various sources of authority. She said that she believed that God is altogether good, merciful and unconditionally loving, that God wants us to live at peace with one another, that God wants us to seek justice and to defend the poor and needy. I told her that her beliefs were a fine example of traditional Unitarian thought and also a good example of Christian humanism at its best.

Then I asked her what I believe are some fairly crucial questions of authority: *Why do you believe God is like this—merciful, just and loving—rather than unreliable or wicked? What is your authority for saying God is one and not the other? And why do you believe that such a God wants us to live a particular quality of life?* "It seems to me," I said to her, "that your doctrine of God and your ethics are borrowed from the Christian faith."

She was puzzled at first and, honestly, a little irritated at my line of questioning. But what I wanted her to think about was this: as our faith matures and becomes our own, we reflect on the various bits and pieces of beliefs we have inherited and picked up along the way. The question of authority is the basic question we all deal with as we evaluate these bits and pieces, as we ask which beliefs are reliable and which are not. I wanted her to examine consciously and critically the sources of her authority for believing what she believed. It's something we could all do a bit more with.

We face the question of authority in the most unexpected places and at the most unexpected times: when we try to determine when it is right or wrong to make a commitment, whether in marriage or in business; as we prepare to teach our children a set of values we believe are worthwhile; or when issues like abortion and homosexuality come home to us and cease to be "issues" at all, becoming instead personal decisions in our own families. Every time we attempt to make a practical decision regarding our beliefs, every time we try to understand who God is and what God wants of us, the question of authority comes into play. Why do we believe this? Why do we care about that? To what will we commit ourselves?

To understand better how this whole very complex business works—and it is important for our study of the basic teachings of the Christian faith that we do understand this better—I want to tell you another story. During the summer of 1827 people left the gloom of Glasgow to vacation along the banks of the Gareloch, as they had done for generations before and still do today. And many of those who vacationed on those hilly shores enjoyed worshiping at the church in the town of Rhu. The young minister there, the Reverend John McLeod Campbell, was a fine preacher. He was also a provocative preacher because he seemed to be saying things that challenged the conventional Scottish religious views of the time, inherited largely from the Westminster statements of faith, the seventeenth-century confession and cate-chisms that served as the doctrinal standards for the Church of Scotland.

When the vacationers returned from their summer holidays, they some-times told their own ministers about what they had heard preached at Rhu. Their ministers also became interested, perhaps provoked is more accurate. Toward the end of 1827 the reports of Campbell's teachings were creating quite a stir in the Scottish religious world. Campbell was invited to the big city of Glasgow to present his ideas. He went. A week later he returned to Glasgow again, having been invited there to preach. Each time colleagues in the Church of Scotland were among his hearers. And each time careful note was taken of what he said.

Now, I'm not going to focus on the substance of what Campbell was preaching. His doctrines were very controversial in his own time, but today not controversial at all. In fact, the Church of Scotland came to share his views—some seventy years after Campbell was convicted of heresy and thrown out of it.

The thing I want to focus on here is the basis for his church's condem-nation of him, because that is what his teachings led to—his condemnation as a heretic, as a teacher of false doctrines. The basis for the condemnation of his teachings was that (to quote the charge against Campbell) they were thought to be "contrary to the Holy Scriptures and to the Confession of Faith approved by the General Assemblies of the Church of Scotland."[6] I want to focus on the basis for his condemnation because it highlights for us the whole question of authority. Why do we believe what we believe? By what authority do we believe in this God and not some other?

Campbell, in his defense before the courts of the Church, said that he based his teachings on the Bible as read in conversation with a variety of creeds and confessions; in dialogue with the writings of Martin Luther, Jonathan Edwards and other great theologians; in light of the voice of other

---

[6]*The Whole Proceedings Before the Presbytery of Dumbarton and Synod of Glasgow and Ayr, in the Case of the Rev. John McLeod Campbell, Minister of Row, Including the Libel, Answers to the Libel, Evidence, and Speeches* (Greenock: R. B. Lusk, 1831), pp. 1-2. Also see Michael Jinkins, *A Comparative Study in the Theology of Atonement in Jonathan Edwards and John McLeod Campbell: Atonement and the Character of God* (San Francisco: Edwin Mellen Research University Press, 1993), pp. 284-303.

Christians in his own community of faith; and in light of his own experience of God's grace. His opponents agreed that Scripture and tradition are
important, indeed, essential. But for them tradition had a more limited
meaning. They said that they must read Scripture through one particular
tradition, through the standard of the Westminster Confession. All other
Christian confessions and all other voices of tradition were of much less (if
any) significance to them.

Campbell had become convinced that the Scriptures and the over-
whelming witness of the great confessions of the church were on his side.
He knew that at certain points his preaching was not precisely in accord
with the Westminster Standards. Nevertheless he felt his heresy trial would
be an excellent opportunity to weigh *this one* confession in the balance
with the Bible, as the Bible had been interpreted through other confessions
and as the Bible had been wrestled with by a variety of theologians and
other persons of faith.

To his astonishment his church did not want to investigate the adequacy
of the Westminster documents but wanted only to discern whether or not
he was a heretic on the basis of those documents. There were moderate
voices among those in the heresy trials, as the appeals went all the way to
the highest court of the Church of Scotland. However, the predominant
tone was set by those who said that the Westminster documents provided
the single, authoritative basis for understanding and interpreting the Bible.
One minister (more extreme than the vast majority) told Campbell that it
was irrelevant bringing the Bible into their deliberations because the Westminster documents provide all we need to know about what the Bible says.

The Bible, in other words, was held by *all* as the highest authority.
Campbell's opponents interpreted the Bible through this single confession,
as though the Westminster Confession had reached the summit of theology
beside which all other statements paled.

Campbell argued for a much richer way of understanding religious
authority. And in this he anticipated our own discussion. Christians are
placed within the context of communities of faith, communities that are not
limited to those immediately contemporary and available to one church or
locale but communities that extend throughout time and that witness in
their abundant variety to the wonder of God and God's enjoyment of variety. Christians in conversation with this variety of communities must bear
the witness of the Scriptures. But the Scriptures do not yield themselves

like a recipe book or (worse) as a book of rules and regulations. Rather, as ethicist James Gustafson has said, through the words of the Scriptures we meet "a Person, the living God. . . . What the Bible makes known [is] . . . a reality, a living presence to whom" we respond. Through the words of the Bible the Spirit of God introduces us to the living Word of God.[7]

Much of this, Campbell said, happens *between the lines of Scripture.* The Word of God, whom we meet by the power of God's Spirit, gives us access to God the Father. We meet the Word of God as we hear the witness of the Scripture in conversation with our faith communities. This is especially important because any particular community, as it submits itself to the living Word of God, is always having its views about God corrected, altered and amended in light of the God to whom it submits itself.

This is where Campbell differed from the Scottish Church of his day. For them, authority was a settled issue—not dynamic, not fluid, not living and alive, but safe, secure, set—and dead. For them, the Bible need only be understood in light of a single tradition, indeed, in light of a single, uniform interpretation of the Westminster Standards.

Campbell knew better. He valued tradition, but he understood tradition as a crowded, diverse, living testimony. For Campbell, as for G. K. Chesterton, "tradition is . . . democracy extended through time . . . giving votes to the most obscure of all classes, our ancestors."[8] Campbell understood what the kirk (church) of his time did not: this obscure class of ancestors to whom we give the franchise to vote is not a uniform and homogeneous voice but a pluralistic, diverse and multiform crowd of voices that must be heard with humility. Tradition draws us into a lively dialogue that must be listened to with one ear while listening with the other for the voice of the Word of God. If we were to diagram the model for authority I am attempting to sketch for you, it might look like figure 3.2. The question of authority is messy in precisely the same way that real life is messy.

Our personal experiences inform our hearing of the Word. But our experiences may be called into question by the experiences of others in our own faith communities and by the experiences of others in the larger church—which we call tradition. We hear the Scriptures through the lenses

---

[7]James Gustafson, cited in Bruce C. Birch and Larry L. Rasmussen, *Bible and Ethics in the Christian Life* (Minneapolis: Augsburg, 1976), p. 23. Gustafson in this context is in conversation with the thought of H. Richard Niebuhr.

[8]G. K. Chesterton, *Orthodoxy* (London: Bodley Head, 1927), pp. 73, 83.

of tradition in all its variety, and we ask of tradition how and in what ways it must be understood in light of our own unique experiences as persons of faith. In all of this the Bible maintains a peculiar relationship to us in our communities of faith and to tradition because God speaks especially through these words by the power of the Spirit. The dynamic relationship between the Christian, communities of faith (contemporary and past), and the Word and Spirit of God is seen vividly in the New Testament itself. We are told in 2 Timothy, for example, that "the Word of God is not chained" (2 Tim 2:9). God's Word, like God's Spirit, is free from human manipulation and control. But God is also vulnerable through his Word in a manner analogous to the incarnation of the Word, in that God allows the Word to be spoken, preached, handled by human beings (2 Cor 1:18-31; Heb 13:7). Yet, however the Word of God meets us, it remains God's own; it nourishes us, abides in us, gives us life and judges us (Jn 14—16; Heb 6:1-9; 1 Jn 2:14).

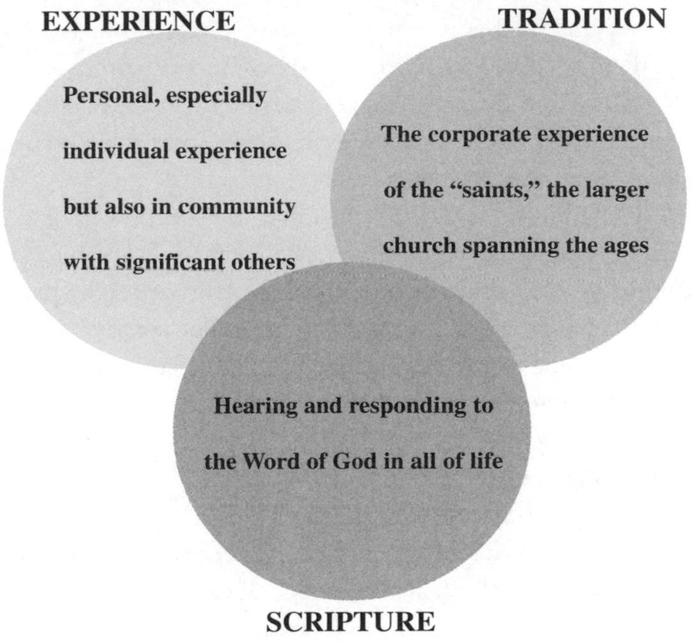

EXPERIENCE   **TRADITION**

Personal, especially

individual experience   The corporate experience

but also in community   of the "saints," the larger

with significant others   church spanning the ages

Hearing and responding to

the Word of God in all of life

SCRIPTURE

Figure 3.2. The spheres of authority

We sometimes find our experiences and the various voices of tradition called into question, at other times confirmed, here challenged and there accepted. We are persons in a matrix of remarkable relationships, attempting to discern the nature of these relationships in light of the God who meets us here and now. And for this reason, it is no accident that this creed begins with the words *I believe in God* rather than words like *God is*.

The statement of Christian faith is anchored in the relationship between an acting human subject in community with other acting human subjects and an object (if you will) transcending all the usual methods of classifying objects. Indeed, this is an object that tenaciously refuses to be an object or to be classified but that turns the tables on us and becomes an *other* subject that makes faith and understanding possible. We are compelled to say, "I believe in God" because we already have said, "I believe in Thee." This is an intimate pilgrimage on which we have embarked as Christians, into the being of a God who is closer to us than we are to ourselves.

Summary. When we say "I believe" (1) we are pledging our allegiance to the God who has revealed himself in Jesus Christ, and (2) we are describing who this God is to whom we have pledged our loyalty. There are then both subjective and objective aspects to our confession of faith. We believe in this God because this God has met us in Jesus Christ by the power of the Holy Spirit. It is for this reason that we are compelled to speak of God in the way we do.

God meets us, as we have said, in Christ by the power of the Spirit, through the spheres of personal experience (both individual and communal), tradition (the corporate experience of the larger church spanning the ages) and the hearing of holy Scripture. It is in the context of these relationships that we seek to live out our pledge of allegiance to God and seek to understand more and more fully who God is.

Homework Assignments

It's showtime! Prepare for your first theology paper.

Francis Bacon, the sixteenth-century philosopher, said (please excuse the gender-exclusive tone of his remarks), "Reading maketh a full man; conference maketh a ready man; and writing an exact man." This is a noble idea, far superior to the alternate muse: "Bacon maketh a full man."

Bacon is right. Reading fills us with ideas. But if all we do is read, our ideas are likely to be a jumbled, undisciplined and poorly examined lot. Through conference (what we would call dialogue or critical conversation) our ideas are shaped, compared with the ideas of others, challenged, supported and made more "ready." But it is only through writing that we become "exact": the words are weighed, the right phrases found, unnecessary or incomplete concepts detected and pared. We've been doing our reading. And we'll do a lot more. This is filling us with ideas. We've been talking through our ideas. We are becoming more ready and able. Now it's time to write.

Your assignment is to write a short paper, an essay to be exact (1,500 words), on any of the following topics:

Why I Believe What I Believe

I Know Whom I Have Believed and Am Persuaded

Knowing God

Talking to God and Talking About God

My Credo

How My Ideas About God Have Changed

What I Did on My Summer Vacation

You should, in your essay, use both general and more specialized sources. In other words, if you are discussing "Why I Believe What I Believe" (the question of authority), start by reading a couple of general articles on authority such as Carl Michalson in *A Handbook of Christian Theology* (New York: Collins, 1979); R. P. C. Hanson in *The Westminster Dictionary of Christian Theology* (Philadelphia: Westminster Press, 1983); and J. Y. Campbell in *A Theological Word Book of the Bible* (New York: Macmillan, 1966), pp. 26-27. Then you can follow this general reading with a little more specific study, looking at people who have dealt with this question in more depth: Daniel L. Migliore, *Faith Seeking Understanding: An Introduction to Christian Theology* (Grand Rapids, Mich.: Eerdmans, 1991); Peter C. Hodgson and Robert H. King, eds., *Christian Theology: An Introduction to Its Traditions and Tasks*, rev. ed. (Philadelphia: Fortress, 1985); Donald K. McKim, *Theological Turning Points: Major Issues in Christian Thought* (Atlanta: John Knox Press, 1988); and Bernard Cooke, *Ministry to Word and Sacraments: History and Theology* (Philadelphia: Fortress, 1976). At this point you do not have to deal with the super heavyweights (Augustine, Athanasius, Aquinas, Luther, Calvin, Barth and the like), but if you want to, you certainly may.

A good essay should (1) demonstrate your ability to handle the subject, (2) indicate your familiarity with the ideas most relevant to the subject, (3) show that you understand problems and major controversies that surround the subject, and (4) exhibit a creative spirit, the ability to discover a new slant on the subject.

I suggest that you take a look at some of the classic essays to see how a lively, informative and provocative essay might look. The recently published *Oxford Book of Essays* might be helpful, but you might also want to look at the essays of G. K. Chesterton, C. S. Lewis, Isaiah Berlin and Ralph Waldo Emerson in particular.

Class 4

I Believe in God,
the Father Almighty,
Creator of Heaven & Earth

"O Lord God, Creator and Giver of life to all souls,
how wonderful is Your kindness and mercy to us,
that You should stoop to visit the poor and humble soul,
and to satisfy her hunger with Your whole Divinity and Humanity!"

THOMAS À KEMPIS (C. 1380-1471)

Q. WHO IS THE GOD WE TRUST?

A. *"God, the Father Almighty, Creator of Heaven and Earth.*

This is our confession of faith. It is in fact a confession that we are compelled to make on the basis of our belief in the God of Israel, the God revealed in Jesus Christ, and not simply some sort of general conclusion we gather from our observations of nature.

We might, looking at nature, draw the same conclusion as Alfred Lord Tennyson: that nature is "red in tooth and claw." And we would be correct. Nature is violent. Nature is about survival. Nature is about eating and being eaten. We might then take a next and not so incredible step to say that nature is, therefore, the creation of a god who is also red in tooth and claw.

Sentimentalism will not do! Those who are honest with themselves must see the world for what it is. Charles Darwin (who was no sentimentalist) looked at nature full in the face and wrote, "What a book a devil's chaplain might write on the clumsy, wasteful, blundering, low, and horribly cruel works of nature."[1] We cannot simply look at the shape of daisies and say that God is the great Maker of daisies and of all things daisy-like, ignoring the pain, suffering and violence of existence. We could just as well look at the terror and horror of existence and gather that God is the author of terror and horror, a relentless sadist.

From the very beginning the creed confesses faith in the God who might not be apparent to some people, some very thoughtful, sensitive and good people. We confess our faith in the God we believe to be "the Father Almighty."

The words "Father Almighty" carry one of the most profound paradoxes in our highly paradoxical faith. Observing the world as it is, some have concluded that God can be either a loving father or almighty, but not both. Indeed someone has said, "If God is good, then God is not all-powerful, and if God is all-powerful, then God is not good." But the creed speaks against much of the evidence presented in the court of nature, and it testifies (on oath) to the existence of a God who is both good and mighty, all-loving and all-powerful. And it does so without shutting its eyes to the evidence.

At the very outset of the creed we raise one of the most difficult questions of life. We confess our trust in the God who is divine Father in love and almighty in power. In other words, we let go of neither the mystery of existence in all its beauty and pain nor the mystery of God's goodness and strength revealed by God's gracious history with Israel and with all creation in Jesus Christ. The creed preserves the mystery against all odds. The creed refuses to reduce the inscrutability of God to easy, pat answers. The creed, through tensions as deep and irrevocable as existence itself, delivers to us the essential questions with which we must wrestle in our life and in our faith. But let's not get ahead of ourselves here.

Let's begin by asking some questions.

Father God?

When we say God is Father, what are we saying? One of the most eloquent discussions of God as Father appears in Hans Urs von Balthasar's little

---

[1]Letter to J. D. Hooker, July 13, 1856, in *Correspondence of Charles Darwin* (Cambridge: Cambridge University Press, 1990), 6:178.

book *Credo: Meditations on the Apostles' Creed,* which he wrote just before he died in 1988. He refers in these meditations to God the Father as the Origin. And he says:

> Herein lies the most unfathomable aspect of the Mystery of God: that what is absolutely primal is no statically self-contained and comprehensible reality, but one that exists solely in dispensing itself: a flowing wellspring with no holding-trough beneath it, an act of procreation with no seminal vesicle, with no organism at all to perform the act. In the pure act of self-pouring-forth, God the Father is his self, or, if one wishes, a "person" (in a transcending way).[2]

To say that God is Father is to describe God in God's unconditioned creativity, God's self-giving, God's eternal fruit bearing, God's bearing of the other purely for the sake of the love God has for the other, God's utterly other relatedness that has no cause than God's own unlimited being in love. We could call God the Origin, and so God is. But God is not a mechanical origin. God is person, one who brings others into being.

To say that God is Father is to look into the very inner life of God and to glimpse there God's eternal outpouring into God's eternally begotten image, the eternal Word who is God.

To say that God is Father is to glimpse the source of that stream of love (who is the Holy Spirit) who flows from the eternal Origin and is returned eternally to that Origin from the imageless image of God (the eternal Son of God).

I am saying all of this to make very clear what we are not saying when we call God Father. *We are not saying that God is Father in a creaturely, biological, sexual or sociological sense.* In fact, what we traditionally call God's "fatherhood" contains in it, as von Balthasar observes, the primal qualities of femaleness and maleness. The fruitfulness of the Father's being gives birth to all that is through the eternal Word by the power of the Spirit. In this we sense the divine "femininity." The seed that fertilizes, that sets in motion this generation of life, is also the originate love of the Father. In this we sense a divine "masculinity." In neither case is God narrowly male or female but eternally the primal origin and the primal ground of both. Human gender finds its origin and its creative force in the character of God the Father.

---

[2]Hans Urs von Balthasar, *Credo: Meditations on the Apostles' Creed,* trans. David Kipp (New York: Crossroad, 1990), p. 30.

We are not saying that we derive our notion of God's fatherhood from our human conceptions of fatherhood. Even in patristic theology (the theology of the church fathers) the primary concern with calling God Father and Son is to preserve the sense of person-relatedness grounded in the Trinity. They were not attempting to ascribe to God the characteristics of human fathers. Which brings us face to face with the whole question of analogy, that is, the way we use human words (signs derived from our creaturely experience) to describe the eternal being of God.

To explain how we talk about God analogically, I'll resort to an explanation I use with confirmation classes, hoping you won't find it too simplistic. There are basically three options we have for using language theologically.

1. We can try to use language *univocally.* Univocal language assumes that there is an *absolute and exact identity* between God and creation (including humanity). Speaking univocally we would observe a woman or a man and say that God is just like the human person, having arms, legs, a tongue, human emotions such as hatefulness, frivolity and so forth. This sort of theological language is undeniably and unabashedly anthropomorphic. That is, it applies or attributes to the divine being precisely those qualities we find in creation.

2. We can try to use language *equivocally.* This means that there is a *fundamental dissimilarity* between God and creation (including humanity). To use language equivocally is to speak symbolically in expressing ideas about God, but with every statement we are also making a very thorough disclaimer to actual knowledge of or information about God.

Obviously both alternatives express certain possibilities: the one expects a complete acquaintance with God, assuming that creation shares the infallible imprint of its Creator; the other respects the infinite qualitative distinction between the Creator and creation, paying homage to God's transcendence by adopting a kind of pious agnosticism. Both must remain real alternatives for everyone who seriously wants to speak of God.

3. A third use of language attempts to steer between the two extremes: *analogy. The Oxford Dictionary of the Christian Church* defines analogy as

(Gk. ἀναλογία orig. a mathematical term denoting proportion, but already used in a more general sense by Plato and Aristotle). In common modern usage the word signifies a resemblance or similarity between objects of discourse. More technically, however, analogy is a linguistic and semantic phenomenon which occurs when one word bears different but related meanings so that its use on different occasions involves neither equivocation nor univocity. . . . In theological circles the general intelligibility of analogy has been cited as a help to understanding how one can significantly refer to God by means of words more usually used of creatures.[3]

That's fairly straightforward, isn't it? Well, yes, except for one thing. From this description of analogy it's not really clear what *the primary point of reference* is for the analogy. We are confronted with some rather daunting choices here:

☐ Does a child look primarily at his or her father to understand what is meant by the fatherhood of God? And if this is true, what of the evil and cruelty of many human fathers? Are we to attribute to God abuse and neglect because some fathers are abusive and other fathers abandon their children? If the human father is the primary reference for understanding God, is our theology not endorsing the disenfranchisement and marginalization of women? And what are we to say of the clearly feminine metaphors and reflections of God that emerge throughout the Bible?

☐ Does the child have to gather a general "idea" of fatherhood from cultural history (if such a thing is possible) and apply this general term to God with the general idea in mind? Yet the world is full of general conceptions for fatherhood and motherhood. Our understandings of fatherhood and motherhood, of the roles of parents and the meaning of families, are culture specific. Can we speak of God truly if all we are doing is attributing to God a variety of experiences arising from various cultures?

☐ Does fatherhood have a primary reference point for the analogy somewhere else? That is to say, theologically speaking, is the reality of fatherhood grounded in the being and action of God as revealed in Jesus Christ in such a way that we can grasp it and speak of it in terms relatively familiar to us, and yet in terms consistent with the nature of the reality we are attempting to describe and thus in tension with our experience and general understanding?

The prize, said Thomas Aquinas, is behind door number three!

---

[3]F. L. Cross and E. A. Livingstone, *The Oxford Dictionary of the Christian Church,* 3rd ed. (Oxford: Oxford University Press, 1997), p. 56.

We must look somewhere else than our own experience of father or any cultural notions of fatherhood to understand what it means to say that God is Father. Specifically, Aquinas said, we must look at the life of Jesus of Nazareth, whom we believe to be the incarnate Son of God, and in this Jesus Christ we are given access (by the power of the Holy Spirit) to the fatherhood of God the Father "from whom all paternity in heaven and on earth is named."[4]

In order to understand what we mean when we confess our faith in God the Father Almighty, we must reflect on God's revelation in Jesus Christ. Only here do we understand God either as Father or Almighty, as a God of love or power. In other words, fatherhood and almightiness are not simply general categories which God and we share. *Fatherhood* and *almightiness* as theological terms are qualities that describe the very being of God and that are understood properly only when we apprehend them in terms of God's revelation in Jesus Christ. To put it another (more technical) way, the prime analogue is the being of God, not our creaturely existence. And that turns the whole business of analogy topsy-turvy and makes it a matter of faith, not simply of natural observation.

This is the point that Aquinas is making. It is also the point that John Calvin and Martin Luther and Karl Barth make, in their own ways. In fact, it's the point that has been made repeatedly by Christian theologians throughout the centuries, though it must also be admitted that Christian theologians have also missed this point repeatedly and egregiously, implying or even maintaining that because God is Father, God is male.

What the Christian faith teaches is that God has established in the realm of creaturely existence an analogous correspondence between God's own being and our humanity through Jesus Christ. And when, by faith, we apprehend Christ as eternal Son (as "God from God"), we are given genuine access to the peculiar quality of fatherhood that God has in relationship to the Son. As one of the fourth-century Cappadocian theologians said, "All things that are the Father's are seen in the Son, and all things that are the Son's are the Father's; because the whole Son is in the Father and has all the Father in himself. Thus the Person . . . of the Son becomes as it were Form and Face of the knowledge of the Father, and the Person . . . of the

---

[4]Ephesians 3:14, cited in Aquinas *Summa Theologiae* 1.1.1.33.2. Also see Etienne Gilson, *The Christian Philosophy of St. Thomas Aquinas* (New York: Dorset Press, Random House, 1956).

Father is known in the Form of the Son."[5] Whatever orthodox Christian theology is saying, it isn't about gender or cultural roles, as Catherine Mowry LaCugna explains: "Gregory answers that *'Father is the name of a relation,'* not the name of an *ousia* [that is, an essence] or *energeia* [an action]. Father is a name that indicates the manner in which the Father is in regard to the Son and vice versa. The names Father and Son reveal to us bloodline and parentage and designate identity of nature between the begetter and the begotten."[6]

God's act toward humanity, an action that is nothing less than the person of Jesus Christ himself, becomes to us the pathway into the eternal life of God, God the divine community. This is our confession of faith in this particular God, the God who has entered into covenant relationship with humanity through the history of Israel and in Jesus of Nazareth. Therefore we confess that through Christ the Son we know God the Father. Hearing the good news of Jesus Christ and his proclamation of the reign of God, the Holy Spirit confronts us by faith with the fatherhood and power of God in God's own terms. I'll return to this idea in just a minute, but before I do, I want us to ask another question.

Almighty God?

When we say that God is almighty, what do we mean? Let's start again from von Balthasar's beautiful meditation on the Apostles' Creed as we try to understand the meaning of the phrase "God, the Father Almighty." He writes:

> When the New Testament refers to [God] in many passages as "almighty," it becomes evident from these that this almightiness can be none other than that of a surrender which is limited by nothing. . . . It is therefore essential, in the first instance, to see the unimaginable power of the Father in the force of his self-surrender, that is, of his love, and not, for example, in his being able to do this or that as he chooses.[7]

The almightiness of God consists in the "superior self-possession of the love which surrenders itself."[8] This conception of might and power runs counter to virtually every conventional human concept. We assume that we

---

[5]See T. F. Torrance, *The Trinitarian Faith* (Edinburgh: T & T Clark, 1988), p. 63.

[6]Catherine Mowry LaCugna, *God for Us: The Trinity & Christian Life* (San Francisco: Harper, 1991), p. 65.

[7]Von Balthasar, *Credo*, p. 31.

[8]Ibid., p. 32.

know what power looks like, don't we? Power, we think, bends others to its control; might manipulates, subdues, forces. That's power, isn't it!

Ah, but there's the rub.

Even as the abused child runs frightened from the concept of the fatherhood of God because of the cruelty he or she has suffered at the hand of a wretched excuse for a father, even as the disenfranchised and marginalized woman rightly lifts her fist in anger against a theology that engenders and enshrines false images of maleness, so also we have looked into the brokenness of the world and seen the terror and brutality of power perverted. So many people have rightly questioned the very idea of God's power because they can see only the worship of worldly manipulation, brute force and vicious control in the name of God.

Such power is not power, *not if God defines power in the life, death and resurrection of Jesus Christ*. Rather, the power of God revealed in Christ is the irresistible force of God's self-surrender, the strength, the almightiness, of God's self-emptying and other-centered love. As Emil Brunner once said, "The almightiness of God and his love do not stand in opposition to one another but in a reciprocal relation."[9] The love of God, as the Scottish writer George MacDonald knew, is itself the consuming fire.[10] Any view of the love of God that does not understand the fierce, burning power of that love, the positive force of that love against sin, evil and death has resigned itself to sentimentalism, because the wrath of God is nothing less than the burning passion of God turned against all those things which threaten to destroy God's good creation.

However, here we have another perplexity, don't we?

If God burns so fiercely against evil, why does God allow the possibility of evil in the first place, and why does God allow evil to continue? Or to return to a question implied from the beginning of this lecture, if God is good, how can God's power *allow* bad things to happen? The problem with trying to answer these questions is this: virtually any answer we try to make ends in reducing the mystery, and so we end up not telling the whole truth about God and the world.

☐ For instance, some people will try to respond to the problem of evil by

---

[9]From Emil Brunner's sermon "The Father Almighty," in *I Believe in the Living God* (Philadelphia: Westminster Press, 1961), p. 35.

[10]George MacDonald, *Creation in Christ*, ed. Rolland Hein (Wheaton, Ill.: Harold Shaw, 1976), pp. 37-46.

saying that evil is an illusion. Evil is apparent, they say, but it is *only appar-ent;* it is unreal.

☐ Others say that evil is simply the necessary shadow and darker shade in the larger picture of life; the reason we are so uncomfortable with it is because we don't see life from a large enough vantage point.

☐ Some of the people who take this view go on to say also that God is the autocratic ruler of the universe from whom all things come directly, and that both good and evil have their source in God (we call this view theo-logical monism).

☐ Others, to the contrary, say that Good and Evil are two virtually equal, opposing powers that are fighting it out for control of the universe (in the-ology we call this view dualism).

☐ Another idea is that though God does not directly create evil, God does permit evil for some greater purpose, perhaps because God values freedom in creation, and evil (as the essential opposition to God's creativity) must be permitted as a genuine possibility in a free universe.

☐ Another form of this view would hold that while God opposes evil (per se), God allows it a place in creation because humanity is strengthened in its struggle against evil.

Ultimately, while resisting the reduction of a question as large as life itself into simplistic answers, the Christian faith has confessed that God assumed into his own eternal Being (in Jesus Christ, in the entire event of his incarnation leading ultimately to the cross) the pain, sorrow and dark-ness of this suffering world, and has taken on the tormented shape of our human brokenness. In this act of utterly selfless love God has defeated evil with the power of love that evil does not know, cannot comprehend and has no power to overcome.

But having said this, we must also admit that we have not answered the "whys" and "wherefores" of evil at all. Our affirmation of faith does not reduce the mystery of creaturely existence, which bears within it the mys-tery of evil, suffering, frailty and sickness (both moral and physical), and sin. But it does tell us that the God we worship has assumed the shape of our suffering humanity in order to deliver us from the darkness and danger that threaten to consume us.

This brings us to consider "the kingdom of God" as the reign and rule of God by that special kind of power that is God's own. As Christians we confess that we only understand clearly the nature of God's power in the

life, death and resurrection of Jesus Christ. And that is supremely paradoxical. God's power is most visible in the helpless and broken figure of
Jesus of Nazareth hanging dying on the cross. But this shouldn't really be
too surprising, should it? Christ himself is the ultimate parable of the kingdom of God he proclaimed. And like the other parables of the kingdom,
this parable turns upside down our assumptions about how the world
works; even our most common values (like fair pay for a day's work and
apparent favoritism toward those who don't deserve our help) are called
into question, and we are cast upon faith alone (see Lk 14:15—16:31).

But there we must leave it amid the fundamental ambiguities of the
Christian gospel because we have before us another phrase, tied to these
we have already considered. And this phrase raises another question that
makes our reflections even more complicated.

Creator God?

What do we mean when we say that we believe in God the Creator? One
of the most startling things Karl Barth had to say (and Barth had a lot of
really startling things to say) is at the opening of his massive study of the
doctrine of creation, a study that runs to 2,270 pages in the English translation of *Church Dogmatics:*

> The insight that man owes his existence and form, together with all the real-
> ity distinct from God, to God's creation, is achieved only in the reception and
> answer of the divine self-witness, that is, only in faith in Jesus Christ, i.e., in
> the knowledge of the unity of Creator and creature actualized in Him, and in
> the life in the present mediated by Him, under the right and in the experi-
> ence of the goodness of the Creator towards His creature.[11]

We find essentially the same thing said in John Chrysostom when he
pulls together the whole witness of the New Testament and reads the story
of creation in light of the fourth Gospel and the Pauline epistles.[12] We find
much the same thing said in John Calvin, who, while placing knowledge of
God the Creator first in his *Institutes,* understands God's creativity as essential to the whole Trinity, so that we know God the Creator through the Son

---

[11]Karl Barth, *Church Dogmatics* 3/1, trans. J. W. Edwards, O. Bussey, and Harold Knight, ed.
G. W. Bromiley and T. F. Torrance (Edinburgh: T & T Clark, 1958), p. 3.
[12]Note especially John Chrysostom, *Homilies on St. John and the Epistle to the Hewbrews* II-V,
The Nicene and Post-Nicene Fathers, ed. Philip Schaff (Grand Rapids, Mich.: Eerdmans,
1983), 14:4-25.

by the power of the Spirit.[13] This is fascinating—and, perhaps, unexpected.

In a sense, these people are asking us to read the Bible *backwards*. It's as though the Bible were a mystery novel. The hints are dropped here and there throughout, but it's only at the end that we discover the *who* in the "who done it." And with that piece of information, when we discover *"who* done it," the whole thing takes on new meaning. The ending makes sense of the whole story.

As James Torrance is fond of saying: we need to read the Bible Christo-logically—not chronologically. He doesn't mean by this that we are to have a narrower view of the divine human drama. No indeed! Rather we have a special and peculiarly Christian perspective on that drama. Understood in this way, we are not arguing for a Christian chauvinism that lords over others its cultic and cultural views. What we have in the Christian faith is a unique perspective on the meaning of the universe because we believe that we know personally the God who has given us, in Christ, the crucial clue we need in order to understand the meaning and goal of life and our place in it.

We are saying that the God who created this universe is not a detached and disinterested deity but *the God of passion*. In fact, God the Creator is the God of *the* Passion, the God revealed in the Passion of Jesus Christ.

☐ The God who created us is the God who sought us with an everlasting love and has drawn us to himself with loving kindness.

☐ The God who sought us is the same God who nurtured the nation of Israel through its rich and tortured history, who widened the circle of covenant to include all humanity.

☐ The creation of heaven and earth, we believe, reflects in its yearning for communion and its dependence on its creator God's own eternal imaging of God's own being in communion, as Father, Son and Holy Spirit.

☐ The earth we walk on, the flesh and bones of which we consist, the air we breath are not dislocated matter but matter grounded in the being of God and matter that God loved so much he would not abandon it to disintegration.

As creatures, we have our being, we live and move in the gracious space and time God created for us. And this time and space is that totality

---

[13]John Calvin *Institutes of the Christian Religion* 1.1.14, ed. John T. McNeill, trans. Ford Lewis Battles (Philadelphia: Westminster Press, 1960).

of creation that God has redeemed in and by the same Word and Spirit through whom God created space and time.[14]

Colin Gunton, in his excellent study *The Triune Creator*, explains that the Christian doctrine of creation in its understanding of creation as the work of God the Father, Son and Holy Spirit teaches us that "God is already 'in advance' of creation, a communion of persons existing in loving relations." Thus "it becomes possible to say that [God] does not need the world, and so is able to will the existence of something else simply for its own sake. Creation is the outcome of God's love indeed, but of his unconstrained love."[15]

Nothing, in other words, caused or forced God to create. God did not even need to create. God creates because it pleases God to do so. Creation is grounded in the delight of God, not in divine compulsion. And because God the Trinity creates out of such freedom and unconstrained love, "creation remains in close relation to God, and yet is free to be itself."[16]

Gunton continues:

> According to the New Testament, creation is *through* and *to* Christ, and this means that it is, so to speak, structured by the very one who became incarnate and thus part of the created order of which we are speaking. It is good because God himself, through his Son, remains in intimate and loving relations with it. Similarly, when Basil of Caesarea described the Holy Spirit as the perfecting cause of the creation, he enabled us to say that it is the work of God the Spirit to enable the created order to be truly itself.[17]

So we say that for us as Christians, even knowledge of God as Creator depends on faith in Jesus Christ through the power of the Holy Spirit. And that is why we are compelled to confess in the very next breath: *And I believe in Jesus Christ his only Son our Lord.* We'll return to the connection between these two affirmations in our next class. However, before moving on from our confession of God as Creator of heaven and earth, there are two other things we need to touch on if only very briefly.

When we say that God is Creator, we mean that God not only made all

---

[14]Claus Westermann, *Creation* (Philadelphia: Fortress, 1974), pp. 113-23.

[15]Colin E. Gunton, *The Triune Creator: A Historical and Systematic Study* (Grand Rapids, Mich.: Eerdmans, 1998), p. 9.

[16]Ibid., p. 10.

[17]Ibid. You may want to look at Basil's theological reflections yourself. His study of the Spirit of God is available in a good English translation, St. Basil the Great, *On the Holy Spirit*, trans. David Anderson (Crestwood, N.Y.: St. Vladimir's Seminary Press, 1997).

things but that God also presently and continually sustains in being every-thing that he made. God did not set in motion a great mechanism from which he was excluded after the beginning point of creation. God's cre-ation is not simply a past occurrence. The Christian understanding of cre-ation is that God *creates* all things that are; indeed, that God creatively holds in being all things through the Spirit and the Word.

One might say then that God, as independent and primal Being, is the ground of all dependent and subsequent being. All things move along because the Prime Mover *keeps on* moving them. But there is a more per-sonal way of looking at this.

G. K. Chesterton, in his own inimitable and playful way, paints a picture of a creation that is reliable and relatively predictable because God takes infinite delight in its regularity. Chesterton says that the regularity and pre-dictability of the universe do not argue against the continuing personal care and creativity of God. To the contrary, God loves routine. And the clue we need for understanding this lies in the nature of children. Chesterton writes:

> The thing I mean can be seen, for instance, in children, when they find some game or joke that they specially enjoy. A child kicks his legs rhythmically through excess, not absence, of life. Because children have abounding vital-ity, because they are in spirit fierce and free, therefore they want things repeated and unchanged. They always say, "Do it again"; and the grown-up person does it again until he is nearly dead. For grown-up people are not strong enough to exult in monotony. But perhaps God is strong enough to exult in monotony. It is possible that God says every morning, "Do it again" to the sun; and every evening, "Do it again" to the moon. It may not be auto-matic necessity that makes all daisies alike; it may be that God makes every daisy separately, but has never got tired of making them. It may be that He has the eternal appetite of infancy; for we have sinned and grown old, and our Father is younger than we.[18]

Obviously this is not technical theological reflection of the kind you might find in a dense, academic book on systematic theology, volume 1, part 2, section 11, subsection B.5 (though the message is similar). Chester-ton's observation is more like poetry. And poetically he gives us a glimpse into the mystery of God's continuous creativity. Our heavenly Father, he tells us, younger by eternity than we, never fails to delight in the routine

---

[18]G. K. Chesterton, *Orthodoxy* (London: Bodley Head, 1927), pp. 106-7.

work of creation. God makes things continuously because God loves the things God makes, and God never tires of loving creation.

Chesterton's God is a lot like Carl Sandburg's God, who is no gentleman but a laborer in overalls, who goes to work "every day / at regular hours . . . and gets / dirty running the universe we know / about and several other universes / nobody knows about but Him."[19] The difference is simply that Chesterton's *God is a workman with the heart of a child.*

The Christian understanding of God as Creator is not of God the detached and uninvolved Watchmaker, as in classical deism and in much popular culture today, who only sees what we are doing from a great distance. God the Creator is intimately, passionately involved in creation continuously from beginning to end and at every nanosecond in between. And if we are to understand this Christian affirmation of creation as a whole as a process of divine creativity, as Jürgen Moltmann has written, "the corresponding doctrine of creation must then embrace creation in the beginning, creation in history, and the creation of the End-time: *creatio originalis-creatio continua-creatio nova.* 'Creation' is the term for God's initial creation, his historical creation, and his perfected creation."[20] All things spring continuously from the God who loves them into existence, loves them redemptively throughout their existence and loves them toward God's final and full purpose.

This brings us to the last thing I want to touch on regarding our confession of faith in God the Creator. When we say that God is Creator, we are saying that all things are endowed with purpose, that all things have meaning and are directed toward an end or a goal that lies beyond themselves. Karl Barth, in a series of lectures on Calvin's catechism, uses the French word *sens* to indicate this end beyond ourselves toward which our lives are directed. The word *sens* signifies both "meaning" and "direction."[21]

This is the idea we get from the outset of the Apostles' Creed. The "goal" of creation in the loving heart of the triune Creator provides creation's "purpose." Indeed, we might say that the most important issue at stake in the doctrine of creation is not the origin of all things but their destiny, the

---

[19]Carl Sandburg, *Honey and Salt* (New York: Harcourt, Brace & World, 1963), p. 39.

[20]Jürgen Moltmann, *God in Creation: The Gifford Lectures (1984-1985): An Ecological Doctrine of Creation* (London: SCM Press, 1985), p. 55.

[21]Karl Barth, *The Faith of the Church: A Commentary on the Apostles' Creed According to Calvin's Catechism* (New York: Meridian, 1958), p. 25.

goal and meaning *(sens)* of creaturely existence. All of this is contained in the affirmation *"I believe in God the Father Almighty, Creator of heaven and earth."* We are created out of God's love, for God's loving purpose. The meaning of human existence, indeed of the existence of all things, lies hidden in the heart of the Creator until God's loving heart is revealed in Jesus Christ. The secret purpose of creation has been unmasked, as it were, in the incarnation of God. So we move on to confess, in our next class, our faith in Jesus Christ.

Homework Assignments

1. *Coming to terms.* In higher trinitarian theology there is a word that describes the special kind of relationship among the persons of the Trinity: the Father, Son and Holy Spirit. The word is *perichoresis*. It is a Greek word that describes, literally, the interpenetration of each person of the Trinity in the other persons. Other theological words that describe the same relationship are *coinherence* or *circumincessio.*

These terms attempt to communicate a profound mystery of Christian theology: the mutual indwelling of the Father, Son and Holy Spirit in one another, and (by extension) the sharing of this divine life and communion that God shares as God with humanity through the Holy Spirit. Ancient teachers of the church such as John of Damascus, Athanasius, the Cappadocian fathers, Hilary of Poitiers and Augustine all provide important aspects of the development of this doctrine. But the doctrine itself is visible even in the New Testament, especially in the writings of Paul and John (note especially the Gospel of John chapters 14-16).

The idea communicated by the word *perichoresis* is crucial but very difficult to handle. We can best deal with it by focusing our attention on the incarnation. When the Word became flesh, God poured out his very life into creation while also and simultaneously taking into his own triune being our humanity in the supreme act of self-abnegation for the sake of others. In this free act of self-surrender God allows us to look into the very heart of his eternal being, into the Father's eternal outpouring *into the Son,* God's giving away of his own self without reservation. This act of self-giving is itself not merely some "it" but is God the Holy Spirit, flowing eternally from the Father to the Son and through the Son to humanity. As the Son in joyful surrender returns this love to the Father, the Spirit eternally returns to the Father, the Origin of all being. (We're talking "eternal" here, so we shouldn't think about chronological sequence at all. God the Father eternally empties and reciprocally is filled by the divine Son [the Word, or divine Self-Expression, or Imageless Image of God].)

The most helpful contemporary studies on the Trinity (and these are studies of a more technical nature) that touch on the subject of *perichoresis* are: Catherine Mowry LaCugna, *God for Us: The Trinity and Christian Life* (San Francisco: HarperSanFrancisco, 1991); Jürgen Moltmann, *The Trinity and the Kingdom of God* (London: SCM Press, 1981); Eberhard Jüngel, *God as the Mystery of the World* (Grand Rapids, Mich.: Eerdmans, 1983); and Thomas F. Torrance, *The Trinitarian Faith* (Edinburgh: T & T Clark, 1988). Let me also suggest a splendid and popularly written book by Thomas Smail, *The Forgotten Father* (London: Hodder & Stoughton, 1980).

2. *Rough and not-so-rough analogies.* We could think of this dynamic relationship in the heart of the triune God through the analogy of love. As the biblical Song of Solomon, St. Augustine, St. Bernard of Clairvaux and others have found, the analogy of love is enormously helpful in reflecting on what we believe about the inner life of God as divine communion. God the Lover (Father), eternally loves God the Beloved (Son). This eternal Love (the Holy Spirit) flows in utterly creative selflessness into the being of the Beloved in free and joyful surrender. God the Beloved eternally returns this Love to God the Lover. And the Love that flows in eternal interpenetration and mutuality from Lover to Beloved and from Beloved to Lover is God the Love, the Holy Spirit. Through the self-giving of Jesus Christ, through God's self-emptying assumption of our humanity, God shares God's own inner life and being in communion with us, uniting us to himself by the Word through the power of the Holy Spirit. Thus the God who is Love brings us into a real participation in the eternal life of God. We shall return to this idea again and again in our classes because it lies at the heart of our Christian faith.

I have found that one of the best ways to catch a glimpse of this doctrine is by contemplating the experience of music. We might think of the webs of relationships that occur in performance as an analogy for the communion shared by God the Father, Son and Holy Spirit, and the way God shares with us this same life. For instance, as the performers in a jazz ensemble play their music, the music flows from them and among them, moving them as they respond to one another. Anyone who has ever played in a good jazz group, and there are few joys as rich this side of heaven, knows exactly what this is like. The joy of the shared music, played by one in response to another, flowing among the members of the ensemble, seeks expression among others, the listeners. Any listener who has any soul at all is moved to respond, tapping feet and anything else that is at hand. The music has a life of its own, a life that draws the musicians together while not diminishing their discrete identities. The music draws the observers into a very real participation in and through the music.

This is a rough analogy, but it is analogy.

3. *Theology and all that jazz.* Your homework is to go to a live musical performance, if at all possible. You may want to make this a field trip for the entire class. Jazz and blues performances are best for understanding the doctrine of *perichoresis*, though a good string quartet will do the trick. If you can't get to a live performance, listen to a good live jazz or blues recording. B. B. King, James Cotton or Bobby Bland would be good choices for blues. There are lots of great jazz artists you might choose, but I recommend Miles Davis because he insisted on a high degree of spontaneity among his musicians.

After the performance either sit down and write out your reflections or talk about them as a group. Here are some questions to get you started.

☐ How does the analogy work? In what ways does a group of musicians in performance reflect the coinherence, the *perichoresis*, of the Trinity?

☐ How were you involved in the act of performance?

☐ How does this reflect analogically our participation in eternal life (the life of God)?

☐ What are some other analogies that might communicate the same eternal reality? What does this analogy say about the worship of God?

Class 5

I Believe in Jesus Christ,
His Only Son,
Our Lord

"'Almighty God, you have made us for yourself,
and our hearts are restless till they find their rest in you.'
Teach us to offer ourselves to your service—
that here we may have your peace,
and in the world to come may see you face to face,
through Jesus Christ our Lord. Amen."

ALTERNATIVE SERVICE BOOK, THE CHURCH OF ENGLAND;

PRAYER BASED ON ONE BY ST. AUGUSTINE OF HIPPO

POPE GREGORY THE GREAT GAVE AUGUSTINE OF CANTERBURY AND HIS FEL-
low missionaries some advice as they set off to evangelize England in 596.
(We'll leave to one side the historical fact that England already had a
vibrant Christian presence.) "My very dear sons, it is better never to under-
take any high enterprise than to abandon it when once begun."[1] As I begin
these lectures on Jesus Christ, these words have returned to my mind
repeatedly, not as a comfort but as a challenge and a goad. With this lecture, as Barth says, "We pass to the heart of the Christian confession."[2]
There's no turning back now for us, even though this subject will demand

---

[1]The Venerable Bede, *A History of the English Church and People*, trans. and ed. Leo Sherley-
Price, rev. R. E. Latham (London: Penguin Press, 1968), p. 67.
[2]Karl Barth, *Dogmatics in Outline*, trans. G. T. Thomson (New York: Harper & Row, Harper
Torchbook, 1959), p. 65.

of us all of the resources we have at hand. To make these lectures more helpful and more comprehensible, I will summarize the main ideas all along the way and will provide some hints to tackling the subject at crucial points.

Faith in Jesus Christ

We begin our study of Jesus Christ by quoting two modern confessions, both from the church in which I serve as a minister of Word and sacrament, the Presbyterian Church (U.S.A.).

The "Confession of 1967" begins with these words:

> The church confesses its faith
> when it bears witness to God's grace in Jesus Christ.

Then, after explaining what is meant by "confessing," it continues:

> In Jesus of Nazareth true humanity was realized once for all. Jesus, a Palestin-ian Jew, lived among his own people and shared their needs, temptations, joys, and sorrows. He expressed the love of God in word and deed and became a brother to all kinds of sinful men. But his complete obedience led him into conflict with his people. His life and teaching judged their good-ness, religious aspirations, and national hopes. Many rejected him and demanded his death. In giving himself freely for them he took upon himself the judgment under which all men stand convicted. God raised him from the dead, vindicating him as Messiah and Lord. The victim of sin became victor, and won the victory over sin and death for all men.[3]

The most recent Presbyterian confession, "The Brief Statement of Faith," speaks of Jesus Christ in this way:

> We trust in Jesus Christ,
>   fully human, fully God.
> Jesus proclaimed the reign of God:
>   preaching good news to the poor
>   and release to the captives,
>   teaching by word and deed

---

[3]Prebyterian Church (U.S.A.), "Confession of 1967," *The Constitution of the Presbyterian Church (U.S.A.): Part I: Book of Confessions* (Louisville, Ky.: The Office of the General Assembly, 1996), p. 262. This is, of course, a fine confession, giving us a valuable glimpse into the meaning and cost of God's incarnation. Unfortunately, it fails to convey the role of Rome in the death of Jesus and the threat of Christ to Roman tyranny. Jesus suffered the fate of many of his countrymen when he died on a Roman cross.

> and blessing the children,
> healing the sick
> and binding up the brokenhearted,
> eating with outcasts,
> forgiving sinners,
> and calling all to repent and believe the gospel.
> Unjustly condemned for blasphemy and sedition,
> Jesus was crucified,
>   suffering the depths of human pain
>   and giving his life for the sins of the world.
> God raised this Jesus from the dead,
>   vindicating his sinless life,
>   breaking the power of sin and evil,
>   delivering us from death to life eternal.[4]

As we've been saying all along, the primary question that we must begin with (over and over again) is the question of *who,* specifically, the theological question "Who is God?"

Today we are asking, *"Who is Jesus Christ?"*

In order to try to answer this question, we must begin in the actuality of the church's faith. There is no place else to which we can resort to answer theologically this question: "Who is Jesus Christ?" And the first thing we see when we begin in the actuality of the church's faith is this: our faith is in this Jesus who we believe to be the Christ, and this one whom we believe to be Christ is Jesus of Nazareth. There is in Christian faith no separating the title *Christ* from the personal name *Jesus.*[5]

It is our faith in Jesus Christ that defines who we are as Christians. Or perhaps I should say, *it is the Jesus Christ of our faith who defines who we are.*

The very name Christian is applied to us by extension. It was someone else's name before it was our name. As Hans Küng observes, "it is a fact too little remembered today that this word [Christian]—which arose in Antioch, according to the Acts of the Apostles—was first used within the context of world history more as a term of abuse than as an honorable title."[6]

---

[4]Prebyterian Church (U.S.A.), "A Brief Statement of Faith," *The Constitution of the Presbyterian Church (U.S.A.): Part I: Book of Confessions* (Louisville, Ky.: The Office of the General Assembly, 1996), p. 275.

[5]*Christ* derives from the Greek Χριστός for the Jewish title "Messiah." The word means, literally, "Anointed One."

[6]Hans Küng, *On Being a Christian,* trans. Edward Quinn (New York: Doubleday, 1976), p. 119.

Küng goes on to note that this "term of abuse" was used also in about A.D. 112 by Pliny the Younger, the Roman governor in the province of Bithynia in Asia Minor. Pliny reported to Emperor Trajan that these "Christians" stubbornly refused to worship the emperor. Instead they recited a hymn antiphonally to this "Christ as to a god," and bound "themselves together by an oath." Pliny seemed especially chagrined with the obstinance of these Christians who would not, for the sake of the empire, renounce their faith in Christ—even on pain of death.[7]

Tacitus, a friend of Pliny, said (in his history of Rome) that "Christians" got their name from a man who was executed during the reign of Tiberius Caesar. The executed man, he says, was called "Christus." We catch other glimpses of Christ and the Christians in the Roman source Suetonius, and in the Jewish historian Josephus. And as Küng says, the one thing we see repeatedly is this: whatever else we may say about Christianity, the Christian movement was from the beginning fundamentally linked to the person called Jesus Christ. That is to say Christianity was from the start neither primarily a worldview nor an idealist philosophy, but a movement of personal allegiance rooted in the faith experience of a particular people in particular places.[8]

When Polycarp, the bishop of Smyrna, was martyred around A.D. 156, the witness he bore with his life was not to a philosophical system but to a person whom he believed to be none other than God in the flesh. Polycarp, a man who lived to be very old and is said by Ignatius to have been personally acquainted with some of the apostles, including John, was marched into the stadium of Smyrna where the Roman proconsul threatened him with death unless he would renounce his faith in Christ.

"Think of your age," beseeched the proconsul, "Swear by the genius of Caesar. Swear, and I will release you; just curse this Christ!"

But Polycarp answered, "For eighty and six years have I served him, and he has never wronged me; how then can I blaspheme my king who saved me?"

And so Polycarp went to his death confessing his faith in Jesus Christ not as a philosophical principle nor as the symbol for a system of morality, but

---

[7]Ibid., pp. 119-20. Also note Henry Bettenson, ed., *Documents of the Christian Church* (London: Oxford University Press, 1959), pp. 3-4.

[8]Küng, *On Being a Christian,* p. 120.

as a person to whom he was loyal unto death.[9]

Now the reason I want us to start our study of the second article of the creed with this confessional and historical discussion is this: When we say that we believe in Jesus Christ, we are saying that our lives have been claimed by another—or an Other. And this other who has laid claim to our lives is identical with a particular man, Jesus of Nazareth, whom we believe to be the Christ and God incarnate.

This Jesus Christ shapes the form, the content and ultimately the goal of our faith. That which we believe and teach and preach is not simply a set of moral precepts that were taught by him, nor merely a set of idealistic principles distilled from his thought. That which we believe and teach is substantially this Jesus Christ himself, in the unity of his person, Son of God and Son of Man.

As Paul says, "I determined to know nothing among you except Jesus Christ, and him crucified" (1 Cor 2:2). This is the substance of the teaching and preaching of the Christian church, a stumbling block, Paul says, to his own Jewish people and foolishness to the Greeks (1 Cor 1:18-25).

From the very beginning of the Christian community this fact has to one degree or another separated us from surrounding communities: We believe ourselves to be confronted personally, historically and eschatologically with the very Godness of God in the humanity of this particular man, Jesus of Nazareth. This is the content of the apostolic message, the *kerygma*. This is the mystery that the great creeds have attempted to preserve without reduction.[10]

Summary. When we turn to the pages of the New Testament, we are struck by the fact that faith in the Christ is inseparable from the Jesus of history. According to the witness of the New Testament, there is (in other words) no getting behind the Christ of faith, the Christ of the church, to a hidden Jesus of history. Jesus Christ remains hidden, but hidden in the unity of Jesus and Christ and hidden in the very midst of revelation. It is the clear witness of the New Testament that there is only this Jesus whom his followers believe to be the Christ and to whom

---

[9]J. B. Lightfoot, ed. *The Apostolic Fathers: Clement, Ignatius and Polycarp* vol. 3, pt. 2 (Peabody, Mass.: Hendrickson, 1989). Also a popular presentation of Polycarp's martyrdom appears in *Christian History* 9, no. 3 (1990): 14-15.

[10]John Leith provides a helpful discussion of this issue in his *Reformed Imperative: What the Church Has to Say That No One Else Can Say* (Philadelphia: Westminster Press, 1988), pp. 48-56.

they bore witness in everything they wrote.

Which brings us to a consideration of one of the most spectacular detours into a dead-end street ever produced in Christendom, a detour that, incidentally, continues to this day to attract many scholars.

The Quest for the Historical Jesus

During and especially in the wake of the Age of Enlightenment, a conviction developed among many religious scholars that there is a Jesus of history buried beneath layers of dogmatic sediment. Christians, for whatever reasons, were thought to have covered over this authentic Jesus of history with elaborate teachings about the Christ of faith.

A variety of biblical scholars, theologians, philosophers and historians took it as their task to restore the Jesus of history by cutting through what they saw as layers of Christian tradition. They believed that eventually they would find the true historical Jesus, a good and moral teacher who preached the ethics of the kingdom of God, who tried to establish this kingdom on earth and whose heroic and tragic death gave his life's work its full meaning, inspiring other people to follow his example.

The quest for the historical Jesus, as it came to be called, began as an attempt to ground faith in history. In fact, historical studies were seen virtually as a sacrament through which we would finally be brought into the presence of the true Jesus. But, while the nineteenth-century search for the historical Jesus began in enthusiasm, it ended in skepticism. Actually there were two endings to this project. The first ending was *described* by Albert Schweitzer; the second was in Schweitzer's own *work*.

The quest for the historical Jesus that Schweitzer described was the search of classical liberal theology for Jesus the great moral teacher. Especially after Immanuel Kant, many of the leading philosophers and theologians saw the value of Christianity as merely an ethical-religious movement.[11] The quest for the historical Jesus was the search for the founder of this movement. But the various attempts to discover the Jesus of history, heroic as they often were, ended in the rather dubious "discovery" of essentially a nineteenth-century moralist (a German-Protestant moralist at that) dressed in the clothes of a first-century Palestinian rabbi. As George

---

[11]See Alasdair Heron's discussion of the philosophical-theological background of this project in his survey *A Century of Protestant Theology* (Cambridge: Lutterworth, 1980), pp. 16-60.

Tyrell, the Roman Catholic scholar, has said, critiquing Adolf von Harnack, the last great representative of the nineteenth-century quest: "The Christ that Harnack sees, looking back through nineteen centuries of Catholic darkness, is only the reflection of a Liberal Protestant face, seen at the bottom of a deep well."[12]

Schweitzer, in his monumental work of biblical criticism, *The Quest of the Historical Jesus*, said that the whole project of trying to discover the historical Jesus of Nazareth (who preached the ethic of the kingdom of God, who founded this kingdom on earth and died to give his work its final consecration) was a doomed project from the outset. The Jesus sought by classical liberalism, Schweitzer wrote, "never had any existence." But Schweitzer was not really throwing out the entire program of searching for a historical Jesus. While he believed that classical liberalism hadn't found the true Jesus of history, there was nonetheless a true Jesus of history to be found, or at least the shadow of such a historical Jesus: a remote, strange, apocalyptic and ultimately unknowable prophet whose real significance is not his moral example but his "spiritual force" compelling us to follow him into conflict with the powers of this world. Schweitzer writes:

> The historical foundation of Christianity as built up by rationalistic, by liberal, and by modern theology no longer exists; but that does not mean that Christianity has lost its historical foundation. The work which historical theology thought itself bound to carry out, and which fell to pieces just as it was nearing completion, was only the brick facing of the real immovable historical foundation which is independent of any historical confirmation or justification.
>
> Jesus means something to our world because a mighty spiritual force streams forth from Him and flows through our time also. This fact can neither be shaken nor confirmed by any historical discovery. It is the solid foundation of Christianity.[13]

The mistake classical liberalism made, according to Schweitzer, was that it supposed the historical Jesus could have more meaning for our time and

---

[12]Tyrell is cited by James C. Livingston, *Modern Christian Thought: From the Enlightenment to Vatican II* (New York: Macmillan, 1971), p. 285. You may want to look for yourself at Harnack, whose popularly written *Das Wesen des Christentums* [literally, "The Essence of Christianity"] (1900) was translated into English (1901) as *What Is Christianity?* trans. Thomas Bailey Saunders (New York: Harper & Row, Harper Torchbook, 1957).

[13]Albert Schweitzer, *The Quest of the Historical Jesus: A Critical Study of Its Progress from Reimarus to Wrede*, trans. W. Montgomery (London: Adam & Charles Black, 1910), p. 397.

could be more relevant to our lives by being presented to us as a man like ourselves. This was a mistake, first, because such a familiar and friendly Jesus *never existed,* and second, because *the spiritual life cannot be created through historical investigation.* Jesus has significance in our time not because he is a familiar figure whom we can imitate in our moral life but because he "spiritually" arises within people.[14]

The Jesus who did exist in the first century remains, Schweitzer said, a stranger, a distant prophet whose dreams we cannot share, "One unknown," virtually nameless and faceless, a man consumed with an apocalyptic vision, who attempted to force the dawning of God's eschatological kingdom with his own death.[15] "Jesus as a concrete historical personality remains a stranger to our time, but His spirit, which lies hidden in His words is known in simplicity, and its influence is direct."[16]

The real historical Jesus was, according to Schweitzer, a complete failure in human terms. He did not accomplish what he hoped to accomplish with his death. He did not usher in God's miraculous and otherworldly kingdom of heaven. He hangs on the cross tragically broken, but, hanging there, he beckons us to follow him. And this Jesus, hidden from the direct glare of historical investigation, reveals himself spiritually "in the toils, the conflicts, the sufferings" that we share in his fellowship, as we follow him.[17]

From around the beginning of the twentieth century, Christian theology was confronted with two rather stark alternatives (at least as outlined by Schweitzer). Either one could dance to the tune of classical Liberalism (whose best teacher Adolf von Harnack was at that time teaching in Berlin) or one could sing the Romantic dirge of Schweitzer (who would soon abandon theological studies and Europe to begin his second career as a saint). From a historical perspective there can be little doubt, based on our best documentary evidence, that Schweitzer's apocalyptic prophet is the more accurate portrayal of Jesus of Nazareth, as contemporary biblical scholars like Bart Ehrman and Dale Allison have recently demonstrated so ably.[18] What is perhaps most fascinating is the way scholars connected with

---

[14]Ibid., p. 399.
[15]Ibid., p. 401.
[16]Ibid., p. 399.
[17]Ibid., p. 401.
[18]Bart D. Ehrman, *Jesus, Apocalyptic Prophet of the New Millennium* (New York: Oxford University Press, 1999); Dale Allison, *Jesus of Nazareth: Millenarian Prophet* (Minneapolis: Fortress, 1998).

the well-publicized Jesus Seminar, most notably John Dominic Crossan and Marcus J. Borg, continue to work out the rather questionable legacy of the classical liberal project.[19]

Nevertheless, the whole quest for a historical Jesus, cast in the image and reflecting the interests of the researchers who search for him, has been called into question at the most fundamental level. Indeed, to many the product of the quest has been judged wishful thinking or even idolatry. Jesus the moral teacher was the product of nineteenth-century moral teachers, a reflection of their faces in the depths of the well they looked down into. Despite Crossan's elaborate methods of tracking the historical Jesus, one may well find in the Jesus of history yet another, though more ironic mirrored reflection of those who search. Schweitzer's Jesus, the strange and unknown millenarian prophet, was certainly closer to the Jesus who walked the dusty roads of Palestine. But as other scholars have noted, the Jesus of the New Testament remains this disappointed prophet only if we refuse to admit the most crucial statements of the Gospels, the rather direct, simple, surprising (and surprised) narratives regarding his resurrection from the dead.[20]

Summary: What many theologians gradually came to see regarding the so-called historical Jesus was this: while there are some things we can learn about the life of Jesus of Nazareth, about his world and his beliefs, there is no getting behind the church's faith in Christ to a historical Jesus prior to or separate from the faith of the Christian community. From the beginning we are confronted with a unified reality, and this unified reality *is* Jesus whom we believe to be the Christ of God.

The Content of the *Kerygma*

The substance of the preaching of the early church (what is called the

---

[19]John Dominic Crossan, *The Historical Jesus: The Life of a Mediterranean Jewish Peasant* (San Francisco: HarperSanFrancisco, 1991); and his *Jesus: A Revolutionary Biography* (San Francisco: HarperSanFrancisco, 1994); Marcus J. Borg, *Meeting Jesus Again for the First Time: The Historical Jesus & the Heart of Contemporary Faith* (San Francisco: HarperSanFrancisco, 1994); also see Luke Timothy Johnson, *The Real Jesus: The Misguided Quest for the Historical Jesus and the Truth of the Traditional Gospels* (San Francisco: HarperSanFrancisco, 1996); and Ben Witherington III, *The Jesus Quest: The Third Search for the Jew of Nazareth* (Downers Grove, Ill.: InterVarsity Press, 1995).

[20]See, for example, N. T. Wright, *Jesus and the Victory of God* (Minneapolis: Fortress, 1996); and his *The Original Jesus: The Life and Vision of a Revolutionary* (Grand Rapids, Mich.: Eerdmans, 1996). For a more detailed analysis of the quests for the historical Jesus see Hans Schwarz, *Christology* (Grand Rapids, Mich.: Eerdmans, 1998), pp. 7-71.

kerygma) with reference to this Jesus whom his followers believed to be the Christ was made up of a clearly discernible pattern of faith statements. Generally, the kerygma of the early church included the following elements of proclamation:

☐ Jesus has inaugurated the fulfillment of the messianic prophecy.

☐ He went about doing good and performing miracles.

☐ He was crucified, according to God's design.

☐ He was raised on the third day and exalted to heaven.

☐ He will return again in judgment.

☐ Because this gospel is true, we should repent, believe and be baptized.

(See Acts 2:14-38; 13:16-41; 15:1-21; 17:1-15; Romans 1:1-17; 10:1-15; 1 Corinthians 15:3-19; and Hebrews 14 for various representations of the *kerygmatic* message of the early church.)[21]

The picture of Jesus that emerges from this holistic presentation (that is, the actual content of the church's preaching) is compelling:

☐ The good teacher who spoke those marvelous words that the Gospel writers collected together as the Sermon on the Mount is the same man who saw himself as the apocalyptic Son of Man coming on clouds of glory.

☐ The person who asked his disciples to take up their crosses and follow him is the same person these disciples say was risen from the dead, an event the disciples seemed as surprised about and as doubtful of as anyone.

☐ There is no separating the words of this teacher from his actions. His life and his teachings were cut from the same bolt of cloth. The *kerygma* presents a garment made up of many threads (miraculous healing, apocalyptic preaching, teaching the kingdom of God, acts of mercy and judgment) woven into a single garment.

Our choices regarding *how* we will see Jesus Christ are therefore somewhat limited. He may indeed have been a heroic apocalyptic failure, as Schweitzer thought, or he may have simply been an obscure Galilean preacher who was put to death by Rome. But the texts we have in hand do

---

[21]C. H. Dodd, *The Apostolic Preaching and its Developments* (London: Hodder & Stoughton, 1936). For varying treatments of the *kerygma* see Robert H. Gundry, *A Survey of the New Testament* (Grand Rapids, Mich.: Zondervan, 1970); Rudolf Bultmann, *New Testament and Mythology: and Other Basic Writings*, ed. Schubert M. Ogden (Philadelphia: Fortress, 1984).

not seem to have left us the option of believing that he was a neo-Kantian moralist. The best sources we have are unabashed proclamations by a group of people who were convinced that this person is nothing less than God, *Kyrios Christos* (Christ the Lord). What we have said about him is said by them.

Dietrich Bonhoeffer explains that in light of this awareness either we can "remain on the historical plane and treat the *Kyrios-Christos* cult as one of a number of similar cults," or we can "pass from historical to dogmatic [i.e., theological] study."[22] And as Bonhoeffer recognizes, the beginning point for this theological study of Jesus Christ as Lord is personal faith in him, faith given by the Holy Spirit in the hearing of the Word of God, and mediated through the witness of the church. Historical studies, though helpful in their way (and they frequently are very helpful), cannot serve as a sacrament by which we have access to Jesus of Nazareth.[23]

Bonhoeffer writes, "There is . . . no way from historical investigation to absoluteness. There is no absolute ground of faith in history." And so, he asks, where is it that our faith gets "its sufficient ground to know, when history is uncertain?" He answers, "There is only the witness of the Risen One to himself, through which the church bears witness to him as the Historical One. By the miracle of his presence in the church he bears witness to himself here and now as the one who was historical then."[24]

The preaching of the community of faith confronts us with this message, a message the content of which is Christ Jesus and him crucified, and hearing this message we stand by the power of God's Spirit in the same relationship to this Jesus Christ as did his original hearers. This Christ, *through* the preaching of the community, makes God's radical and comprehensive claim on our lives, even as God claimed the lives of those who lived centuries before us.

In this century the most persuasive attempt to present this view was made by the New Testament theologian Rudolf Bultmann, though in this

---

[22]Dietrich Bonhoeffer, *Christ the Center* (New York: Harper & Row, 1966), p. 72.

[23]For careful and critical analysis of various aspects of the context of Jesus (and for a sense of how helpful historical studies of Jesus can be), see Raymond E. Brown, *The Death of the Messiah: From Gethsemane to the Grave,* 2 vols. (New York: Doubleday, 1994); E. P. Sanders, *The Historical Figure of Jesus* (London: Penguin, 1993); Robert Eisenman, *James the Brother of Jesus* (London: Penguin, 1997); Anthony J. Saldarini, *Matthew's Christian-Jewish Community* (Chicago: University of Chicago Press, 1994).

[24]Bonhoeffer, *Christ the Center,* p. 75.

Bultmann is similar to Søren Kierkegaard, the early Karl Barth (in his controversial commentary *The Epistle to the Romans*) and most evangelical Christian preaching.[25] We can call this the "crisis model of faith." In this model the preaching (*kerygma*) of the Christian community bears witness to Christ's life and words. God creates a hearing for this proclamation among us at a particular moment (or at various particular moments throughout our lives). The moment God creates this hearing for the Word is called the "moment of crisis" (or in evangelical Christianity, the "conversion experience"). God graciously gives us faith in the hearing of the proclamation of Jesus Christ. And through faith this very same Jesus Christ (through the Holy Spirit) lays claim to our lives. (See figure 5.1 for a diagram of this model of faith.)

Kierkegaard observed that those persons who saw Jesus in the flesh have no advantage over those of us who only hear the proclamation because *faith comes through hearing the gospel.* And through hearing the gospel in faith we encounter Christ Jesus himself. To return to Paul again, we learn that even those who knew Jesus of Nazareth in the flesh and who believed in him as Christ and Lord no longer knew him "after the flesh," but by faith. (2 Cor 5:16). Those who knew Jesus in the flesh might know him "after the flesh" and still not know *who* he is. By the same token, those who now hear the proclamation of Jesus Christ crucified, though they never saw Jesus in the flesh, by faith may penetrate to a full understanding of who he is as he lays claim to their lives.[26]

Summary. This is the focal point for our theological inquiry. The reality of our faith in Christ presses upon us the responsibility of understanding who this one is who confronts us and claims our lives for God.

---

[25]Karl Barth, *The Epistle to the Romans*, trans. Edwyn C. Hoskyns (London: Oxford University Press, 1933). The second edition of *Romans* burst on the theological scene in 1921, launching Barth's career in academic theology and what became known as the theology of crisis.

[26]Søren Kierkegaard, *Philosophical Fragments/Johannes Climacus*, ed. and trans. Howard V. Hong and Edna H. Hong (Princeton, N.J.: Princeton University Press, 1987). "If the believer is the believer and knows the god by having received the condition from the god himself, then in exactly the same sense someone who comes later must receive the condition from the god himself and cannot receive it at second hand, because, if that were the case, then the second hand would have to be the god himself, and in that case there is no question of a second hand. But if the one who comes later receives the condition from the god himself, then he is a contemporary, a genuine contemporary—which indeed only the believer is and which every believer is" (p. 69).

The Christological Controversies

There are basically two ways to approach the study of Jesus Christ (at least, so goes the conventional wisdom). Either we can approach the doctrine of Christology from *below* or from *above*. That is, either we can approach Jesus Christ by discovering who he was historically and existentially— studying his words and actions, his historical existence, his humanity, and the effects of belief in him on the Christian community—and then attempt to ascend to his divinity, or we can begin with his divinity—his eternal being as the second person of the Trinity, as the eternally begotten image of the Father—and only subsequently attempt to descend to his humanity and the existential effects of belief in him. The Synoptic Gospels (Matthew, Mark and Luke) are usually cited as examples of the former (Christology from below), while the Fourth Gospel (the Gospel of John), the Pauline Epistles and the epistle to the Hebrews are cited as examples of the latter (as Christology from above).

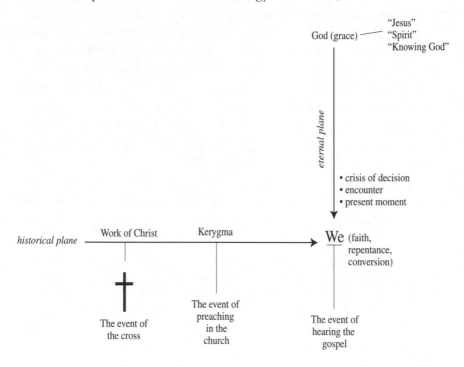

Figure 5.1. The existential (evangelical) model of Christian faith and relationship with God (as seen in Bultmann, Kierkegaard, early Barth and evangelical Christianity). Adapted from James B. Torrance, *Worship, Community and the Triune God of Grace: The Didsbury Lectures* (Carlyle, U.K.: Paternoster, 1996), p. 14.

In fact, based on what we have already observed, Christology is properly done from below and above at the very same time. Though the narrative character of the Synoptic Gospels is more what we might call biographical in style, though they are clearly something quite different from biographies, and the Johannine writings are perhaps more typically theological in tone, and the Pauline Epistles are, in turn, more consciously theological, ethical and topical, and the book of Hebrews is highly liturgical, yet in all these sources the object is the same—to bear witness to the reality of God's self-revelation in Jesus Christ. Any Christology, if it is to remain true to the total witness of holy Scripture, is at once from below and above. Of course, that is what our confessions of faith are saying too.

"A Christian," as Karl Barth once observed, "is one who makes confession of Christ. And the Christian confession is confession of Jesus Christ the Lord."[27] We recognize this fact when we say, "I believe in Jesus Christ." We are making a faith statement, a claim or assertion that is grounded in our belief, our trust in the God revealed in Jesus Christ. But, having said this, we are left with the daunting task of understanding what we have said. We are compelled to ask, over and over again, in different ways and from different perspectives, this single, unavoidable and most crucial question: *"Who is this Jesus Christ whom we confess as the Lord?"*

From its beginning the Christian community has been reflecting on the meaning of this question, the question that is enshrined in our earliest confession of faith, "Jesus Christ is Lord" (Rom 10:9; Phil 2:11; cf. 1 Cor 8:6). And from the beginning we have had countless controversies concerning what this confession means.

The title Lord (Greek, *Kyrios*), without a doubt, was no ordinary title of respect for those Jewish men and women who were the first followers of Christ. *Kyrios* was that word used in the Greek translation of the Jewish Scriptures, the Septuagint, in place of the holy and unspeakable name of the Lord God, YHWH (we've filled in the missing vowels to make the name "Jehovah" or "Yaweh," but in point of fact, because the ineffable name is sacred, it cannot be uttered, no one really knows what the vowels were). *Kyrios*, in other words, stands in for the sacred name of the Lord. A Greek-speaking Jewish follower of Jesus, like Paul for example, would not lightly place the title *Kyrios* on his lips. Even more solemnly would he

---

[27]Barth, *Dogmatics in Outline*, p. 65.

apply it to the human Jesus who had met his death at the hands of Rome. Yet this title is applied to Jesus by Christians who, like Paul, understood its deepest meaning.

"Who is this Jesus Christ?" they asked.

"*He is the Lord,*" they answered.

From the very outset of the New Testament, this is the antiphonal message that meets us. And the complicated and highly technical controversies that occupied the church for much of its first six centuries have their origin here in these most basic questions:

☐ If the Lord God is one, how can Jesus be God?

☐ If God is eternal and immutable, how can God become flesh in this Jesus who suffered and died?

☐ How can Jesus Christ, at the same time, be a human being and God's eternal Son, both a creature and the divine Word through whom all things are created and sustained in being?

These questions and others were posed from the time of the early church. The ways they were answered shape who we are and what we believe today. And the mistakes that were made in trying to provide answers to these questions are also still with us. For instance:

☐ Something of the fear of the world and human flesh that plagued Docetic Gnosticism and caused Christians influenced by Gnosticism to split the earthly Jesus from the heavenly Christ is still with us in some New Age expressions of Christianity and in a lot of Christian churches that would rather worship a transcendent deity than follow a God who became flesh.

☐ The tendency of the Ebionites to reduce Christianity to a set of rules is not unknown in our time. For some people (some very "enlightened" people) Christianity is a topflight morality and little more, founded by a great moralist and teacher.

As we go through our discussion, we will notice other parallels between the ancient heresies and some modern and often venerable expressions of the Christian faith. The discussion that follows is a fairly detailed historical-theological sort of description. In other words, one may tend to get bogged down in it a bit. If you do get bogged down and are trying to figure out why in the world this guy is telling me all this stuff, you may want to go directly to the section titled "What Does It All Mean?" Then you can work back through the historical-theological details with a little better perspective. With that in mind, here goes.

Docetism and Ebionitism. The two earliest heresies in the Christian church resulted from trying to understand the relationship between Jesus and God. In one case (Docetic Gnosticism), the divinity of Jesus Christ was preserved at the expense of his humanity. In the other case (Ebionitism), Jesus Christ's humanity was safeguarded at the expense of his divinity.

The Gnostic movement (if we can properly call it that) predated the beginning of the Christian faith. Its name reflects the Greek word for knowledge *(gnosis)*, and refers to the Gnostic belief that their adherents possessed a secret knowledge hidden from most humanity, a knowledge the possession of which gave (or was) salvation. The Gnostics believed that the eternal realm of the spirit alone is good and that the material world of existence is evil. Thus the Docetic Gnostics, those Christians influenced by Gnostic doctrines, using various theological formulae, said that Jesus Christ only *appeared* or *seemed* to be human (the word *docetic* comes from the Greek *dokeō,* meaning "I seem") but that he was really fully divine all along. For Jesus Christ to be truly human would mean that he was tainted by the evil of the material world. The incarnation, according to Docetic thought, was essentially an elaborate charade. Some Gnostic Christians said that the divine Son only dressed up in human flesh but did not *become* flesh and blood. Others said that the divine spirit or "Christ" came to rest upon the human Jesus at his baptism and departed from him prior to the crucifixion (thus the cry, "My God, My God, why hast thou forsaken me?") because it was unthinkable that God could suffer (suffering and changeability were features of the material world, not of the eternal realm).

Another contrasting solution to the relationship between Jesus and God was provided early on by the Ebionites, a Jewish-Christian sect (the name means "poor ones") that believed that the divinity of Jesus Christ threatened Judaic monotheism. While the Gnostics affirmed some form of the divinity of the Son while denying his actual humanity, the Ebionites believed the exact opposite; they affirmed the humanity of the Son while denying or playing down his divinity. Jesus of Nazareth was, they reasoned, a great teacher, a prophet, the Messiah promised by God. But, according to these early Christians, also known as the Judaizers, Jesus of Nazareth is merely human.

Both Docetic Gnostics and Ebionites were countered by the church's earliest writers. Much of the New Testament, especially Luke's Gospel and the

Gospel according to John, the book of Acts, Paul's letters and the epistle to the Hebrews, carry a countermessage to the Ebionites. And Gnosticism drew considerable fire specifically from the first epistle of John (see 1 Jn 1:1-4). Irenaeus of Lyons (c. 130-c. 200; see his *Against Heresies,* book 5) decisively countered his Gnostic opponents in his theology, the church's first.[28]

Justin Martyr, our first apologist, and the rise of Logos theology. In the second century, especially through the work of the brilliant apologist Justin Martyr (c. 100-c. 165), what has come to be called "Logos Christology" developed as a means of handling the extremely intricate questions around the relationship of Jesus and God, especially in conversation with the surrounding culture.

Justin was accused by his learned neighbors of blasphemy because he worshiped Jesus Christ as God. Drawing on John's Gospel and carefully relating its description of the divine Logos to the already familiar Stoic philosophical category of the Logos (the rational principle that pervades the universe), Justin was able to explain that the divine Logos that creatively permeates and gives order to the universe has uniquely become flesh in this man Jesus Christ. Thus to worship Christ is not to blaspheme against God but to recognize God in the flesh.

Justin did what all good apologists do.[29] He explained the Christian faith in terms and modes of thought comprehensible to his culture in the hope that he might convince others of the rationality or reasonableness of Christianity. In the early nineteenth century, in the context of German culture

---

[28]With reference to Docetism and other Gnostic variations see Henry Chadwick, *The Early Church* (London: Penguin, 1967), pp. 32-41; David Christie-Murray, *A History of Heresy* (Oxford: Oxford University Press, 1976), pp. 21-32; Elaine Pagels, *The Gnostic Gospels* (New York: Random House, 1979). On Ebionitism see Christie-Murray, *History of Heresy,* pp. 13-20; Robert Eisenman, *James the Brother of Jesus* (New York: Penguin, 1997). A fascinating resource on these and other heretical movements in the early church is Arland J. Hultgren and Steven A. Haggmark, *The Earliest Christian Heretics: Readings From Their Opponents* (Minneapolis: Fortress, 1996).

[29]The word *apologist* refers to those who make a case for the Christian faith, defending what we believe and commending it to those who do not share our beliefs. As such, the apologist does not say, "I'm sorry." Rather, he says, "We believe this. . . . Let me explain why." The earliest apologists countered claims among non-Christians that Christians are cannibals (because of their misunderstanding of the Lord's Supper, the eating of the "body of Christ" and the drinking of his "blood"), that we indulge in illicit sexual practices and orgies (because of their misunderstanding of the meaning of the *agapé,* or love, feasts) and that we are atheists (because we deny the existence of the classical Greco-Roman pantheon). Apologists traditionally have dealt with cultural, social, philosophical and moral defenses of the Christian faith, seeking a common ground for understanding with non-Christians.

under the influence of Immanuel Kant, Friedrich Schleiermacher did much the same thing in his *Speeches on Religion to Its Cultured Despisers*.[30] In the next century, apologists like C. S. Lewis, in his famous radio talks,[31] and Reinhold Niebuhr, for example, in his early book *Does Civilization Need Religion?* articulated the Christian faith in terms appropriate to twentieth-century popular and intellectual culture in Western Europe and North America.[32]

Sabellius and Paul of Samosata. Between the late second and the early third centuries, two potentially influential views developed: those represented by Sabellius and by Paul of Samosata. In both cases the attempt was made to answer the various questions raised in the incarnation by reducing the mystery of God to a simple "one size fits all" formula.

We know very little about Sabellius. Scholars tend to place him in Rome with like-minded Christian thinkers such as Noetus and Praxeas in the early third century. What we do know about is his rather disastrous attempt to explain the relationship of Jesus Christ to God.

Sabellius employed what later came to be known as modalism, or modalist monarchianism, a view that so emphasized the oneness of God that the three persons of the Trinity became merely successive functions of the one God, or "modes of being." Each mode is in turn temporarily assumed by God, one after the other. In other words, God is not *eternally* Father, *eternally* Son, *eternally* Spirit, but is Father, Son and Spirit in succession, one mode following another.

The idea is similar to the ancient Greek theater in which one actor plays several parts by putting on different masks. Interestingly (and this is a fact you may want to file somewhere), the various characters played by these actors were given the name *persona*. Christ, in this view, is the second mode of being (the second *persona*), which the singular God assumes. God remains hidden behind the various masks he wears at various times. This suggests that God changes his "character" depending on when he appears and to whom. You can still get a whiff of this old heresy when someone

---

[30]His *Reden über die Religion* was actually published in 1799, but the English translation, *On Religion: Speeches to Its Cultured Despisers*, did not appear until 1893; the two stand like bookends around the nineteenth century. A good English edition is that translated by John Oman, published in 1958 by Harper & Row.

[31]Subsequently collected and published as *Mere Christianity* (New York: Macmillan, 1952).

[32]Reinhold Niebuhr, *Does Civilization Need Religion? A Study in the Social Resources and Limitations of Religion in Modern Life* (New York: Macmillan, 1928).

says that we don't worship the God of the Old Testament but the God of the New Testament.

The second view put forth during this period came from Paul of Samosata. He also attempted to answer the questions posed in the incarnation by reducing the mystery to a simple equation. Paul, who also lived in the third century and served as bishop of Antioch, taught that God consists of a closely knit trinity of Father, Wisdom and Word. This Godhead formed an absolute unity, a single *hypostasis,* as he called it (don't forget this word either) until creation. Paul's Christology, or doctrine of Christ, anticipated that of Nestorius (fifth century). Paul said that at the incarnation, the divine Word came upon the human being Jesus of Nazareth, and rested on him. But this divine Word was completely separate from the human Jesus and was not identifiable with him. Thus one could say that Jesus was different from the prophets of the Old Testament—but *only in degree.* Jesus, in other words, was merely a human being under the powerful influence of divine inspiration.

Arius versus Athanasius. We have already alluded briefly to the fourth century controversy between Arius (c. 250-c. 336) and Athanasius of Alexandria (c. 296-373). Arius held the view that "the Son of God" is a creature and is accorded the title of Son only honorifically. There was, according to the Arius, a time when the Son did not exist. Like all creatures, he was created out of nothing by God. Thus knowledge of Jesus Christ does not provide knowledge of God. The Son of God might be considered a perfect creature, in the view of Arius, and perhaps he could be considered in some sense "divine," as long as we understand the term to signify his participation in God's grace. But the Son is not of the same nature or essence as God, who is eternally transcendent, immutable, immortal, without beginning, all wise, all good, sovereign and self-existent. Jesus Christ was flesh and blood. He participated fully in the realm of mutability. Jesus Christ might not be entirely like human beings because of his unique status among creatures and his role in relation to God, but neither is he fully God. He is something else, some other order of being altogether, a sort of demigod, neither fully God nor fully human.[33]

The Greek language in which the debate with Arius and his followers was carried out provides us with the terms that became the signature of the

---

[33]J. N. D. Kelly, *Early Christian Doctrines,* rev. ed. (London: A & C Black, 1977), pp. 226-30.

controversy: Arius insisted that the Lord Jesus Christ and God the Father were of utterly different essences, though some of his followers (those known as semi-Arians) compromised by saying that Jesus Christ was of *similar essence* with the Father (thus, *homoiousias: homoi* means "similar"). Athanasius and the orthodox party (which eventually won the day at the Council of Nicea), by contrast, said that Jesus Christ is of the *same essence* as God the Father (thus, *homoousias: homo* means "same"). This crucial distinction is preserved in the Nicene-Constantinopolitan Creed (in its received form, A.D. 381) and comes to us via the Western form of the creed, as we have it in most of our hymn books, prayer books and books of confession:

> We believe in . . . one Lord Jesus Christ, the only-begotten Son of God, begotten of His Father before all worlds; God of God; Light of Light; very God of Very God; Begotten, not made; Being of one substance with the Father, by whom all things were made; who for us men and for our salvation came down from heaven and was incarnate by the Holy Ghost of the Virgin Mary, and was made man, and was crucified also for us under Pontius Pilate. He suffered and was buried, and the third day he rose again according to the scriptures . . . (The Nicene Creed)

We have already noted how Arius undercut the simple biblical understanding of revelation. The New Testament said that when we have seen Jesus Christ, we have seen the Father. Arius *could not* and indeed *did not want* to make such a statement. Athanasius and the orthodox party, by contrast, wanted to dispel all doubt on this point. When we have seen Jesus Christ, the Son of God, we have seen the Father, they said, because the Father and the Son share the very same essential being. And this Jesus Christ whom we believe to be "very God" is also and not one bit less "very human," God in the flesh—God in *our* flesh.

Perceptive theologians, like Gregory of Nazianzus (329-389), indeed also saw the threat of Arian theology to the Christian understanding of atonement, a threat that understood that if Jesus Christ is not God, atonement is impossible, and that if Jesus Christ is not human, atonement is not effective. His famous phrase is "What remains unassumed is unhealed." Jesus Christ himself, Gregory understood, is the atonement of God and humanity. But if Jesus Christ is not both fully God and fully human, then there is no *at-one-ment* between God and humanity.

Patristic writers, like Gregory (and his colleagues Gregory of Nyssa and

Basil the Great), understood the human person as essentially sin-sick, in need of healing that only God can provide. And the healing we need cannot be the result of the doctor writing a prescription or recommending that his patient get some rest. For them the atonement was a case of the doctor becoming the patient in order to heal the patient's sickness. Only God could do this because only God had the healing power that would rid our humanity "of what ails us." But if God did not actually become fully human, then God's healing power would not touch and heal our condition, or would (at very least) leave a part of us untouched and unhealed.

Apollinarius. Gregory's comments on the atonement help clarify why the teaching of Apollinarius (310-c. 390) was declared heretical by the church. Apollinarius worked with an anthropology (a conception of humanity, from the Greek word *anthropos* meaning "man") that divided the human person into discrete parts of body and spirit. We call this a dualistic view of humanity. Using this dualism of body and spirit, Apollinarius said that Jesus had a human body. But in place of a human mind, Jesus had the divine Logos.

Of course, again the church understood the importance of the patristic message: *what remains unassumed is unhealed.* The Christ of Apollinarius did not actually have to deal with the temptations arising from our human minds and spirits, only those arising from the frailty of our earthly bodies. In other words, the humanity of Jesus was not really *our* humanity at all. The teachings of Apollinarius were, therefore, condemned by the Council of Constantinople (381).

The Antiochenes. As in so much of life, in the history of Christian theology one swing of the pendulum frequently calls for another. Thus a contrasting approach to understanding the divine humanity of Jesus Christ was provided by what we call the Antiochene school (named after the city of Antioch). Under the leadership of Diodore of Tarsus (d. c. 390), his pupil Theodore of Mopsuestia (c. 350-428) and Theodore's student Nestorius (d. c. 451), this school of theological thought developed, as Donald McKim has said, a "Word-human framework" that "presupposes a complete and independent human nature for Jesus."[34]

The Antiochenes were so determined to preserve the reality of Christ's

---

[34]Donald McKim, *Theological Turning Points: Major Issues in Christian Thought* (Atlanta: John Knox Press, 1988), p. 36.

purely human experience that they divided the divinity from the humanity in him almost to the point of making Christ into two separate persons. They were especially offended by the term *Theotokos* (which is Greek for "God-bearer"). The term was used in worship to refer to Mary, the mother of Jesus, because she "bore God" in giving birth to Jesus Christ. They felt that calling Mary the "God-bearer" compromised Christ's full divinity. The Council of Ephesus (431) condemned the views of the Antiochenes. And the term *Theotokos* became a part of the church's enduring liturgy.

An interesting historical footnote: Although the views of Nestorius were condemned, his followers formed a separate branch of Christendom. Known as "Assyrian Christians," they survived into the twentieth century and are remembered today for their missionary endeavors on behalf of their version of Christian faith.

The pendulum swings again; for every action there is an opposite and equal reaction.

Eutyches. The archinmandrite of a large monastery in Constantinople, Eutyches (c. 378-454) reacted violently to the Antiochene Christology. He maintained that in the person of Christ Jesus there was only a single, divine nature. Jesus Christ is truly God, but the humanity of Jesus Christ is not our humanity. Thus the unity of the person of Jesus Christ is preserved, but the atonement lies shattered. Once again the soteriological (related to the doctrine of salvation) problem arose: Christ, in the incarnation, though he was fully God did not take on our full humanity, and so he did not heal and redeem us.

Eutyches was deposed and exiled at the Council of Constantinople (in 451). The theological party that developed following Eutyches holds what is known as a Monophysite Christology (from the Greek *monos,* meaning "only one," and *physis,* "nature"). This christological view is still predominant among some Eastern Orthodox branches of the church. As some theologians in the Anglican Church have recently noted, Monophysite Christology is also fairly common in their communion, though they are certainly not alone. Like so many of the ancient heresies, this one has never really gone out of style.

Chalcedon. All of these christological debates led up to and culminated in the great Council of Chalcedon, which in A.D. 451 produced one of the most important statements of faith in the history of the church. Much of the language used in the prior debates was put to use again, sometimes in new and surprising ways.

The declaration of the council held the following views regarding Jesus Christ:

1. Jesus Christ is fully and perfectly God and fully and perfectly human; the Chalcedonian statement of faith says Christ was "consubstantial with the Father in his Godhead, and with us in his manhood."

2. The divine-humanity of Jesus Christ was manifest 'in two natures without confusion, change, division, or separation."

3. The difference between the human and the divine natures in Jesus Christ "is in no sense abolished by the union" of the two natures.

4. The "properties of each nature are preserved intact, and both come together to form one person (prosōpon) and one hypostasis."

Henry Chadwick explains, "The formula was a mosaic of phrases from different sources."[35] Drawing on a number of writers and employing and combining familiar terms often in new ways, the council emphasized the oneness of Christ's person (Jesus Christ) and the indissoluble duality and harmonious communication of the natures (divine and human):

To emphasize the oneness of Jesus Christ, it employed the terms hypostasis and prosōpon (both of which mean "person" and are used together to stress the oneness of Christ's person).

The Greek term hypostasis literally meant "something standing under." The word went through a long evolution of meanings, which gets much too complicated to go into here. But after the Council of Nicea a clear distinction was made between ousia, meaning "substance" or "essence," and hypostasis, which had come to mean "person." And so the orthodox trinitarian formula common in the Latin West, "one substance, three persons," was given the Greek equivalent of, "one ousia, three hypostases."

The term hypostasis was even used more technically in the development of Christology when Cyril of Alexandria (d. 444) formulated his conception of a "hypostatic union" of the divine and human natures in the one person of Jesus Christ in opposition to Nestorius, who maintained a distinction of two hypostases (human and divine) in Christ Jesus.[36]

---

[35]Henry Chadwick, The Early Church (London: Penguin, 1967), pp. 203-4.

[36]For clear and much more detailed treatments of the development of these doctrines see Kelly, Early Christian Doctrines, pp. 310-43; Edward R. Hardy, Christology of the Later Fathers (Philadelphia: Westminster Press, 1954); Alan Richardson, Creeds in the Making: A Short Introduction to the History of Christian Doctrine (London: SCM Press, 1935); and G. L. Prestige, Fathers and Heretics (London: SPCK, 1940).

What Does It All Mean?

The point of this long and at times tortuous struggle over terminology was really very simple and *very* important, for all its subtlety. As T. F. Torrance has observed, the desire of Cyril of Alexandria (and this applies in general to other orthodox theologians of the time) was to say "the union of God and man in the incarnation of the Son was substantive and hypostatic, constituting an indivisible unity."[37] These theologians wanted there to be no misunderstanding on this point. The one we are dealing with when we are dealing with Jesus Christ is both God and human in a *single personal reality*.

The purpose of the Chalcedonian Definition, or the Symbol of Chalcedon, as it is variously called, was therefore to preserve from reductionism the mystery of the person of Jesus Christ in his full divine humanity. It reads:

> We . . . teach men to confess one and the same Son, our Lord Jesus Christ the same perfect in Godhead and also perfect in manhood; truly God and truly man, of a reasonable [rational] soul and body; consubstantial [*homoousian,* coessential] with the Father according to Godhead, and consubstantial [*homoousian,* coessential] with us according to the Manhood; in all things like unto us, without sin; begotten before all ages of the Father according to the Godhead, and in these latter days, for us and for our salvation, born of the Virgin Mary, the Mother of God, according to the Manhood; one and the same Christ, Son, Lord, Only-begotten, to be acknowledged in two natures [*in duo physisin*], inconfusedly, unchangeably, indivisibly, inseparably; the distinction of natures being by no means taken away by the union, but rather the property of each nature being preserved, and concurring in one Person [*prosōpon*] and one Subsistence [*hypostasis*], not parted or divided into two persons, but one and the same Son, and only begotten, God the Word, the Lord Jesus Christ, as the prophets from the beginning [have declared] concerning him, and the Lord Jesus Christ himself has taught us, and the Creed of the holy Fathers has handed down to us.[38]

Summary. What was at stake in the debates that raged during these early centuries of the church's development was nothing less than the integrity of the two central teachings of the Christian faith: God's self-revelation in Jesus Christ and the atonement of God and humanity. The ques-

---

[37]T. F. Torrance, *Theology in Reconciliation* (London: Geoffrey Chapman, 1975), p. 160.
[38]Philip Schaff, ed., *The Creeds of Christendom, with a History and Critical Notes: The Greek and Latin Creeds,* rev. ed., ed. David Schaff (Grand Rapids, Mich.: Baker, 1983), 2:63.

tion that confronted these early theologians is the same question that continues to confront us to this day, the same question we started with: Who is Jesus Christ?

In regard to *revelation,* the questions the church was asking were: When we encounter Jesus Christ, have we indeed beheld the very heart of God? Does Jesus Christ reveal the hidden God? Is this revelation reliable and true? In regard to the *atonement,* the questions were: If Christ is not *human,* how can Christ redeem *us?* And if Christ is not *God,* how can he *redeem* us? The answer to both of these questions, in light of these earliest controversies, was

☐ Jesus Christ is none other than the Lord; in the mystery of his humanity, fully human; in the mystery of his divinity, fully God; both fully God and human, yet fully one real person meeting us.

☐ Jesus Christ is neither merely an appearance of humanity nor only the semblance of the divine, but the divine Word become flesh, Emmanuel (God among us).

☐ When we encounter Jesus Christ, we have truly encountered God.

☐ God in Jesus Christ became human, and in our flesh overcame our sin and death.

The early confessions, using the language and thought forms of the Greek-speaking world, tried to stake out the boundaries of the debate and to hold on to the mystery of the God-Human, given the limitations of their language and the controversies in which they were embroiled. In all of this often bewildering history of christological development, we can take comfort in knowing that the greatest minds of the ages have confessed their inability to express these mysteries in human terms, even while they have labored to do so.

Augustine fittingly said, "God is greater and truer in our thoughts than in our words; [and] he is greater and truer in reality than in our thoughts."[39]

The Lordship of Jesus Christ

Before moving on from our discussion of "God's Son, our Lord," we need to return again to the earliest Christian confession to pick up one more aspect of what it means when we say, "Jesus Christ is Lord."

We have already noted that this is a confession of the Godness of Jesus

---

[39]Augustine of Hippo *De Trinitate* 7.4.7.

Christ. But it is also a confession of the singularity of Christ as Lord. This takes us both backwards into the deepest memories of the people of Israel and forward into the church's confrontation with every power that vies for its singular allegiance to the God revealed in Jesus Christ.

Many of the abstract theological discussions we get into about how God can be Trinity, one and yet three, originate in a profound misunderstanding of the singularity of divine Being. To get a handle on this it would be helpful to go back to the basic confession of faith for the Jewish people: the *Shema.*

We find this confession of faith in Deuteronomy 6:4. *"Shema yisra'el YHWH [adonai] 'elohenu YHWH [adonai] 'ehad,"* which is usually translated, "Hear, O Israel, the LORD is God, the LORD is one." (Note that YHWH, the name of the Lord, is not spoken; instead *adonai,* the Hebrew word for divine Lord, is used.) But as a confession of faith, the *Shema* represents much more a pledge of allegiance than any sort of a metaphysical assertion. Thus the translation of this passage in the New Revised Standard Version is much closer to the spirit of the original Hebrew. This translation reads, "Hear, O Israel: The LORD is our God, the LORD alone." The *Shema,* in other words, echoes the First Commandment: "I am the LORD your God, who brought you out of the land of Egypt, out of the house of slavery; you shall have no other gods before me." The confession is not demanding us to take up a metaphysical position on the existence of supernatural beings; it is laying claim to our lives in the name of the Lord. The *Shema* literally calls us *to hear,* to be attentive to and to submit ourselves to the Word of YHWH, the Lord God.

The religious crime of blasphemy was fundamentally a form of idolatry, allowing something other than the Lord to own the place of highest esteem in our lives. As Paul Tillich observed, idolatry is to allow anything other than the Lord our God, *YHWH adonai*—the God who delivered us out of the land of Egypt, from the house of bondage—to become our "ultimate concern."[40]

In the Old Testament there is a wealth of theological language about the complex character, the infinite variety and depth of the being of the Lord God. ☐ God is the speaker whose Word brings all things into existence.

---

[40]Paul Tillich, *Dynamics of Faith* (New York: Harper, 1956), pp. 2-3.

☐ God is the creative Spirit brooding like a storm over the face of the primordial deep.

☐ God is Elohim, mysteriously multiple in acts and being.

☐ God is YHWH, sweeping across legend and history like fire in a dry wilderness.

☐ God is the voice coming upon the prophets giving them utterance.

☐ God is the eternal Wisdom guiding the steps of the righteous.

☐ God is the multiform guest dining with Abram at the oaks of Mamre.

☐ God is the mysterious stranger wrestling with Jacob on the banks of the Jabbock river.

☐ God is the extravagant Lover who woos and pursues the beloved.

☐ God is the mighty king who alone calls the people to justice.

☐ God is the gracious Author of the law, the Judge, the Father, the grieving Parent, the estranged Spouse.

The God of the Old Testament *never was* Spinoza's puny, skinny, simplistic little god, the bare monad of rationalism and deism. My point is simply this: the fundamental teaching of Christ's lordship does not pose primarily a problem for logic but a problem for loyalty. The God of the Old Testament is none other than the God revealed in Jesus Christ. At last we find the truth that was hinted at, estimated, hoped for, that God is an eternal *plerosis* of being, a fullness of ever-springing life overflowing. And this overflowing God who meets us in Jesus Christ demands this confession of us that is older and deeper than our memories: *"The Lord is God, the Lord alone."* This is essentially the same confession we make as Christians: *"Jesus Christ is our Lord."*

This is the confession that so bewildered and angered Pliny the Younger, the sophisticated Roman senator and governor of Bithynia and Pontus under Emperor Trajan. Christians ought to be punished, he said, whatever it is they believe or do, if for no other reason than because of their stubborn obstinance. They simply will not confess Caesar's priority over their lives as all beneficiaries of Roman rule ought.

All of which brings us into the twentieth century via another of the great confessional statements of the church, the Declaration of Barmen (1934), which declared to the whole world, in the context of the rise of totalitarian regimes (especially the Nazi regime in Germany) that tried to claim for themselves their subjects' ultimate allegiance that Christians have one Lord, one Master, one Leader, Jesus Christ.[41] Robert McAfee Brown says something in his book *Unexpected News* that I had been sensing for quite some time but had not been able to put into words. And I doubt if he and I are the only ones who are thinking this. He says that it just may be time for a confessing church or a Barmen Declaration of our own. "There cannot be two highest allegiances but only one," Brown writes.[42]

"The Lord Jesus Christ is our God, the Lord alone!" This is what the Barmen Declaration is saying in the face of Adolf Hitler and those like him. We belong to this God, the Lord God revealed in the history of Israel and culminating in the life, death and resurrection of Jesus Christ, and we belong to this God, body and soul, in life and in death—and we belong to no other.[43] The Declaration of Barmen resounds off the walls of our battered history like a theological oath of fealty. It spells out the practical implications of that most fundamental Christian confession: *"Jesus Christ is Lord."* We will have no other gods before the Lord—therefore, our knees will not bend in worship or servitude to Hitler or any other tyrant. The Declaration spells out this oath of loyalty to the Lord God in the clearest terms possible so there will be no mistake about what we are saying:

> Jesus Christ, as he is attested to us in Holy Scripture, is the one Word of God whom we are to hear, whom we are to trust and obey in life and in death. . . . Just as Jesus Christ is the pledge of the forgiveness of all our sins, just so— and with the same earnestness—is he also God's mighty claim on our whole life; in him we encounter a joyous liberation from the godless claims of this world to free and thankful service to his creatures.[44]

Summary. This is the essential message that comes to us as Christians from the Scriptures of the Old and New Testaments. We believe that the

---

[41]The "Theological Declaration of Barmen," principally written by Karl Barth, was adopted by the confessing church in Germany in 1934. The best English translation of the confession appears in John Leith, *Creeds of the Churches: A Reader in Christian Doctrine from the Bible to the Present,* 3rd ed. (Atlanta: John Knox Press, 1982).

[42]R. M. Brown, *Unexpected News: Reading the Bible with Third World Eyes* (Philadelphia: Westminster Press, 1984), p. 59.

[43]I am paraphrasing here another great confession of Protestant evangelicalism here, "The Heidelberg Catechism," which begins with the question "What is your only comfort, in life and in death?" and answers, "That I belong—body and soul, in life and in death—not to myself but to my faithful Savior, Jesus Christ." *The Heidelberg Catechism with Commentary,* foreword by Allen O. Miller, M. Eugene Osterhaven, Aladar Komjathy and James I. McCord (New York: Pilgrim Press, 1979).

[44]"Theological Declaration of Barmen," in *Creeds of the Churches: A Reader in Christian Doctrine from the Bible to the Present,* ed. John Leith, 3rd ed. (Atlanta: John Knox, 1982). p. 520.

God who delivered the nation of Israel has shown us his very innermost heart in Jesus Christ. When we know Jesus Christ, we know God the Father Almighty, the Lord God of Israel who spoke through the prophets. When Jesus Christ addresses us, we believe we are addressed by none other than the God of Abraham, Isaac and Jacob. His claim on us is absolute and comprehensive. We belong to the Lord, Jesus Christ, utterly and completely, body and soul, in life and in death.

Homework Assignments

1. *Mapping.* This week we are going to become acquainted with an extremely helpful learning device: conceptual mapping. Professional educators sometimes refer to this as semantic webbing, and although the term may seem slightly jargonish, the activity is extremely enjoyable and helpful. I have used this learning tool in a variety of settings with a variety of students, and it has never failed to help clarify thinking on complex subjects.

Mapping works like this: most of the time when we hear a lecture or read a chapter in a book, our brain is trying to organize the ideas we encounter. Mapping (or semantic webbing) actually brings to visual form— on paper—this organizational work.

For instance, this week, in the most technical part of our session, I was talking about the way the early church attempted to interpret the implications of the incarnation, God becoming a human in Jesus Christ. We heard about Docetism, Ebionitism, Justin Martyr, Sabellius and Paul of Samosata, modalistic monarchianism, Arius and Athanasius, Apollinarius, the Antiochenes, Eutyches, the Council of Chalcedon, and a whole bunch of other stuff. Unless we want this list to just lie there like pages from an ancient telephone book, we are going to have to sort through it all. That's where mapping comes in handy. A map will help us picture what we are figuring out. For instance, let's map the pendulum swings of the early christological controversies that we heard about in the lecture (see figure 5.2).

Your first assignment in mapping is a good deal simpler than mapping the christological controversies of the early church. Your assignment is to map (or draw a conceptual picture of) the quest for the historical Jesus from its beginning to its dead end—including the significance of the *Kerygma* (remember what Bonhoeffer said) and the essential confrontation with Jesus Christ that we see in Kierkegaard and others (notice the "existential [evangelical] model of Christian Faith"). Anything else you want to

throw in—or any further light you'd like to throw on the whole subject—
will be most welcome.

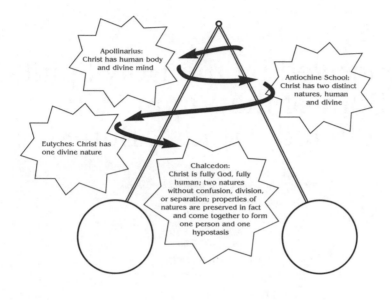

Figure 5.2. The pendulum swings of patristic Christology

Use crayons, colored markers or pencils, whatever you fancy. Have fun!

2. *Our oath of allegiance.* In the last section of this session, we dealt
with the idea that the *Shema* is a sort of pledge of allegiance (rather than a
statement of abstract metaphysics). If this is indeed what the *Shema* is saying, that *the Lord is our God, the Lord alone,* then, speaking negatively,
what are we saying about other things (other gods) that are *not* God? What
are some of the other things that may try to claim the place of God in our
allegiance? How can we deal faithfully with these competing loyalties?

3. *Before we leave this session behind.* Make sure you understand all new
words and concepts. Go back through and conduct a little review of the
most important points. Notice especially the summaries at the end of each
subsection.

Class 6

Conceived by the Holy Spirit, Born of the Virgin Mary, Suffered, Dead & Buried

"Merciful God, I ask that thou wilt grant me,
as thou pleasest,
to seek earnestly,
to investigate carefully,
to know truthfully,
and to present perfectly,
to the glory of thy name, amen."

THOMAS AQUINAS

RECENTLY I WAS READING A LETTER BASIL THE GREAT (C. 330-379) WROTE TO "a fallen virgin," as the address of the letter states. The letter is a brilliant example of pastoral care in the ancient catholic church.[1] It closes with these words:

> The Lord wishes to cleanse you from the trouble of your sickness and to show you light after darkness. The good Shepherd, Who left them that had not wandered away, is seeking after you. If you give yourself to Him He will not hold back. He, in His love, will not disdain even to carry you on His own shoulders, rejoicing that He has found His sheep which was lost. The Father stands and awaits your return from your wandering. Only come back, and while you are yet afar off, He will run and fall upon your neck, and, now that

---

[1]I am using the term "ancient catholic church" here in the way John Leith uses it: "the church of the first five centuries." John Leith, *The Church: A Believing Fellowship* (Atlanta: John Knox Press, 1981), p. 29.

you are cleansed by repentance, will enwrap you in embraces of love. He will clothe with the chief robe the soul that has put off the old man with all his works; He will put a ring on hands that have washed off the blood of death, and will put shoes on the feet that have turned from the evil way to the path of the Gospel of peace. . . . If any of those who think they stand find fault because of your quick reception [back into the fellowship of the Church], the good Father will Himself make answer for you in the words, "It was meet that we should make merry and be glad for this" my daughter "was dead and is alive again, was lost and is found."[2]

I quote this passage today to make the following point: From the age of the ancient catholic church, we are provided with a portrait of the character of God that finds its source and content in the life of Jesus Christ, and, more, that understands who this Jesus Christ is on the basis of the writings of the New Testament.

God, for Basil, is clearly pictured as the searching shepherd, the parent eager to forgive. The character of God is made known, Basil says in another letter, in Jesus Christ, the physician of our souls who, stooping to our sickness and breathing in the foul breath of our sin, heals us from our disease.[3] Our knowledge of God's character is grounded, Basil tells us, in the manger, in a carpenter's shop in Nazareth, in the death of this man named Jesus.[4]

But in time this elegantly simple understanding of God was largely pushed out of the picture by competing views. In order for us to understand what we mean when we say we believe in "Jesus Christ, who was conceived by the Holy Ghost, born of the Virgin Mary, suffered under Pontius Pilate, was crucified, dead, and buried," we are going to take a historical detour to the land of Martin Luther.

Martin Luther Meets Jesus

Martin Luther came to the religious life via a thunderstorm on a sultry day

---

[2]Basil the Great, "Letter XLVI," in *St. Basil: Letters and Select Works*, Nicene and Post Nicene Fathers, second series, ed. Philip Schaff and Henry Wace, trans. Blomfield Jackson (Grand Rapids, Mich.: Eerdmans, 1983), 8:152.

[3]Basil the Great, "Letter VIII: To the Caesareans," in *St. Basil: Letters and Select Works*, Nicene and Post Nicene Fathers, second series, ed. Philip Schaff and Henry Wace, trans. Blomfield Jackson (Grand Rapids, Mich.: Eerdmans, 1983), 8:115.

[4]I recommend the excellent though difficult to find book on Christology by Dietrich Ritschl, *Concerning Christ: Thinking of Our Past, Present and Future with Him* (Richmond, Tex.: Well Spring Center, 1980), especially chap. 3, "Who Is He?"

in 1505. He was then, as the church historian Roland Bainton explains, a student, twenty-one years old, returning to the University of Erfurt following a visit with his family. Quite suddenly a bolt of "lightning struck him to earth." Bainton writes:

> In that single flash he saw the denouement of the drama of existence. There was God the all-terrible, Christ the inexorable, and all the leering fiends springing from their lurking places in pond and wood that with sardonic cachinnations they might seize his shock of curly hair and bolt him into hell.[5]

In a flash Luther cried out to his father's patron saint (the patron saint of miners), "St. Anne help me! I will become a monk."

Now the thing I want us to concentrate on in this session is not Luther's vocation but his *vision of God*, which is so well phrased in Bainton's description of "the terror of the Holy." Luther casts about him to understand who God is and what God is like, and he sees reflected in the piety of his age an absolutely almighty God, a vengeful and wrathful God of blood and fury, whose Son, Jesus Christ, sat upon the rainbow of the covenant with his sword in hand, the Judge all-terrible.[6]

Later Luther, a young monk, would tremble in terror in the presence of Jesus Christ. He tried to remember all of his sins so he might confess them and be forgiven. But his memory was faulty, and he feared that he might die with unnoticed and unconfessed sins on his soul, and be cast into the fires of hell, where the flame is not quenched and the worm never dies. God, he believed, was unknowable and unknown, dwelling in heaven inaccessible. We approach him, he felt, but his majesty overpowers and shatters us.

Some of Luther's Roman Catholic teachers tried to help him. John Staupitz tried to teach Luther that God is love and that the response God desires of us is love. But, Luther asked, "Love God?" How can we love a God who sits enthroned in heaven arbitrarily consigning the damned souls to the flames of hell?[7]

---

[5]Roland H. Bainton, *Here I Stand: A Life of Martin Luther* (Nashville: Abingdon, 1950), p. 25.
[6]Ibid., p. 29.
[7]Indeed as Bainton (*Here I Stand*, pp. 43-45) shows and as others such as McGrath have demonstrated, some of Luther's key insights are not only shared by his teachers, notably John Staupitz, but were medieval commonplaces; for example, Luther's "recognition of the pastoral significance of the wounds of Christ, and the insight that penance begins with the love of God." Alister McGrath, *The Intellectual Origins of the European Reformation* (Oxford: Basil Blackwell, 1987), p. 114.

The very sight of a crucifix terrified Luther like a lightning bolt. He fled from the vengeful Son of God and sought protection in the merciful mother, the Virgin Mary. His despair grew ever deeper as he reflected on his understanding of the atonement. He believed that all humanity is sinful and rightly should be damned by an absolutely righteous and just God. But God showed his capacity for mercy by arbitrarily choosing a few sinners for heaven while also showing his capacity for justice by arbitrarily damning all others to hell. Both groups are consigned to these eternal destinations, heaven or perdition, on the basis of God's whim. "This appears iniquitous, cruel and intolerable in God," he wrote. "I was myself more than once driven to the very abyss of despair so that I wished I had never been created. Love God? I hated him!"[8]

It was at this point that something really unexpected happened. Luther was assigned the job of teaching the Bible. And in order to teach the Bible he had to make careful study of it. In 1513 Luther began a series of lectures on Psalms. In the fall of 1515 he began lecturing on Romans. Throughout 1516-1517 he taught Galatians.

These studies of the Bible proved to be fundamentally transformative for Luther. Gradually he came to see that his understanding of God was woefully inadequate. Jesus Christ had assumed a preassigned role in his theology, but Luther had never seen Christ as he was, in light of Christ's own life as presented in the Gospels. The entire being of God had played a preassigned role in Luther's larger theological scheme, but God had never been understood by Luther in light of the simplicity of the Bible's own message. Intently studying Scripture, Luther discovered that God indeed is love, as Staupitz had tried to tell him. And furthermore, the God of the Bible is revealed in Christ's death on the cross, a death that is God's supreme self-offering for the sake of all persons.

"What a new picture of Christ!" Bainton writes. (Of course, it wasn't really a new picture of Christ. But it was new for Luther.) Bainton continues:

> A new view also of God is here. The All Terrible is the All Merciful too. Wrath and love fuse upon the cross. The hideousness of sin cannot be denied or forgotten; but God who desires not that a sinner should die but

---

[8]Bainton, *Here I Stand*, p. 44. Though Carter Lindberg's use of the term "covenantal theology" is unhelpful, he provides some helpful insights into Luther's frightening vision of a God unimpressed by his piety. Carter Lindberg, *The European Reformations* (Oxford: Basil Blackwell, 1996), pp. 69-70.

that he should turn and live, has found the reconciliation in the pangs of bitter death. It is not that the Son by his sacrifice has placated the irate Father; it is not primarily that the Master by his self-abandoning goodness has made up for our deficiency. It is that in some inexplicable way, in the utter desolation of the forsaken Christ, God was able to reconcile the world to himself. . . . How amazing that God in Christ should do all this; that the Most High, the Most Holy should be the All Loving too; that the ineffable Majesty should stoop to take upon himself our flesh, subject to hunger and cold, death and desperation. We see him lying in the feedbox of a donkey, laboring in a carpenter's shop, dying a derelict under the sins of the world. The gospel is not so much a miracle as a marvel, and every line is suffused with wonder.[9]

The linchpin of Luther's new theological insight is his theology of the cross. It grew from his biblical studies, his wrestling with the work of Augustine and his reflections on German mystics such as John Tauler. Luther places the theology of the cross *(theologia crucis)* over against what he terms a theology of glory *(theologia gloriae)*.[10] For instance, during the Heidelberg Disputation, Luther argues:

He deserves to be called a theologian . . . who comprehends the visible and manifest things of God seen through the suffering and the cross. So . . . in John XIV [:8] where Philip spoke according to the theology of glory: "Show us the Father." Christ forthwith set aside his flighty thought about seeing God elsewhere and led him to himself, saying, "Philip, he who has seen me has seen the Father" [John XIV:9]. For this reason true theology and recognition of God are in the crucified Christ.[11]

God reveals *who God is,* Luther says, *in complete vulnerability by placing himself in the hands of humanity, in surrendering to suffering and death*. What this means, as Paul Althaus writes, is that "the knowledge of God is not theoretical knowledge but rather a matter of [a person's] entire existence." Which means that theology of the cross is theology by faith. Its objectivity is wrapped in an absolute subjectivity. Remember what we mean by subjectivity: the passionate surrender of the self to the God we know in Christ. So Althaus continues:

---

[9]Bainton, *Here I Stand*, p. 48

[10]See Jürgen Moltmann's excellent article, "Theology of the Cross" in *The Westminster Dictionary of Christian Theology*, ed. Alan Richardson and John Bowden, rev. ed. (Philadelphia: Westminster Press, 1983), pp. 135-37.

[11]E. G. Rupp and Benjamin Drewery, eds., "The Heidelberg Disputation, April 1518," in *Martin Luther: Documents of Modern History* (London: Edward Arnold, 1978), p. 28.

We cannot view the cross as an objective reality in Christ without at once knowing ourselves as crucified with Christ. The cross means: God meets us in death, in the death of Christ, but only when we experience Christ's death as our own death. The death of Christ leads us to an encounter with God only when it becomes our death. Contemplating the death of Christ necessarily becomes a dying together with him.[12]

In other words, God's revelation of himself is hidden in the mystery of Jesus Christ even as God's hiddenness is revealed in Jesus Christ. To meet God in Christ means to come to the outer banks of human understanding, beyond which we cannot venture on our own. This faith-knowledge is a gift purely and completely. And it carries in itself a warning against making theology into a playground of idle speculation. God meets us in Christ, and in Christ God calls us to follow through the cross in which we die to the world and through which the world is given its life.

Luther's theological reflections return us to an earlier tradition that largely (though not entirely!) had been abandoned. The concern of this earlier tradition, traced through the fathers of the church (e.g., Basil of Caesarea), was centered in discovering the character of God through the sufferings of Jesus Christ. But to understand what this means we need to look at the other great Reformer of the sixteenth century, John Calvin, because Calvin understood something that few others seem to have understood: *The whole life of Jesus Christ* "was nothing but a sort of perpetual cross."[13] Our knowledge of God, Calvin says, is linked inextricably to our fellowship with Christ in his suffering through the power of the Holy Spirit.

James Torrance provides another diagram (see figure 6.1) describing this relationship of the knowledge of God understood as a participation in God's own life. This is the perspective we find in John Calvin (and others such as the mature Karl Barth).[14]

James Torrance's diagram graphically illustrates the manner in which we are drawn into the life (and the living, experiential knowledge) of the triune God: our present relationship with Jesus Christ (the fellowship or communion we enjoy with him) is possible because through faith, Christ shares with us,

---

[12]Paul Althaus, *The Theology of Martin Luther* (Philadelphia: Fortress, 1966), p. 28.

[13]John Calvin *Institutes of the Christian Religion* 3.8.1. Also see John Leith, ed., *John Calvin: The Christian Life* (New York: Harper & Row, 1984), pp. vii-xv, 14.

[14]James Torrance, *Worship, Community and the Triune God of Grace* (Carlyle, U.K.: Paternoster), p. 15.

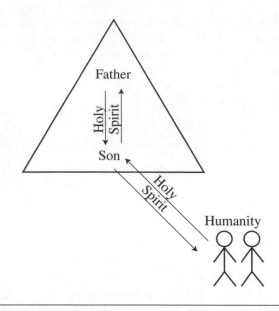

Figure 6.1. Trinitarian model of relationship of God to humanity (mature Barth, John McLeod Campbell, Athanasius). Adapted from James B. Torrance, *Worship, Community and the Triune God of Grace* (Downers Grove, Ill.: InterVarsity Press, 1996), p. 30.

as the living Word of God, the gift of the Holy Spirit. This is the same Spirit with whom Jesus was filled, moved, even driven (Mt 3:13—4:1; Mk 1:9-12). This is absolutely crucial to understand. It is the same Spirit, the Spirit of Christ, who shares with us that relationship of trustful reliance on God the Father that was the essence of Jesus' human life on earth (Eph 2, 4). Torrance represents this movement of God's grace with the arrows moving from the inner life of God (Relationship 1: between Father and Son through the Spirit) toward humanity (Relationship 2: through Christ by the Holy Spirit God relates to us). Correspondingly, Jesus Christ, as the perfect high priest of God and Mediator, brings us *(in and through himself)* even now into the very presence of God the Father through the Spirit (Heb 5—6). Observe how the arrows in his diagram run from humanity in Christ through the Holy Spirit to God the Father. Thus he illustrates what Calvin meant when he said, "For the Son of God became man in such a manner that he had God in common with us. . . . And the reason why [God] is our God, is that [God] is Christ's God, whose members we are."[15]

---

[15]John Calvin, "Commentary on Ephesians," in *Calvin's New Testament Commentaries: Galatians, Ephesians, Philippians and Colossians*, ed. David W. Torrance and Thomas F. Torrance, trans. T. H. L. Parker (Grand Rapids, Mich.: Eerdmans, 1965), p. 134.

We are united to Jesus Christ ("bone of his bone, flesh of his flesh") by the Spirit of God in such a way that we fully participate in his humanity, a humanity that consists in an utter and complete dependence on God. Through the only begotten Son of the Father, God graciously adopts us as children and shares with us the eternal life that belongs to God as holy Trinity through the power of the Holy Spirit. We return again by yet another route to that teaching of the ancient church we call "the wonderful (or glorious) exchange," *mirifica commutatio:* the Son of God became the Son of Man so that we children of humanity might become children of God. As Trevor Hart has written so beautifully, "The Son of God has taken our humanity and has 'joined' it to his eternal divinity, healing it from its broken state, and conforming it to his creative will. He has put to death the old sinful humanity and has raised up a 'new man' in its place, living out a life of fellowship and sonship in his humanity, in relation to the Father and the Spirit."[16] *Mirifica commutatio* indeed.

The Self-Emptying God

Both Martin Luther and John Calvin, in the process of taking us back to the teachings of the ancient church, bring to mind one of the church's earliest hymns, a hymn Paul preserves for us in his letter to the Philippians. The Greek text provides the very rhythm of the hymn, but the force of the hymn is not altogether lost in translation:

> Let the same mind be in you that was in Christ Jesus,
> who, though he was in the form of God,
> did not regard equality with God
> as something to be exploited,
> but emptied himself,
> taking the form of a slave,
> being born in human likeness.
> And being found in human form,
> he humbled himself
> and became obedient to the point of death —
> even death on a cross.
> Therefore God also highly exalted him
> and gave him the name

---

[16]Trevor Hart, "Humankind in Christ and Christ in Humankind: Salvation as Participation in Our Substitute in the Theology of John Calvin," *Scottish Journal of Theology* 42, no. 1 (1989): 83.

that is above every name,
so that at the name of Jesus
    every knee should bend,
    in heaven and on earth and under the earth,
and every tongue should confess
    that Jesus Christ is Lord,
    to the glory of God the Father. (Phil 2:5-11)

Paul says, in quoting this hymn, what Calvin also says centuries later, *that the whole life of Christ was a sort of perpetual cross,* a perpetual suffering, a perpetual humiliation from beginning to end. Or to use the biblical phrase, *"heauton ekenōsen,"* (from which we get the theological term *kenosis*) that is, Christ "emptied *himself"* (Phil 2:7). This teaching is at the heart of the entire New Testament witness to Jesus Christ.

Echoes of *kenosis* (Christ's self-emptying) reverberate like thunder throughout the New Testament.

□ The Synoptic Gospels (the Gospels according to Matthew, Mark, Luke) speak of the "Son of Man" who "came to seek out and save the lost" (Lk 19:10) even at the cost of his own life (Mt 17:22-23; Mk 9:30-32; Lk 9:43-45). This is the message of *kenosis.*

□ The writer of the first epistle of Peter builds his entire message around the theme of Christ's self-emptying love, understanding that Christ trusted himself wholly and utterly to the Father rather than trusting himself to his own strength (1 Pet 2:23). Here we see the mystery of *kenosis* grounded in the heart of the Trinity.

□ When we read the prologue to the Gospel according to John and hear of a light that overcomes the darkness, of the glory of God revealed in the divine Word who has pitched his tent among us, we hear the language of *kenosis.*

□ In 2 Corinthians 8:9 we read "For you know the generous act of our Lord Jesus Christ, that though he was rich, yet for your sake he became poor, so that by his poverty you might become rich." This is the good news of *kenosis.*

□ Paul speaks of the wisdom of the world made foolish by the vulnerable, self-emptying wisdom of God and the vain strength of the world unveiled in its impotence by the power of God that appears (to all the world) to be but weakness (1 Cor 1:18-25). Here we see the power of *kenosis* revealed in all its paradoxical splendor.

It is not too much to say that the fullness of God consists in God's self-emptying, God's power to give up God's very life for the sake of others, indeed of *every* other. It is this which we see in the incarnation: Christ empties himself for the sake of humanity, and in this act of supreme self-surrender Christ affirms the fullness of God's almighty love.

Irenaeus (c. 130-c. 200), the first great theologian of the Christian church, grounded his doctrine of the atonement in the self-emptying of God. Irenaeus says that the humanity we lost as "Adam" has been recovered for us in Christ "being the Word of God, descending from the Father, becoming incarnate, stooping low, even to death, and consummating the arranged plan of our salvation."[17] Irenaeus provides his version of what Calvin would later call *mirifica commutatio* ("the wonderful exchange"): "Our Lord Jesus Christ . . . through his transcendent love, [became] what we are, that he might bring us to be even what he is himself."[18] We will talk more about this teaching soon when we turn our attention specifically to the doctrine of the atonement.

The theologian in the twentieth century who grasped most fully the implications of the self-emptying, or *kenosis,* of Christ was P. T. Forsyth. In this he stands shoulder to shoulder with the Reformers Luther and Calvin. He says that when we encounter Jesus Christ, we are faced with the God "whose infinite power took effect in self-humiliation, whose strength was perfected in weakness, who consented not to know with an ignorance divinely wise, and who emptied himself in virtue of his divine fulness."[19]

This is where von Balthasar's observations on God the Father come back to us with such force, helping us to understand the character of the God revealed in Jesus Christ. If you remember, von Balthasar said that *God's fatherhood consists in God's eternal outpouring, God's self-emptying into another, the Son.* God the Father, he said, is "a flowing wellspring with no

[17]Irenaeus, *Against Heresies,* ed. Alexander Roberts and James Donaldson, The Ante-Nicene Fathers (Grand Rapids, Mich.: Eerdmans, 1981), 1:446.

[18]Ibid., p. 526. See also James Torrance, "The Ministry of Reconciliation Today: The Realism of Grace," in *Incarnational Ministry: The Presence of Christ in Church, Society, and Family,* ed. Christian D. Kettler and Todd H. Speidell (Colorado Springs, Colo.: Helmers & Howard, 1990), pp. 130-31. I have already referred to his Didsbury lectures, published as *Worship, Community and the Triune God of Grace.*

[19]Peter Taylor Forsyth, *The Person and Place of Jesus Christ* (London: Independent Press, 1909), p. 294.

holding-trough beneath it. In the pure act of self-pouring-forth, God the Father is his self."[20]

This is precisely what we see in Jesus Christ, isn't it?

The Son of God, through the power of the Holy Spirit, empties himself, gives himself away. Freely and unreservedly Christ pours himself out for others, "taking the form of a slave, being born in human likeness. And being found in human form, he humbled himself and became obedient to the point of death—even death on a cross." Jesus Christ, whose whole life was a sort of perpetual cross, shows us the character of this God whose power, whose wonder and glory, is revealed in self-emptying love. Christ's life of complete trust in and utter dependence on God the Father through the power of the Holy Spirit reflects the very inner life of God, the communion that is God.[21] Our speculations about how God might be this and not that, our abstractions, rambling pontifications and the speculations to which a theology of glory might aspire are denied any place of legitimacy here. But an understanding of the character of God is, we believe, available to us by faith in the crucified Christ.

All of which brings us back again to the phrase of the creed that demands our attention today: I believe in Jesus Christ "conceived *by* the Holy Spirit, *born of* the Virgin Mary."

The Holy Spirit, which we believe is the mutual, divine love of the Father and the Son, that self-emptying love, the gift of God's very life that eternally flows out from the Father to the Son and is returned in the form of the Son's adoration of the Father, flows out also from God into God's creation, indeed into God's human creatures, in the person of Jesus Christ by the power of God's Spirit. This is the miracle of participation in the life of God that the Johannine writer breathlessly describes with such passion and clarity in what is sometimes called Christ's high priestly prayer for his disciples in John 17.

So when we say that Jesus Christ was conceived by the Holy Spirit, we are saying that the same self-emptying love that flows eternally from the Father to the Son and from the Son to the Father flows now into our

---

[20]Hans Urs von Balthasar, *Credo: Meditations on the Apostles' Creed*, trans. David Kipp (New York: Crossroad, 1990), pp. 30-31.

[21]Geoffrey Wainwright is, I believe, entirely correct in saying that this *kenosis* of the Son corresponds to the "eternal perichoresis by which, according to highly developed trinitarian theology, the divine Persons empty themselves into one another and receive each other's fulness." Wainwright, *Doxology: The Praise of God in Worship, Doctrine and Life: A Systematic Theology* (New York: Oxford University Press, 1980), p. 23.

humanity and has created in our humanity a genuinely new possibility, so new that it cannot be signaled by anything less than this virgin birth. This affirmation in the creed acts as a signpost pointing to what Barth has called "the mystery and miracle of Christmas,"[22] that event which stands uniquely among historical and human events and is distinguished from these events with the statement of belief in Christ's virgin birth we find in the creed.[23] But let's not lose sight of the central teaching of the creed here, that God selflessly emptied himself for the sake of his creation, not because of any need in himself but in the free expression of his own unconditional love.[24]

Augustine (354-430) clearly has the mystery of God's self-emptying love in mind when he speaks of the birth of Christ. In reflection on the incarnation, Augustine writes:

And now, with what words shall we praise the love of God? What thanks shall we give? He so loved us that for our sakes He, through whom time was made, was made in time; and He, older by eternity than the world itself, was younger in age than many of His servants in the world; He who made man, was made man; He was given existence by a mother whom He brought into existence; He was carried in the hands which He formed; He nursed at

[22]Karl Barth, *Dogmatics in Outline*, trans. G. T. Thomson (New York: Harper & Row, Harper Torchbook, 1959) p. 95. A more detailed description of Barth's understanding of the phrase, "conceived by the Holy Spirit, born of the Virgin Mary" appears in *Church Dogmatics* 1/1, pp. 485-86. Barth explains here that the teaching of the church does not say that the Holy Spirit is the father of the man Jesus or that the Virgin Mary is the mother of the Son of God ("the man Jesus has no father [just as He has no mother as Son of God]"). Rather, "What is ascribed to the Holy Spirit in the birth of Christ is the assumption of human existence in the Virgin Mary into unity with God in the mode of being of the Logos. That this is possible, that this other, this being as man, this flesh, is there for God, for fellowship and even unity with God, that flesh can be the Word when the Word becomes flesh, is the work of the Holy Spirit in the birth of Christ."

[23]Again Barth is most helpful here. He explains that the purpose of the statements about the virgin birth in the Bible (Mt 1:18-25 and Lk 1:26-38) and in the creeds is to point toward "the One who was and is and will be the Son of God." The purpose of these statements is not to explain "how he became this." The virgin birth "is the sign which accompanies and indicates the mystery of the incarnation of the Son, marking it off as a mystery from all the beginnings of other human existences." For a fuller treatment, see *Church Dogmatics*, 4/1, p. 207.

[24]A basic, and enjoyable, discussion of this concept of divine love is provided in Mary Ann Fatula, *The Triune God of Christian Faith* (Collegeville, Minn.: Liturgical Press, 1990), pp. 23-26. You might also enjoy the rather more technical studies presented by Colin E. Gunton, *Theology Through the Theologians* (Edinburgh: T & T Clark, 1996); Anthony Kelly, *The Trinity of Love: A Theology of the Christian God* (Wilmington, Del.: Michael Glazier, 1989); and as has already been mentioned, Catherine Mowry LaCugna, *God for Us: The Trinity and the Christian Life* (San Francisco: HarperSanFrancisco, 1991).

breasts which he filled; He cried like a baby in the manger in speechless infancy—this Word without which human eloquence is speechless.[25]

Jesus Christ, a man born of a woman, is the love of God in the flesh. He is, Karl Rahner said, "the miracle of the possibility of the free gift." Christ is, again in Rahner's words, "the incomprehensible obvious."[26] And to this miracle of free, self-emptying divine love, to this "incomprehensible obvious," we bear witness with these words in the creed, "conceived by the Holy Spirit, born of the Virgin Mary."

The essential issue at stake in this phrase of the creed, as T. F. Torrance explains, is that "the Incarnation was the coming of God to save us in the heart of our fallen and depraved humanity, where humanity is at its wickedest in its enmity and violence against the reconciling love of God." We need to be absolutely clear on this point. Christ in his incomprehensible, self-emptying love took upon himself "our fallen human nature, our actual human existence laden with sin and guilt, our humanity diseased in body, mind and soul in its estrangement or alienation from the Creator."[27] In the depths of our humanity (our *fallen* humanity) Christ, by the power of the Holy Spirit, accomplished our atonement with God, cleansing us and healing our fundamental brokenness and alienation. And now, by the power of this same Spirit, we are given a genuine participation in our new humanity in Jesus Christ.[28]

The Lord of Lost Causes
The eucharistic liturgy of the Scottish Episcopal Church contains a postcommunion prayer that expresses the good news of the gospel better and

---

[25]Augustine of Hippo, "Christmas: The Word of God Cannot be Explained by Man," in *Twenty Centuries of Great Preaching: An Encyclopedia of Preaching,* ed. Clyde E. Fant Jr. and William M. Pinson Jr. (Waco, Tex.: Word, 1971), 1.1.137.

[26]Karl Rahner, *Theological Investigations* (London: Darton, Longman & Todd, 1966, 1974), 9:109-17, 119-20. Also cited in the anthology of Rahner's work, *A Rahner Reader,* ed. Gerald A. McCool (New York: Crossroad, 1987), see sections on "Incarnation" and "Trinity."

[27]Thomas F. Torrance, *The Mediation of Christ,* rev. ed. (Colorado Springs, Colo.: Helmers & Howard, 1992), pp. 39-46. From the fifth century on, Latin theologians began rejecting this teaching. Instead they taught the idea that the Son of God assumed "a humanity in its perfect original state" from "the Virgin Mary." Both Roman Catholicism and much of Protestant orthodoxy inherited this view of the incarnation. The result has been that the atonement became generally a matter of "external relations between Jesus Christ and sinners," as Torrance says. Jesus, in this view, bore the penalty for sinners and his perfect account of sinlessness was transferred to their bankrupt account.

[28]The classic statement of this doctrine appears in Athanasius, *De Incarnatione* (Oxford: Oxford University Press, 1971), pp. 155-59.

more beautifully than any other prayer I have ever heard. It says:

> Father of all, we give you thanks and praise
> that when we were still far off
> you met us in your Son, and brought us home.
> Dying and living, he declared your love,
> gave us grace, and opened the gate of glory.
> May we who share Christ's body live his risen life;
> we who drink his cup bring life to others;
> we whom the Spirit lights, give light to the world.
> Keep us firm in the hope you have set before us,
> so we and all your children shall be free,
> and the whole earth live to praise your name;
> through Christ our Lord. Amen.[29]

The same teaching is expressed in the opening sentences of Karl Barth's study of the doctrine of reconciliation. It is one of the most evocative passages in Barth's massive work:

> The subject-matter, origin and content of the message received and proclaimed by the Christian community is at its heart the free act of the faithfulness of God in which He takes the lost cause of man, who has denied Him as Creator and in so doing ruined himself as creature, and makes it His own in Jesus Christ carrying it through to its goal and in that way maintaining and manifesting His own glory in the world.[30]

God makes himself the Lord of *our* lost cause, taking upon himself our ruin and making it his own. In the depths of Christ's divine humanity God heals our disease, transforming our curse into blessing. This is the good news to which the New Testament writers give witness in a variety of ways.[31]

---

[29]Scottish Episcopal Church, *Scottish Liturgy*. This liturgy is drawn from "The Order for Holy Communion, Rite A" in *The Alternative Service Book 1980* (Church of England, 1982), p. 144.

[30]Barth, *Church Dogmatics* 4/1, p. 3.

[31]Before making our very brief sketch of the Christian teaching of atonement, and because this area of theological reflection is so crucial to Christian doctrine, let me suggest the following bibliography, beginning with a few general texts then going on to the more purely constructive theological studies of the atonement. You can hardly do better than F. W. Dillistone, *The Christian Understanding of Atonement* (London: SCM Press, 1968) for an excellent and wonderfully written general text, supremely readable and thorough. Also, Paul S. Fiddes, *Past Event and Present Salvation: The Christian Idea of Atonement* (Louisville, Ky.: Westminster John Knox, 1989); L. W. Grensted, *A Short History of the Doctrine of the Atonement* (Manchester. U.K.: Manchester University Press, 1920); and John McIntyre, *The Shape of Soteriology* (Edinburgh: T & T Clark, 1992). Now for the more constructive studies: Irenaeus, *Against Heresies* (absolutely fundamental reading!); Anselm of Canterbury, *Cur deus homo (Why God Became Man)*; Thomas Aquinas, *Summa Theologica*, IIIa. Q46; John Calvin, *Institutes of the Christian Reli-*

☐ The writer of the Fourth Gospel (arguably the most technical trinitarian theologian of the New Testament) tells us that "God so loved the world he gave his only begotten Son that whosover believes in him should not perish but have everlasting life."

☐ The Synoptic Gospels, as we have already seen, place in the mouth of Jesus the prediction of his death—and his resurrection. And examples such as the parable of the vineyard (Mk 12:6) clearly show that the purpose of Christ's mission to humanity is redemptive.

☐ Paul, writing prior to all of these sources, gives expression to the belief in the earliest Christian communities that Jesus Christ died and rose again to save humanity from sin, the curse and death (Rom 5; 1 Cor 15; 2 Cor 4:3-15; 5:16-21; Col 2).

☐ The imagery of the New Testament, especially the epistle to the Hebrews, is reminiscent of the history of Israel: their *deliverance* from bondage, their *redemption* or *ransom* by the kinsman-redeemer, their *forgiveness* through the blood of sacrifice, and their *priestly inclusion* in the person of the high priest. Even the name Jesus speaks the promise of salvation; this *Joshua* (the name Jesus in Hebrew) is the deliverer of his people,

---

gion 2, "The Knowledge of God the Redeemer in Christ," and his commentaries on Ephesians and Hebrews; Jonathan Edwards, *The Great Christian Doctrine of Original Sin Defended* and *A History of the Work of Redemption* (Yale University Press publishes the critical edition of Edwards's work); also see miscellaneous remarks, "Of Satisfaction of Sin" (Edwards represents the high water mark of a type of Calvinist soteriology, though not the only type). John McLeod Campbell, *The Nature of the Atonement* (Grand Rapids, Mich.: Eerdmans, 1996); originally published in 1856, this is perhaps the most extraordinary and important book written on the subject of the atonement; R. C. Moberly, *Atonement and Personality* (London: John Murray, 1911); Horace Bushnell, *The Vicarious Sacrifice* (London: Dickenson, 1880); R. W. Dale, *The Atonement* (London: Congregational Union, 1898); Albrecht Ritschl, *The Christian Doctrine of Justification and Reconciliation,* vol. 3, *The Positive Development of the Doctrine* (Edinburgh: T & T Clark, 1900), this is volume three of Ritschl's monumental study; James Denney, *The Death of Christ: Its Place and Interpretation in the New Testament* (London: Hodder & Stoughton, 1907), and *The Christian Doctrine of Reconciliation,* Cunningham Lectures for 1917 (London: Hodder & Stoughton, 1917); H. R. Mackintosh, *The Christian Experience of Forgiveness* (London: Nisbet, 1927); P. T. Forsyth, *The Work of Christ* (London: Independent Press, 1910); Donald E. Baillie, *God Was in Christ: An Essay on Incarnation and Atonement* (New York: Scribner's, 1948); Gustaf Aulén, *Christus Victor* (New York: Macmillan, 1969); Emil Brunner, Dogmatics, vol. 2, *The Christian Doctrine of Creation and Redemption,* (Philadelphia: Westminster Press, 1952), and his *The Mediator* (London: Lutterworth, 1934); Colin E. Gunton, *The Actuality of the Atonement* (Edinburgh: T & T Clark, 1988); Lesslie Newbigin, *Sin and Salvation* (London: SCM Press, 1956); and Karl Barth, *Church Dogmatics* 4/1, 2, 3, 4, *The Doctrine of Reconciliation.*

"the one for the many." He becomes "the suffering servant," the whole people of Israel represented in a single person who is wounded for our transgressions, in whose stripes we are healed.

It is no exaggeration to say with C. S. Lewis that "the central Christian belief is that Christ's death has somehow put us right with God and given us a fresh start." But, as Lewis continues, "theories as to how it did this are another matter."[32]

We need to expand just a little on Lewis's statement, however. The most basic affirmation of faith we can make is that Christ suffered, died and rose again *for us*. The early Christian community saw the incarnation, from birth to death, as *a single whole reality*. Christ did not simply die for us, in other words. Christ was *born* for us. Christ *lived* for us. Christ suffered, died *and was raised* for us. In Christ we have been at-oned with God. But how this happened is indeed "another matter." The conventional way to look at this teaching of the church is to say that there are a number of theories about how the atonement takes place. This is the point Lewis is making.

Approaching the subject of the atonement via the conventional theories, we can survey the historical development of this doctrine and the way various approaches to understanding the atonement have stressed different biblical motifs. For instance, we have already alluded to both Irenaeus and Athanasius. Both stress the whole life of Jesus Christ, the incarnation of God, as a complete event in their understandings of the atonement.

Irenaeus sets the atonement within the biblical framework contrasting Christ with Adam. He says that the humanity we lost in Adam is recovered for us in Jesus Christ. Christ is himself the New Creation injected into the old world of brokenness and alienation. Thus Christ, as the New Creation, sums up or *recapitulates* the whole history of the old world, including the old creation of humanity in himself, in his own history. *Christ became what we are,* Irenaeus tells us, *so that Christ might bring us to be even what he is.* Human history is, in Christ, not simply reversed and restored to God's original intention, it is re-created. All that is is given new birth, a radical new creation, by God's sovereign act in Christ.[33]

---

[32]C. S. Lewis, "The Perfect Penitent," in *Mere Christianity* (London: Collins, 1952), p. 52.

[33]Irenaeus *Against Heresies* bk. 5. His exact term for this "recapitulation" is the Greek word *anakephalaiosis,* which is rendered not altogether satisfactorily by the Latin *recapitulatio.* The idea is not, as the Latin seems to suggest, merely a repetitious recapitulation but is

Athanasius (c. 296-373) takes this essential framework and expands it with his characteristic style and subtlety. Athanasius's most famous phrase is "He became man that we might be made divine." He meant by this that through Christ we share in the very life of God, *the eternal life shared by God the Father and God the Son in and through God the Spirit.* He is not suggesting that we cease to be creatures or that we become deities. What Athanasius does affirm is our real participation by faith in the *character* of God (the self-giving, kenotic, love of the other), which is revealed in Jesus Christ. The essential issue at stake in the atonement, for Athanasius (as for Irenaeus), is the incarnation of the Word of God. The atonement is not simply something God does; it is who God is in the incarnation.

The fact that God in Jesus Christ has taken on our flesh is itself the heart of the at-onement (the reconciliation, the bringing together) of God and humanity for both of these early Christian thinkers. Taking on our human flesh God accustoms the Spirit to dwell in humanity, and God creates the capacity in our humanity to receive the divine life. Our death and corruption are overcome in the divine humanity of Jesus Christ. Death, Athanasius says, spent its full force on the Lord's body, and in his resurrection death was rendered impotent. The death and resurrection of Jesus Christ are for us the *arche zoes,* the origin and fountain of that life that is new in its very being. Athanasius also, and even more fully than Irenaeus, speaks of the "redemptive exchange" (the *mirifica communtatio,* the "wonderful exchange"). "O marvel at the loving-kindness of the Word," Athanasius writes, "that for our sakes he is dishonored that we may be brought to honor."[34]

In Athansius we catch a glimpse of an earlier theologian he regarded very highly, Origen (c. 185-c. 254). Origen proposed a model of the atonement in which the death of Christ was a "ransom" paid to Satan, who had acquired authority over fallen humanity because of the debt humanity owed for its transgressions. This view, sometimes called the ransom theory, was largely rejected by the church, at least in Origen's version, though we do hear hints of it (in somewhat modified forms) in some of the Latin theologians. An idea frequently retained is that Jesus Christ served as a sort of

---

a once-for-all-time restoration in Jesus Christ of the marred and defaced image of God in God's human creatures.

[34]Athanasius "On the Incarnation," in *Christology of the Later Fathers,* ed. Edward R. Hardy (Philadelphia: Westminster Press, 1954), p. 88.

bait that the powers of evil took. The powers of evil thought this was their chance to destroy God by killing God in the flesh. But when they took the bait and put Christ to death, they did not realize they had also swallowed the hook. Christ died, but when Christ entered death (or when death entered Christ), he overwhelmed death and destroyed its power forever. Paul Fiddes ably critiques Origen's view of the atonement, observing that even apart from the "vexed question of whether the devil could actually have rights, which later theologians such as Anselm and Abelard vehemently denied, . . . [Origen's approach] treats sin as a kind of impersonal debt rather than an active power in human existence here and now."[35]

Behind this conception of atonement there lies an important biblical understanding that is more familiar to us under the term *redemption.* Words like *redeem, ransom, purchase,* familiar to us from the church's hymns as much as the church's confessions, speak of practices in the ancient world from which the Bible emerged. The words *redeem* or *ransom* are grounded in "the practice of buying something which formerly belonged to the purchaser, but has for some reason passed out of his possession."[36] The theological idea of redemption reflects its common usage; at times the theological brushes past the common with such grace that one finds it hard to distinguish between the two. Thus in Isaiah 43:3 God tells Israel that he has paid a ransom for their deliverance from captivity: "For I am the LORD your God, the Holy One of Israel, your Savior. I give Egypt as your ransom, Ethiopia and Seba in exchange for you."

The concept of redeemer, which became so important in the church's understanding of Jesus Christ, has its roots in the Hebrew law, which allows a kinsman-redeemer to purchase the freedom of a family member who had sold himself into slavery to a resident alien (see Lev 25:47-55). The provision in the law is theological, as we are told in verse 55. The people of Israel belong to the Lord; they are the Lord's servants because the Lord delivered them from Egyptian bondage. Thus God's claim on the people of Israel is prior to anyone else's claim. All of these themes of redemption and ransom are drawn together in the New Testament understanding of Christ as "the Son of Man" who "came not to be served but to serve, and

---

[35]Fiddes, *Past Event*, p. 131.
[36]F. J. Taylor, "Redeem," in *A Theological Word Book of the Bible,* ed. Alan Richardson (New York: Macmillan, 1962), p. 185.

to give his life a ransom for many" (Mk 10:45; Mt 20:28). Preserved in the Christian understanding of redemption and ransom is the purpose of redemption, the costly restoration and deliverance of those who belong to God. This idea is present even in Origen, though in recent years aspects of this view of the atonement have been more fruitfully explored by Gustaf Aulén and in the popular writings of C. S. Lewis, for instance in his children's book *The Lion, the Witch and the Wardrobe.*[37]

The next major theory of the atonement was developed in the high Middle Ages. Being so closely identified with the peculiarities of that feudal age, it is difficult to understand why it remains so popular. Anselm (c. 1033-1109), the archbishop of Canterbury and the greatest theologian between Augustine and Aquinas, developed what we call the satisfaction theory.

Anselm, in his *Cur Deus Homo,* understands sin primarily as an offense against the infinite dignity of God. God, for Anselm, seems to have been the ultimate feudal overlord or king. And this infinite monarch demands (for the sake of the order of his kingdom) that appropriate satisfaction be made for the injury to his dignity. But of course such satisfaction must be infinite because the dignity offended is the dignity of God, the infinite being. Humanity cannot accomplish the infinite and cannot make the necessary satisfaction for the injury it has caused to God's dignity. Yet only a human being could pay the penalty to satisfy divine justice because humanity owed the penalty (enshrined in this view is a version of the patristic idea that the "unassumed remains unhealed"). Christ, the infinite Son of God, therefore became the finite Son of Man, took the place of humanity and paid the penalty, thus satisfying divine justice through his death. He being God and human paid the penalty for our sin; thus the perfect dignity of God was retained while the offenses of humanity were forgiven.

This view of the atonement was adapted into what might be called a "mercantile" model in which the payment of the penalty was stressed (certainly there is also something here of the biblical concepts of redemption and ransom too), and Christ's perfect moral achievements and his perfect satisfaction were transferred from his account to the account of the "elect." The theory was also adapted into a more "forensic" or "legal" model (the so-called penal substitutionary theory) in which the legal side of this transaction was emphasized, the view that our redemption consists in a "legal fiction" by

---

[37]C. S. Lewis, *The Lion, the Witch and the Wardrobe* (London: Macmillan, 1950).

which the benefits of the work of Christ are accounted to us as though they were ours, though they in fact are not. The great scholastic theologian Thomas Aquinas (c. 1225-1274) concurred with Anselm in believing that the satisfaction model is the way God actually went about atoning for humanity's sin. But he says that God was not bound to act in this way and might very well have redeemed humanity through some other means.[38]

Protestant orthodoxy has frequently given priority to these views. We see these ideas expressed throughout the Puritan writers, in the writings of John Owen for example, and in America's great theologian Jonathan Edwards. It was this view of the atonement that the Scottish theologian John McLeod Campbell countered in his brilliant study *The Nature of the Atonement*. We will return to Campbell in a few moments.

Anselm's younger contemporary *Peter Abelard* (1079-1142) developed an alternative to the Anselmian model of the atonement in which Jesus Christ, his suffering and death in particular, calls for a moral and affectional response in humanity, a response of the individual's life to the self-giving love of God. As L. W. Grensted observes, Abelard's "central thesis is the Cross as the manifestation of the love of God, and to the thought of this love he continually returns." Grensted continues, "The justification of man is the kindling of this divine love in his heart in the presence of the Cross." When we, in imitation of Christ, love others we share in his freedom "from the slavery of sin" and "attain to the true liberty of the sons of God."[39]

In contrast to Christian thinkers like Bernard of Clairvaux, who saw human individuals largely as passive observers or recipients of God's love, Abelard believed that when a person witnesses what God in Christ has done on the cross, his "eyes are opened to see the greatness of a love which came near to him even when he was its enemy."[40] According to F. W. Dillistone, Abelard's understanding of the atonement "marks the transition from an outlook which saw God dealing with humanity *as a whole*, either through a legal transaction or through a mystical transfusion, to one in which the ethical and psychological qualities of *the individual within the community* began to receive fuller recognition."[41] To dismiss

---

[38]See Thomas Aquinas *Summa Theologia* 3.46, "The Passion of Christ," especially the second article, in contrast to Anselm.

[39]Grensted, *Short History of the Doctrine*, pp. 103-4.

[40]Dillistone, *Christian Understanding*, pp. 324-25.

[41]Ibid., p. 325.

Abelard's view of the atonement out of hand as religious subjectivism is to miss his "profound psychological insight . . . that nothing is more powerful to move the will from its apathetic acquiescence in some sinful habit than the sight of the One Who actually suffered on account of our sins and bore their penalty in His death."[42] Abelard's emphasis is certainly on the response of the individual. It is therefore subjective. But it is precisely this subjectivism that provides his view with a personal intensity that recovers the vital power of the gospel to change lives. In a sense, Abelard grasped something very close to an understanding of "evangelical repentance" in which a person is drawn to repent because he or she hears the good news of the greatness, the power and beauty of God's love—in contrast to merely a "legal repentance," in which one is driven to repent because one becomes terrified of the punishment God threatens to inflict on those who do not.[43]

---

[42]Ibid.

[43]See James Torrance, "Covenant or Contract: A Study of the Theological Background of Worship in Seventeenth-Century Scotland," *Scottish Journal of Theology* 23, no. 1 (1970): 51-76, in which he observes the use of these terms among "seventeenth-century divines" who distinguished between "(a) *legal repentance*—where the form is 'If you repent, you will be forgiven' . . . 'This do and thou shalt live!' and (b) *evangelical repentance*—where the form is 'Christ has done this for you, therefore repent!' " (p. 57). Torrance returns to these issues in his enormously influential essay "The Contribution of McLeod Campbell to Scottish Theology," *Scottish Journal of Theology* 26, no. 3 (1973): 295-311 At the risk of getting a bit ahead of myself, it may be helpful here to note a similar contrast in John Calvin's understanding of repentance: for Calvin, repentance is the gift of God; it is synonymous with our conversion by the regenerating power of the Spirit. Incidentally, in this context Calvin makes clear that God "wills the conversion of all, and directs exhortation to all in common" (*Institutes* 3.3.21). The trust that God gives us to find in Christ the fulfillment of God's purpose for our humanity and God's particular will for each of us impels us to turn (repent) toward God and to be transformed (converted) by the Holy Spirit. According to Calvin, repentance is not merely a matter of seeing our legal failings in light of a code of rules and of deciding to conform our behavior more closely to the law, but by faith of seeing in Christ the true humanity for which we were created and of receiving the new life that God alone can give. Thus the contrast (which Torrance notes) between *legal* and *evangelical* (evangelical referring to the "evangel," i.e., the gospel or good news) repentance. All aspects of our repentance and faith, including, for example, "fear of God," "mortification" (putting to death the "old self"), "vivification" (being made alive in Christ), "rebirth," and "sanctification," should be understood as gifts of God. (*Institutes* 3.3.5-10). Indeed Calvin, in speaking of the sacrament of the Lord's Supper, says (and his comments relate closely to the matter of evangelical repentance), "By this [Christ] declares himself to be the bread of life, of which those who eat will live forever [Jn 6:48, 50]. And to do this, the Sacrament sends us to the cross of Christ, where that promise was indeed performed and in all respects fulfilled" (*Institutes* 4.17.4). We are made to participate by faith in the life of Christ (the positive aspect of repentance/conversion that consists in turning to God) through the hearing of the gospel and (he says "more

The *moral exemplary model* of the atonement (which to some degree is grounded in Abelard's thought) was given powerful expression by Hastings Rashdall (1858-1924) in his Bampton Lectures of 1915. Rashdall, in these renowned lectures, surveys the history of the doctrine of the atonement and presents (as the view he attributes to Abelard *and* Origen) a doctrine of the atonement he feels is more appropriate to modern Christendom (and I think it's appropriate to underscore *modern* here). He writes, "The death of Christ . . . justifies us, inasmuch as through it charity is stirred up in our hearts."[44] In other words, when we contemplate that which Jesus Christ did for us, when we see the cost of his love for humanity, we are compelled to respond ethically, to live a life consistent with Christ's. His love evokes our own.

This moral exemplary model, like the Abelardian approach to which it is indebted, is often described as a subjective view of the atonement and is contrasted to so-called objective views of the atonement. Let's take a moment to contrast the two just a bit. An objective view of the atonement understands reconciliation as being accomplished totally by God in what Jesus Christ did on behalf of humanity. It does not, in other words, depend on our subjective response for its efficacy. The subjective view, by contrast, places its weight more on what we do in response to Christ. In the twentieth century we saw a tremendous emphasis on objective views of the atonement (e.g., by Karl Barth, Emil Brunner and Gustaf Aulén, each in his own distinctive way) over against more subjective views of the atonement (as seen here in Rashdall and also in Friedrich Schleiermacher). As we shall see, a more complete understanding of the atonement neglects neither the subjective nor the objective.

During the Reformation the two most important developments in the doctrine of the atonement were (as you might expect) in the theologies of Martin Luther and John Calvin. Both were elaborations on what we call the *substitutionary* model of the atonement. Luther (1483-1546) reiterated Christ's substitution, Christ's standing in for humanity. We can hear in the

---

clearly") by receiving in faith the Lord's Supper: "For it assures us that all Christ did or suffered was done to quicken us [i.e., to give us life]; and again, that this quickening is eternal, we being ceaselessly nourished, sustained, and preserved throughout life by it" (*Institutes* 4.17.5). Also see John Calvin, "The Necessity of Reforming the Church," in *Calvin: Theological Treatises,* ed. J. K. S. Reid (Philadelphia: Westminster Press, 1954), pp. 197-202.

[44]Hastings Rashdall, *The Idea of Atonement in Christian Theology* (London: Macmillan, 1919), p. 438.

background of Luther's reflections on the atonement the thought of Anselm like the thrumming of a double bass beneath a Brahms symphony. But in contrast to Anselm, Luther's idea is a substitution that is not simply a matter of juggling the accounting books (that is, not simply "external" to our essential humanity, as though Christ bore the legal penalty for humanity that was later transferred from his account to ours). For Luther, Christ in taking on himself our humanity *became* sin for us (reflecting Paul's insight: "For our sake [God] made him to be sin who knew no sin, so that in him we might become the righteousness of God" [2 Cor 5:21]). Christ, *who is himself without sin,* identified so completely with us in our sin, in our alienation from God, he put himself in our place so utterly and profoundly that *he was made sin for us;* and now when God looks at us, God no longer sees us but Christ in our place.[45] Remember Basil the Great: Christ, the Great Physician, assumes not only the role of the patient—but takes into himself the very sickness—so that he can heal humanity.

John Calvin (1509-1564), if anything, actually goes beyond Luther in his understanding of substitution. Calvin sees Jesus Christ as both the complete substitution and the full representative for humanity.[46] Calvin beautifully expresses this idea of substitution/representation in his commentary on the epistle to the Hebrews, drawing on the biblical image of the high priest.[47] As mentioned earlier, Calvin draws on the insight shared by Irenaeus and Athanasius to see in Christ the "wonderful exchange." *Christ became what we are so that we might become what he is.* Calvin means by this that Christ took on our human nature (in all its weakness) to enable us to share in the truly human nature of Jesus Christ (in his complete reliance upon God through the Holy Spirit).[48] Humanity, according to Calvin, was created for grace; humanity was originally created for trustful dependence on God. We are meant to enjoy the reality of our reliance on God, to revel in this reality, this

---

[45]See, for example, Luther's *Commentary on Galatians* and also J. M. Campbell's discussion of Luther, *The Nature of the Atonement,* chap. 2.

[46]Calvin *Institutes* 3.11.2, 21-23; 3.12.1-21; cf. 2.8.59, and 2.16.

[47]John Calvin, *Hebrews and I and II Peter,* ed. David W. Torrance and Thomas F. Torrance, trans. W. B. Johnston (Grand Rapids, Mich.: Eerdmans, 1963); see parallel developments in *Calvin's Commentary on Ephesians,* chaps. 1 and 2. See also the development of this insight in *Institutes* 2.15.6.

[48]Calvin *Institutes* 4.17.2.

fact.[49] Humanity's fall (Gen 3) does not relate the failure of humanity to diligently obey the minutiae of a legal code. Genesis tells the story of a failure of trust. Humanity, created for joyful trust and loving fellowship with its Creator, fell into independence and distrust, and therefore disgrace.[50] Thus it is through faith in Christ that we can now participate by the power of the Spirit in that genuine and complete restoration of trust in God by which Jesus lived—and for which we were created.[51] But, as if this were not enough, there is even more to Calvin's view of the atonement.

In Jesus Christ, Calvin says, *all parts of our salvation are complete.* Every aspect of the life that God intends for humanity is fully and finally fulfilled and made real in our humanity by Jesus Christ. Everything God intended us to be was accomplished and is now given to us as God's gift by faith in Jesus Christ. Calvin uses the language of a variety of models of the atonement and places all of them in a radically substitutionary framework.[52] For Calvin this doctrine springs from the biblical understanding of the high priesthood of Jesus Christ (as we see in Calvin's moving commentary on the epistles to the Hebrews). Christ represents our humanity, restored to trust and trustful dependence on God, in the presence of God the Father. In a real sense, for Calvin we stand in the person of Jesus Christ as Christ intercedes with God the Father on our behalf. Thus our atonement is not simply a transfer of salvific credits from one account to another. Our atonement in Christ is dynamic and living—and real. Calvin's thought on the atonement actually transcends the rather limited approach of the "theories" of atonement, pressing the various aspects of the atonement toward a more inclusive incarnational framework and grounding our understanding of the atonement in that adoration and worship of God that Christ now renders

---

[49]You can see a direct connection between the nineteenth-century German Reformed theologian Scheiermacher and John Calvin at precisely this point. Schleiermacher understands the essence of Christian faith as the feeling or intuition of our utter dependence on God; Calvin understands faith as a living, existential, trust in the God on whom we depend for life. For Calvin the stress is on the objective fact of God's upholding all things (the ground of our trust); for Schleiermacher the stress is on our subjective intuition of dependence.

[50]One of the most helpful interpreters of Calvin on this point was Holmes Rolston III. My choice of phrases here is deliberately reminiscent of his interpretation of Calvin. See his *John Calvin Versus the Westminster Confession* (Richmond, Va.: John Knox Press, 1972), which is the popular version of his Ph.D. thesis at New College, Edinburgh.

[51]Calvin *Institutes* 2.12.2.

[52]Calvin *Institutes* 2.17. n.

on our behalf. We will come back to these reflections after our discussion of the theories.

In the twentieth century Gustaf Aulén (1879-1977), the Swedish bishop and theologian, provided a revised reading of early Christian theology (especially of Irenaeus) and of Luther in what became known as his *Christus Victor* model of the atonement (or as he also calls this view, the "classic" or the "dramatic" idea of atonement). Though Aulén fails at some critical points in his historical-theological analysis, he is helpful in recovering a perspective on the atonement that has been neglected—the idea that in Jesus Christ, God has achieved victory over and has vanquished the powers of evil. The central theme of this atonement motif is, in his own words, "the idea of the Atonement as a Divine conflict and victory; Christ— *Christus Victor* [the victorious Christ]— fights against and triumphs over the evil powers of the world, the 'tyrants' under which mankind is in bondage and suffering, and in Him God reconciles the world to Himself."[53] This heroic perspective on the atonement, which recaptures something of the warrior God in a modern age both rent by violence and distrustful of images of God that might glorify (or apotheosize) such violence,[54] has been popularized in C. S. Lewis's Chronicles of Narnia, in his Space Trilogy and in the writings of Lewis's friend Charles Williams.[55]

Aspects of the Atonement: Toward a More Inclusive Framework

As I said when we began this lecture, the conventional method of looking at the doctrine of the atonement has been to speak of a variety of "theories" of the atonement, as though the meaning of the salvation Christ brings to us could be boiled down to this or that single theory. In fact, the biblical witness is far richer than this approach allows, and the richness of the biblical witness gives rise to a wealth of theological reflection.

---

[53]Aulén, *Christus Victor*, p. 4.

[54]See, for example, Erich Zenger, *A God of Vengeance? Understanding the Psalms of Divine Wrath,* trans. Linda M. Maloney (Louisville, Ky.: Westminster John Knox, 1996); Mary E. Mills, *Images of God in the Old Testament* (Collegeville, Minn.: Michael Glazier/Liturgical Press, 1998); Michael Jinkins, *In the House of the Lord: Inhabiting the Psalms of Lament* (Collegeville, Minn.: Liturgical Press, 1998).

[55]F. W. Dillistone provides a helpful discussion of this model of the atonement in "The Unique Redemption," chap. 3 of *The Christian Understanding of the Atonement* (London: SCM Press, 1968), pp. 76-114. His historical-theological analysis is more accurate than Aulén's, and he takes far more material into his synthesis.

A more helpful way of looking at the meaning of Christ's life, death and resurrection would be to see the *various aspects of atonement* (what the theories are trying to get at) *in a more inclusive incarnational framework.* This is suggested, in fact, by Irenaeus, Athanasius, Calvin, Luther (to some extent) and even more fully by John McLeod Campbell, to whom we will now turn our attention.

There are things the various theories of the atonement are trying to teach us but that easily get lost in the shuffle if we see them as separate and discrete theories, especially as opposing theories from which we must choose the "right" one. If we could see them as aspects of a larger and more comprehensive reality, we would do much better. Each aspect of the atonement to a greater or a lesser degree has some value. But we must not lose sight of the issue as a whole: *What Jesus Christ did for us he did in the depths of his unique divine humanity, in uniting our humanity with the life of God in himself.*

Yet even here there is need for careful qualification and clarification.

While we can say that Jesus Christ righted the universal wrong, fulfilled the terms of absolutely righteous divine justice and kept the promise of our being that we failed to keep, it is necessary also to insist that Christ's atonement is not a matter of legal fictions or satisfying the bloodlust of a vengeful God. And it is here, as I mentioned earlier, that John McLeod Campbell (1800-1872) can be of service to us. Campbell understood and appreciated the various aspects of the atonement while placing them in a larger, more inclusive incarnational framework.

What he did is deceptively simple.

Campbell said that Christ did not come to change the mind of an angry God but to reveal the loving heart of God toward all God's rebellious children. Campbell said that the filial relationship to God for which we were originally created, the reality of our being children of God that we have forgotten in our life-destroying and dissolute existence in the far country, has been restored fully to us in Jesus Christ, the Son of God and Son of Man. In teachings reminiscent of early Christian theologians Campbell emphasized the idea that the triune God in Jesus Christ became what we are so that we might share in his quality of life.

Whereas so much theology, in the spirit of Anselm and post-Calvin Calvinism (the sort of Calvinism that tried to "out-Calvin" Calvin and so lost the evangelical passion and warmth of Calvin's thought), had emphasized what Campbell called the "retrospective aspect of the atonement," which had become little more than a backward-looking preoccupation with our salvation from the penalties of sin, Campbell reminds us that the true *retrospective aspect* of the atonement is freedom from the bondage to sin itself. God's purpose for us is nothing less than delivering us from slavery to sin in order to deliver us to a real participation in *eternal life,* not merely life in the sweet hereafter but the quality of life in relationship to and for others that Christ lived by trusting in God the Father through the power of the Holy Spirit. This involves what Campbell called the *prospective aspect* of the atonement, the continuing experience of God's life and character that Christ shares with us through his atonement.

Christ went into the far country and *became the prodigal Son* so that he might return us (in himself) to the Father's house. According to Campbell the heart of God the Father sought to provide in Jesus Christ an atonement for humanity's sin simply because God yearned to return humanity to himself. Christ became human so that he could, as Campbell says, pronounce a perfect "Amen" to God's judgment on our sin. Only God could understand the "hatefulness" and destructiveness of our sin; only Christ as God could feel that divine grief God feels toward sin when God sees creation ruined by the independence and disgrace of our sin. As true Son of God, Christ condemns our sin in our flesh while he also extends in himself grace and mercy to all sinners. As true Son of Man, Christ confesses our sin and repents of our sin for us while he alone rightly responds obediently in our humanity to God, opening the way for us to follow him in the power of his Spirit into the life that is eternal in quality. Jesus Christ is both God's yes to humanity and God's no to the sin that destroys our humanity—a yes and a no spoken from the very heart of God the Father through the divine Spirit. To put it another way, the atonement of God and humanity is an event in the depths of the Trinity, in the very inner life of God, an event the reality of which God shares with us now as we follow Christ in the world by the power of the Spirit.[56]

---

[56]There is no substitute for reading John McLeod Campbell's study of the atonement, *The Nature of the Atonement,* though his writing style makes for slow going. James Torrance's introduction to the new printing of this classic provides an excellent overview of Campbell's thought. See John McLeod Campbell, *The Nature of the Atonement,* introduction by James B. Torrance (Grand Rapids, Mich.: Eerdmans, 1996). Also of interest may be Michael Jinkins, *Love Is of the Essence: An Introduction to the Theology of John McLeod Campbell* (Edinburgh: St. Andrew Press, 1993); and my more technical study, *A Comparative Study in the Theology of Atonement in Jonathan Edwards and John McLeod Campbell: Atonement and the Character of God* (San Francisco: Mellen University Press, 1993).

In Christ, Campbell tells us, *we* have repented and returned to God. *In Christ we* have died and our sins are nailed to his cross. *In Christ we* have descended into hell, and *we* have left there our disobedience and distrust, our independence and inauthenticity, our brokenness, our alienation, guilt and disgrace, this accursed living-death we have vainly tried to live apart from God. *In Christ we* are raised again to new life, and now *we* stand *in Christ* in the very presence of God the Father almighty. The birth, life, suffering, death, resurrection and ascension of Jesus Christ are a seamless garment, a single divine-human reality, in the church's teaching.

The One who suffered and died has risen from the dead; the One who is risen was born to suffer and die. And all he did, he did in revealing God the Father's love toward a world that had rebelled against God, that had forgotten God, that had replaced God with its foolish gods. What Jesus Christ achieved for us in his humanity, in his life of utter trustfulness in God, he achieved in living as much as in dying and as much in dying as in rising from the dead. We must understand, as Lesslie Newbigin has said, *the resurrection of Jesus Christ is not the reversal of a defeat, but the proclamation of a victory.*[57]

This is especially crucial as we reflect on Campbell's understanding of the atonement. Christ's whole life and being is God's atonement. He lived and died and rose again so that God might give us Christ's quality of life, that character which God intended us to share by the power of the Spirit. The resurrection, then, is God's stamp of approval on the eternal quality of life Jesus lived, a quality of life that culminates in the cross. The victory of Jesus Christ, then, is his living *this quality of life in this kind of world* (in a world that rejects and crucifies eternal life); and this life that is victorious in death is answered by God's thundering Yes! God's ultimate Amen in the resurrection of Jesus Christ.

All of this we attempt to hold on to in the teaching of the Christian church because to do less would be untrue both to the complexity of the gospel and the complexity of human life. And so we close this session with another beginning, by remembering the first question and answer exchange of the Heidelberg Catechism (1563), which we have already noted in another context:

---

[57]Lesslie Newbigin, *Foolishness to the Greeks: The Gospel and Western Culture* (London: SPCK, 1986), p. 127.

Q. What is your only comfort, in life and in death?

A. That I belong—body and soul, in life and in death—not to myself but to my faithful Savior, Jesus Christ, who at the cost of his own blood has fully paid for all my sins and has completely freed me from the dominion of the devil; that he protects me so well that without the will of my Father in heaven not a hair can fall from my head; indeed, that everything must fit his purpose for my salvation. Therefore, by his Holy Spirit, he also assures me of eternal life, and makes me wholeheartedly willing and ready from now on to live for him.[58]

We are "wholeheartedly willing and ready from now on to live for him," because Christ has in our humanity lived for us. As the church confessed with Paul, "I have been crucified with Christ; and it is no longer I who live, but it is Christ who lives in me. And the life I now live in the flesh I live by faith in the Son of God, who loved me and gave himself for me" (Gal 2:19-20).

Summary. Jesus Christ is the at-onement of our humanity with God. In his supreme act of self-giving love, God has taken upon himself our sin and death, and the fear of sin and death, so that we might know eternal life, God's quality of life.

Homework Assignments

1. *Coming to terms.* It's important to know the meanings of the words we use and why we use a particular word in a particular context instead of some other word. The Christian faith uses a variety of words to describe the reality of what God has done for us in Christ: *salvation, deliverance, liberation, redemption, ransom, reconciliation, atonement, justification* and *sanctification.*

Write a definition paragraph (250 words) on each of the above words; explain the basic meanings of each word as these meanings have emerged in its usage, noting the word's origins, its biblical uses, its use in the history of the church and the ways it is now used to convey shades of meaning that distinguish it from the other words.

2. *Connections.* This lecture says that there is a real connection between the self-emptying life of Jesus Christ and the inner life of God the Father, Son and Holy Spirit. What does this mean to you?

---

[58]Question one of *The Heidelberg Catechism with Commentary*, foreword by Allen O. Miller et al. (New York: Pilgrim, 1979), p. 17.

3. *Reflections on the cross.* What does it mean to say, as John Calvin does, that the whole life of Jesus Christ was "a sort of perpetual cross"? Does this mean that Jesus was always suffering and never happy? We are given the impression that Jesus joyfully did the will of God and seems to have enjoyed life. Is joy somehow different from happiness? What do you think? What else might Calvin have been getting at?

4. *Aspects of the atonement.* The various theories of the atonement are attempts to picture the reality of what God has done for us in Christ. Each theory uses ideas available at a particular time and place to express the unexpressible mystery of divine love. Thus Anselm's picture of the atonement reflects feudal society, and Hastings Rashdall's reflects the idealistic aspirations at the beginning of the twentieth century. Which of the historic theories seems to you most helpful? Which seems least helpful? Realizing of course that all our attempts are only of limited value (because of our limited outlooks), how would you picture the reality of what God has done for us in Christ (the atonement)?

Class 7

Our Humanity
in Light of Jesus Christ

"O Lord, thou hast searched me out, and known me.
Thou knowest my down-sitting, and mine up-rising;
thou understandest my thoughts long before.
Thou art about my path, and about my bed, and art acquainted with all my ways.
For lo, there is not a word in my tongue, but thou, O LORD, knowest it altogether.
Thou hast beset me behind and before, and laid thine hand upon me.
Such knowledge is too wonderful and excellent for me, I cannot attain unto it.

PSALM 139:1-5 KJV

"O God, by whom the meek are guided in judgment, and light riseth up in
darkness for the godly; Grant us, in all our doubts and uncertainties,
the grace to ask what thou wouldest have us to do,
that the Spirit of Wisdom may save us from
all false choices, and that in thy light we may see light, and in thy straight path
may not stumble; through Jesus Christ our Lord. Amen."

BOOK OF COMMON PRAYER

TODAY'S SESSION FORMS SOMETHING OF A PARENTHESIS WITHIN OUR LARGER study of Jesus Christ. The question we will grapple with today is a biblical question we are asking of God: "What are human beings that you are mindful of them?" (Ps 8:5).

It is a very big question, inquiring into the nature of this creature that is so close to us yet so for away, which is "made . . . a little lower than God" and "crowned . . . with glory and honor" (Ps 8:5). Perhaps this knowledge of ourselves really is "too wonderful" for us, as the psalmist says.

Certainly Shakespeare's well-worn words praise humanity, but even his perceptive verse fails to do more than accentuate the questions. "What a piece of work is a man! How noble in reason! how infinite in faculty! in form, in moving, how express and admirable! in action, how like an angel! in apprehension, how like a god! the beauty of the world! the paragon of animals! And yet, to me, what is this quintessence of dust?" (*Hamlet,* 2.2.).

Abraham Heschel, a Jewish scholar and one of the finest and most sensitive theological minds of the twentieth century, wrestled with this question. In his essay "What Is Man?" Heschel asks, "What is human about a human being?" He writes:

> We know that man is more similar to an ape than an ape is to a toad. We are told that "man has not only developed from the realm of animals—, he was, is, and shall always remain an animal." But is this the whole truth about man? Is this an answer to the question, "What do I see when I see a man?"[1]

With characteristic humor he reports reading a college textbook in which the human being is described as "an ingenious assembly of portable plumbing. . . . What glory to be a man!" Heschel exclaims. Then more seriously, he says that we ought not to laugh off such a description because it reveals a basic attitude that many people entertain about our humanity. He continues, "Is it not right to say that we often treat man as if he were made in the likeness of a machine rather than in the likeness of God."[2] Heschel's comment rings as true today in the age of computer analogies as it did in the age of when most machines went "clatter" and "clank."

Heschel then mentions in passing a description of humanity that appeared in the *Encyclopaedia Britannica.* It read, "Man is a seeker after the greatest degree of comfort for the least necessary expenditure of energy." In as far as it goes, this is an accurate statement. There are, of course, many such descriptions and definitions of humankind to be had based on observations of humanity at its best and at its worst. And speaking of humanity at its worst, hardly pausing, Heschel turns to a more sinister (one might even say demonic) attempt to define the human person. He writes, "In pre-Nazi Germany the following statement of man was frequently quoted: 'the human body contains a sufficient amount of fat to

---

[1]Abraham Heschel, "What Is Man?" in *Between God and Man: An Interpretation of Judaism,* ed. Fritz A. Rothschild (New York: Free Press, 1959), p. 233.
[2]Ibid.

make seven cakes of soap, enough iron to make a medium-sized nail, a sufficient amount of phosphorus to equip two thousand match-heads, [and] enough sulphur to rid one's self of one's fleas.' Perhaps," Heschel writes, "there was a connection between this statement and what the Nazis actually did in the extermination camps: to make soap of human flesh."[3]

Of course there was a connection, as Heschel understood only too well.

The first step toward the abolition of humanity is the reduction of humanity. Then comes the degradation and destruction of humanity. It is only a very small step from saying that Mrs. Fleischmann is the sum of her chemical parts to reducing Mrs. Fleischmann to chemical ash. Heschel says it best: "As descriptions of one of many aspects of the nature of man, these definitions may indeed be correct. But when pretending to express his totality of meaning, they contribute to the gradual liquidation of man's self-understanding. And the liquidation of the self-understanding of man may lead to the self-extinction of man." When we address ourselves to the mystery of humanity, we have reached the boundaries of science because, he tells us, "the depth and mystery of a human being is something that no science can grasp."[4] Until we become aware of "the sacred image" of our humanity, we shall merely be restating half-truths and oversimplifications. Heschel himself directs the earnest searcher for the truth about humanity to look at the Bible, to see humanity created in the image of God, humanity as dust of the earth, humanity as object of God's concern.[5]

Byron Sherwin, Heschel's biographer, helps us to sharpen our question even further. He writes:

> Aristotle had defined man as a variety of animal. For Aristotle, man is a "political animal," a "civilized animal," an "imitative animal." Scholastic philosophy had accepted Aristotle's other definition of man as a "rational animal." Benjamin Franklin defined man as a "tool making animal."
>
> While Heschel does not reject the zoological validity of classifying man as a variety of animal, he does insist that zoologically oriented definitions of man are *too* limited, too incomplete. Though man may be an animal, he is more than an animal. To define man only as an animal is to dehumanize man.[6]

We are animals. Certainly this is true. But is this all we are?

---

[3]Ibid.
[4]Ibid.
[5]Ibid., pp. 233-34.
[6]Byron Sherwin, *Abraham Joshua Heschel* (Atlanta: John Knox Press, 1979), p. 26.

Imagination Enough to See What Is There

We have been saying since the beginning of this course that we are persistently tempted to reductionism in regard to God—tempted to reduce the complexity, the depth, the profound mystery of God to easy formulas. We must now say that this temptation is no less true with regard to our own humanity. Even that which seems most familiar to us is not. There are heresies against the mystery of humanity as surely as there are heresies against the mystery of God.

At the heart of our creaturely existence lies inscrutable mystery. Our familiarity with ourselves only aggravates the situation, teasing us as though we are caught in a game of hide-and-seek with our own mischievous souls. As Reinhold Niebuhr said at the beginning of his classic inquiry into the nature of humanity, "Man has always been his own most vexing problem."[7]

We so easily move from observations about various aspects of our humanity (such as observing our wonderful capacity for reason) to final, comprehensive definitions of human nature (such as that of Boethius, who defined the human being as a "rational substance"). The transition is all too easy and all too false both in its simplicity and in its comprehensiveness.

As Christians we have a rather peculiar responsibility when it comes to anthropology (which is the technical name for the study of humanity or "the doctrine of man," as it once was called) because our understanding of humanity is given its shape and content by our peculiar theological reflection. Our theological perspective, like that of Heschel's, would insist that we are not merely animals, though certainly we are that. Thus if confronted with a purely biological definition of humanity, we find ourselves agreeing in as far as this definition might go yet wanting to go well beyond it.

On the other hand, when either a Marxist or a full-blooded capitalist tells us that a human being is essentially an economic unit—whether they mean by that a worker or a consumer—we exercise our theological prerogative by saying categorically, "No!" A human being is not essentially an economic unit, neither just a laborer nor a consumer. Ironically both Marxism and capitalism have this in common, this tendency to reduce ontology (that is, being) to economy. And in the face of both, Christian faith attempts

---

[7]Reinhold Niebuhr, *The Nature and Destiny of Man: A Christian Interpretation*, vol. 1, *Human Nature* (New York: Charles Scribner's Sons, 1941), p. 1.

to affirm and to preserve the mystery of our humanity against the threat of reduction.[8]

A moment ago I alluded to Boethius and his conception of the human being as a "rational substance." An inspiring vision, isn't it? But this is very similar to the vision of human nature we find in René Descartes and in the rationalism that developed following his lead. Theologian Colin Gunton says, "For Descartes, the person is the thinking thing, the intellectual reality to which all other human experiences ultimately reduce."[9]

"I am," says Descartes, "a mind." The individual mind exists in isolation from other individual minds, defining itself in terms of its own rational capacity. The individual mind is only loosely related to a body, to *any* body.

This view was handed along to us in Locke's rationalistic empiricism (though Locke saw his work largely as a critical rebuttal of Descartes) and was refined and given moral content in the doctrines of Immanuel Kant. This view of the human being as an isolated and individual rational entity, a mind dwelling in a body (separate from other minds dwelling in bodies), is fundamental to most of the Western philosophical, religious, scientific, political and ethical thought of the modern period. It represents the zenith of alienation as persons sense their assunderedness from themselves, from one another, from the world around them and from "the rational principle" behind the existence of this world (if such a "rational principle" can be assumed to exist).[10]

From our peculiar perspective as Christians, again we are called on by our faith to speak clearly a word of reconciliation into the midst of alienation.

---

[8]*Ontology* is the technical term for the study of being. The term is derived from the Greek *ont-*, meaning "that which is," in combination with *logos*, meaning "word." In context I am using the word to describe our essential being, who we are, as closely connected with why we are. The primary purpose of our being is not economic. The purpose of our existence is "to glorify God and enjoy him forever." We do this by reflecting God's character in community with one another. Secondarily we may express God's glory through economic endeavors. But we are not merely what we produce, nor is our worth as persons grounded in our ability to multiply capital.

[9]Colin Gunton, "The One, the Three and the Many: An Inaugural Lecture in the Chair of Christian Doctrine," a paper read at King's College, London, May 14, 1985), p. 3.

[10]I would encourage the reader wishing to pursue this line of thought to see another book by Colin Gunton, *Enlightenment & Alienation: An Essay Towards a Trinitarian Theology* (Basingstoke, U.K.: Marshall Morgan & Scott, 1985).

But how do we do this? We are surrounded by questions upon questions.

☐ I know that a human being is an animal. But what does it mean to be *this particular kind* of animal?

☐ I know that a human being is marvelously made up of a variety of parts, at times machinelike, at times computerlike, at times broken, at times whole. But what does it mean to be a human being, *whose sum is so much greater than the parts?*

☐ I am aware that a human being derives pleasure and meaning from being engaged in different sorts of activities: working, playing, creating. But what does it mean to be a worker, to be a player, to be a creator, to be created in the image of God?

☐ I think, but my *rationality* isn't detached from my *being*. And *my* being is somehow in relationship with *your* being. But I don't understand how. What does it mean to be in relationship? To be constituted in such a way that relationship is absolutely crucial to being human?

I am reminded of something that G. K. Chesterton says in the introduction of his own excursion into anthropology, the book that many consider his best, *The Everlasting Man*. Chesterton says that when we are trying to gain an understanding of truth, "we must try to recover the candour and wonder of the child; the unspoilt realism and objectivity of innocence. Or if we cannot do that, we must try at least to shake off the cloud of mere custom and see the thing as new, if only by seeing it as unnatural. . . . We must invoke the most wild and soaring sort of imagination; the imagination that can see what is there."[11]

Somehow we must be given a clear vision of that reality—our own humanity—which is closer to us than any other but which remains mysteriously hidden from us; we must be given a vision of who we are, a vision that is hidden by our own selves. We need a revelation of our humanity as surely as we need a revelation of God.

Our humanity, in other words, *is a question the answer to which eludes us.* This was in part what Paul Tillich was getting at when in his study of Christ he discussed his "method of correlation." Tillich explained that the human being "in the conflicts of his existential situation" provides the question that we must try to answer in Christian theology. But our "analysis of the human predicament" does not provide the answer, only the question.

---

[11]G. K. Chesterton, *The Everlasting Man* (London: Hodder & Stoughton, 1925), p. 9.

The answer to the question posed by our human existence is "the divine self-manifestation," God's self-disclosure. Or to put it another way, Tillich continues, "Man is the question, not the answer. . . . He cannot avoid asking [the question], because his very being is the question of his existence." But "God is manifest only through God. Existential questions and theological answers are independent of each other." And yet our existential questions demand answers that are unavailable within the bounds of our creaturely existence.[12]

The problem with Tillich's excellent analysis is this: I'm not really sure it is altogether true either to life or the teachings of the Christian church. I'm not sure Tillich is seeing with "that most wild and soaring kind of imagination," as Chesterton called it, "the imagination that can see what is there."[13]

What is there in the midst of our existential situations is a good deal more confusing, complex, ambiguous and hidden than this description given by Tillich. Even if *a* question is being posed by our human existence, I'm not sure it is altogether the right question or the most helpful question or that it is being asked in a way that is answerable. Often the questions our existence poses are voiced in contorted and distorted ways, in untrue ways, in ways that predetermine answers that are foreshortened, hopelessly skewed and obscure. As we have been saying from the beginning, the quality of our questions determines the quality of our answers. And the questions we pose in our shattered human existence seem hopelessly inadequate. We seem altogether unable in the contradictions of our existence to pose the question that our existence demands. But if we have the imagination of faith to see *what is there* in Jesus Christ, we can comprehend that the question of human existence has been given voice in the incarnation, in the life of the one who "is there only for others," the one who for our sake adequately poses the question our existence demands but that we are unable to articulate for ourselves.[14]

In one of his most memorable aphorisms Kierkegaard says that life can

---

[12]Paul Tillich, *Systematic Theology,* vol. 2, *Existence and the Christ* (Chicago: University of Chicago Press, 1957), pp. 13-14.

[13]Chesterton, *Everlasting Man*, p. 9, emphasis mine.

[14]Dietrich Bonhoeffer, from notes he made for a book he never got to write (July-August 1944), *Letter and Papers from Prison*, ed. Eberhard Bethge (1953; reprint, New York: Macmillan, 1971), p. 381.

only be understood backwards, but it must be lived forwards.[15] We need a place to stand, a vantage point from which we can survey human life so that we can ask the right questions pertaining to our existence and ask them well. Living our lives "forwards" we lack the necessary perspective to ask the questions our existence demands us to ask. We need to see our lives "backwards," with the benefit of perspective, in order to ask the questions that will make sense of it all. Which brings us back again to Jesus Christ. We believe we have found in Jesus Christ one whose life poses the questions demanded by our human existence. Looking back over our humanity, through him, we believe we are given the necessary perspective to see our humanity in a way we cannot see ourselves living forwards.

The Specificity of Jesus Christ

The beginning point for our anthropology then is not our own experience but Jesus Christ in whom God discovers to us our humanity. The one who, in his revelation of God's character, embodies the answer to the questions posed by our human existence is also the one who, in his revelation of our humanity, poses the questions in a way that can and must be answered. To understand this twofold revelation we are compelled to look at the specificity of the Synoptic Gospels and to the theological reflections of our earliest theologians (Paul, and to the author of the Fourth Gospel and the epistles of John) in order to understand the truth about our human nature, rather than trying to build up a general conception of humanity based on our experiences.

We are seeking to understand who we are, not simply the processes through which we have attained to this physiological or psychological or sociological status. Our sciences are quite helpful in providing clues to the riddles of *how,* but even the most widely based analyses of humanity and human cultures are unable to comprehend the questions of *who* and the *why* of our existence.

---

[15]Kierkegaard's actual comment was "It is perfectly true, as philosophers say, that life must be understood backwards. But they forget the other proposition, that it must be lived forwards." See Patrick Gardiner's reflections on this idea in his *Kierkegaard* (Oxford: Oxford University Press, 1988), p. 90. Also note the way Kierkegaard relates this idea to the life of Christ in a journal entry from April 14, 1838: "Life can only be explained after it has been lived, just as Christ only began to interpret the Scriptures and show how they applied to him—after his resurrection." Robert Bretall, ed., *A Kierkegaard Anthology* (Princeton, N.J.: Princeton University Press, 1946), p. 10.

When we begin in this way, attempting to understand our humanity in light of Jesus Christ by addressing ourselves to the specificity of the Jesus Christ we meet in the Gospels and in the reflections of the earliest Christian communities, we are confronted by a human being who (with utter clarity of consciousness) draws his life from God and who lives his life for others, a human person who lives in union with God, and in union with God is truly who he is in his humanity. Let's rehearse some of the events we learn of Jesus Christ in the Gospels.

In his baptism Jesus identifies fully with humanity (Mt 3:13-17; Mk 1:12; Lk 3:21-22) by presenting a picture of emptying himself for the sake of others. In loving submission to the love of God he humbles himself, as we have already observed, "taking the form of a slave, being born in human likeness and being found in human likeness, he humbled himself and became obedient to the point of death."[16] For our sake he became like us. And as he who was without sin humbled himself for the sake of others, identifying with our humanity in our sin (in our willful rebellion against God, our unrighteousness and frailty) and submitting himself to baptism for the remission of our sins, "he saw the heavens torn apart and the Spirit descending like a dove on him." And the voice from heaven spoke to the Son, "You are my Son, the Beloved; with you I am well pleased" (Mk 1:11).

And straight away this same Spirit who confirmed Christ's self-emptying identification with humanity "drove him into the wilderness" where he was tempted by Satan (Mk 1:12-13). He was tempted with the fundamental temptations of humankind—to rely on himself, to defy God and to worship something in place of God (Mt 4:1-11; Lk 4:1-13). In the simplicity and directness of these passages we are confronted with the humanity of Christ, his vulnerability, childlike trustfulness, and adoration and love of God. His strength lies not in claiming exceptional power for himself but precisely in his complete reliance on God and his unwillingness to make his own way or to turn aside from his heavenly Father.

Jesus returned to Galilee, following these remarkable events, Luke says, "in the power of the Spirit" (Lk 4:14). And perhaps this could be the single phrase descriptive of his quality of life as a whole: *in the power of the Spirit.*

---

[16]Michael Green makes much the same point in his *Baptism: Its Purpose, Practice and Power* (Downers Grove, Ill.: InterVarsity Press, 1987), pp. 38-39. The implications of this insight are evident in Karl Rahner's *Meditations on the Sacraments* (New York: Seabury, 1977), pp. 1-15.

If so, what we see in Jesus is a humanity fully human precisely in the way God originally intended humanity to be, in complete reliance on God, in trustful, grateful openness to God's power and God's future rather than in arrogant independence and vain distrust. And this is the same humanity to which Jesus Christ calls us by the Spirit.

His first recorded appearance as a teacher in the local synagogue is most significant in this regard. He opened the scroll and found the place in Isaiah where it was written, "The Spirit of the Lord is upon Me, because He anointed Me to preach the Gospel to the poor. He has sent Me to proclaim release to the captives, and recovery of sight to the blind, to set free those who are downtrodden, to proclaim the favorable year of the Lord." Closing the scroll he sat down, "and the eyes of all in the synagogue were fixed on Him. And he began to say to them, 'Today this Scripture has been fulfilled in your hearing.' And all were speaking well of Him, and wondering at the gracious words which were falling from His lips; and they were saying, 'Is this not Joseph's son?'" (Lk 4:17-22 NASB). Jesus consciously began his teaching ministry by appropriating Isaiah's proclamation of a "favorable year," a time of great reversals of fortune. And here we see the living parable of the humanity Jesus revealed to be *true* humanity, a humanity over which God reigns as sovereign.

Jesus said to the congregation, "This day has this Scripture been fulfilled in your hearing." He speaks, and the new era dawns. I think we might go so far as to say that Jesus is himself the personal embodiment of the Lord's *kairos* (the Lord's time, the "fullness of time"). His life is none other than God's time. In his coming Jesus Christ overwhelms the merely chronological. He turns back on itself the developments of *chronos* time, preaching good news to the poor, setting captives free, giving sight to the blind and uplifting the downtrodden. Those who have made themselves first, according to the standards of mere chronology, find themselves at the end of the line in the Lord's era of *kairos*. The humanity that measures its successes on the plain of chronology finds itself measured by another standard in the "favorable year." And this new era that Jesus embodies dawns by the power of the Spirit, not by the power of the flesh.

This is what we see throughout Jesus' ministry, isn't it?

Jesus breaks through the moral, social, economic, racial, tribal, political and religious boundaries set by the standards of every present age:

☐ in the calling of his disciples, the fishermen, a tax collector, a political zealot

☐ in the extension of his fellowship to sinners, publicans and prostitutes

☐ in his parables of the kingdom (which are verbal pictures of the human life he embodied)

☐ in casting out demons and in healing the sick (by which he announced God's sovereignty over human life)

☐ in forgiving sinners (by which he joined together that privilege to judge, which is God's alone, and the opportunity to release people from guilt, which is an opportunity also facing each human being).

The hatred he inspired among the powers and principalities of this world (who in the end took his life) bears eloquent witness to the grandeur of his vision of humanity.[17] We see in Christ that human dignity is bestowed not by the powers of the present age but by the God to whom we entrust our life, which is another way of saying that our humanity is the gift of grace, not of works. Jesus Christ is the true person of faith. His humanity is our humanity as it is meant to be, not grasped in greed or fear but graciously received from the hand of God.

This message beckons so clearly back to the Genesis narrative of the Fall, in which evil whispered in our ears the message of distrust. Trust is the essential issue at stake in the saga of humankind—not obedience to legal pronouncements per se but childlike reliance on God. Our obedience to the Word of God is an expression of our trust in God, not a condition we must meet prior to being admitted to relationship with God.

In the story of the Fall the serpent tells humanity that the God who created us and who sustains us and who placed us in the Garden and gave us everything we need cannot be trusted, that this God is jealously denying us something that is good for us. So humanity declares its independence on the basis of a fundamental distrust of God, and the dull litany of disgrace becomes the theme of human history.

The Gospel narratives we have just brought to mind show us a stunning reversal of this sad story. The account of Jesus' baptism parallels the story of creation and Fall. The creative Word identifies with created humanity, and the voice from heaven that had pronounced creation *Tov! Good!* confirms Jesus' mission: *Tov! Tov!* "This is my Son, the Beloved, in whom I am

---

[17]See Ellis Rivkin, *What Crucified Jesus?* (Nashville: Abingdon, 1984).

well pleased." Then comes the temptation in the wilderness, paralleling the temptation in the Garden, the temptation to grasp in creaturely independence and fear, to mistrust and to displace God. But Christ does not stumble and fall as humanity does; in himself he raises up our humanity to the highest position in creation, the place of trust in God.

Paul and the Johannine author draw us to reflect even further on the implications of this insight into Christ's humanity and ours. Karl Barth has said that "Jesus Christ," for Paul, "is the secret truth about the essential nature of man."[18] Commenting on Romans 5:1-11 and the relationship between Adam (as the name for our humanity as we see ourselves only in light of our history) and Christ (God's revelation of our true nature), Barth continues:

> Christ stands above and is first, and Adam stands below and is second. So it is Christ that reveals the true nature of man. Man's nature in Adam is not, as is usually assumed, his true and original nature; it is only truly human at all in so far as it reflects and corresponds to essential human nature as it is found in Christ.[19]

The story of the Fall of humanity in Adam and Eve forms the essential backdrop for Paul's reflections on Christ. For that reason it might be helpful to recount the story of the Fall from the book of Genesis, chapter three. The story of the Fall begins intriguingly, as though we are walking onto a stage already set, an action already in motion: "Now the serpent was more crafty than any other wild animal that the LORD God had made. He said to the woman, 'Did God say, "You shall not eat from any tree in the garden"?' The woman said to the serpent, 'We may eat of the fruit of the trees in the garden; but God said, "You shall not eat of the fruit of the tree that is in the middle of the garden, nor shall you touch it, or you shall die".' But the serpent said to the woman, 'You will not die; for God knows that when you eat of it your eyes will be opened, and you will be like God, knowing good and evil.' So when the woman saw that the tree was good for food, and that the tree was to be desired to make one wise, she took of its fruit and ate; and she also gave some to her husband, who was with her, and he ate. Then the eyes of both were opened, and they

---

[18]Karl Barth, *Christ and Adam: Man and Humanity in Romans 5*, trans. Thomas A. Smail, Scottish Journal of Theology Occasional Papers 5 (Edinburgh: Oliver & Boyd, 1956, 1963), p. 41.

[19]Ibid., p. 43.

knew that they were naked; and they sewed fig leaves together and made loincloths for themselves" (Gen 3:1-7). Fast on the heels of these events comes God's discovery of humanity's disobedience, the consequences of the refusal to trust God alone, the blaming of one another and of God, then the whole sad, monotonous story of anger, wrath, violence and pain, enmity, and alienation from God, others, creation and self—the whole sad litany that becomes subsumed under the name of Adam, humanity, created male and female, created for community, created to delight and glory in fellowship with God and one another but turned instead toward brokenness and sin.

Dietrich Bonhoeffer, in his lectures on creation and the Fall, comments on the story:

> The Bible does not seek to impart information about the origin of evil but to witness to its character as guilt and as the unending burden that humankind bears. To pose the question about the origin of evil as something separate from this is far from the mind of the biblical author. Yet when the question is posed in the way that the biblical author poses it, the answer cannot be unequivocal or direct. It will always contain two sides [das Doppelte]: that I as a creature of God have done what is completely opposed to God and is evil, and that just for that very reason this constitutes guilt and indeed inexcusable guilt. It will therefore never be possible simply to blame the devil who has led one astray; instead this same devil will always be precisely in the place where I, as God's creature in God's world, ought to have been living and did not wish to live. It is, of course, just as impossible to accuse creation of being imperfect and to blame it for my evil. The guilt is mine alone: I have committed evil in the midst of the original state of creation.[20]

Were this account of our Fall, our failure, to be the only or even the primary thing that we must say about our humanity, then there would be little joy in being human. This is why Karl Barth is so insistent that we understand Paul's bold theological move, Paul's extraordinary insight into the grace of God in Jesus Christ. Think again of Barth's statement: "Jesus Christ is the secret truth about the essential nature of man." The deep, hidden secret about our humanity is not that we are descended from Adam, it is not that we have in our family tree a fratricidal character like Cain, nor is it that our family closet is full of skeletons that rattle in the dark, which we

---

[20]Dietrich Bonhoeffer, *Creation and Fall: A Theological Exposition of Genesis 1—3*, ed. John W. De Gruchy, trans. Douglas Stephen Bax (Minneapolis: Fortress, 1997), p. 105.

must keep hidden at all costs. No indeed. Jesus Christ is our family secret. This is the heart of Paul's gospel, and it turns the Fall on its head.

Christ identifies so completely with our humanity that we come to discover our true identity only in and through him. Christ is, to use Paul's expression, *the one for the many* or *the one for all.* Who Christ is, he is for all humanity and not merely for the Jewish nation and certainly not for the members of some Johnny-come-lately Gentile cult. And the humanity Christ reveals is unlike the dull, monotonous Adamic humanity, characterized by its distrust of God, its vacuous self-reliance, its estrangement from self and subordination of others. The humanity that Christ reveals and to which Christ invites us is characterized by Paul as eternal life, as we have already noted, that quality of life that flows from the Spirit of Christ, the new life that pronounces as dead "the old man," the resurrected life that owes its power not to the strength of the flesh but to the power of the Spirit. And as possessors of this life we are drawn into the relationship with God that Jesus Christ enjoyed. As Paul says, "For you did not receive a spirit of slavery to fall back into fear, but you have received a spirit of adoption. When we cry, 'Abba! Father!' it is that very Spirit bearing witness with our spirit that we are children of God, and if children, then heirs, heirs of God, and joint heirs with Christ" (Rom 8:14-17).

Even as Christ's ministry of reconciliation broke through the various boundaries of the present age in the name of the reign of God (as we saw in the Synoptic Gospels), participation in his life by the power of the Spirit (union with Christ) places us under a new and comprehensive vision of humanity in which "there is no longer Jew or Greek [no racial or cultural boundaries], there is no longer slave or free, [no political or economic boundaries], there is no longer male or female [no gender-based boundaries]; *for all of you are one in Christ Jesus"* (Gal 3:28). All identities and relationships are utterly transformed by our union with Christ. As Marcus Barth reminds us in his study of the epistle to the Ephesians, Jesus Christ in his cross and resurrection has " 'broken down' (or abolished)" the various walls of division between humanity and God, and between us and others, and between us and the life to which God calls us in Christ. But we should not stop here, he says.

> To confess Jesus Christ is to affirm the abolition and end of division and hostility, the end of separation and segregation, the end of enmity and contempt, and the end of every sort of ghetto! Jesus Christ does not bring victory to the

[person] who is on either this or that side of the fence. Neither rich nor poor, Jew nor Greek, man nor woman, black nor white, can claim Christ solely for himself. All bear the stigma of "the old man that perishes in deceitful desires" (Eph 4:22; 2:2-3;) whereas in Christ "the two are created one new man" (2:15). So Christ's victory is for both; it cannot be divided.[21]

The sign and seal of the new life God gives us is our baptism into Jesus Christ, our identification with him who identified with us (Eph 4:1-16), a baptism that is the sign and seal of our death, both to sin and to our old humanity in Adam, in the death of Christ: "for you have died, and your life is hidden with Christ in God" (Col 3:3). Thus Christ is not only head of the church, Christ is also Lord of all creation (Col 1:15-20), even those who do not know or who do not yet recognize that Christ is the hidden name of our humanity.[22]

The writer of 1 John presses home the belief that the "eternal life that was with the Father" was "revealed to us" (1 Jn 1:2-3). God reveals the character of his eternal life, his "perfect love," in "sending his Son into the world so that we might live through him." Though "the world" (as we know it in our experience) does not comprehend or value the eternal life and perfect love embodied by Jesus Christ, yet this life, this love, is stronger than the darkness and death of "the world" (1 Jn 3:11-17; 4:7-12). God shares his character with those who "abide in him," and these persons are born of God to live in the world for the sake of others (1 Jn 4:13-16).

The contrast in the Fourth Gospel between God and the world, light and darkness, truth and falsehood, life and death is grounded in the fact that Jesus Christ reveals to us "the Way," which does not make itself known in the usual commerce of the present age. The discourse attributed to Jesus in chapters 13-17 of the Fourth Gospel comprises the most astounding and soaring trinitarian reflection in the whole of Scripture. But it arises from the very simple belief that God gave himself for the sake of creation and that in this divine self-giving, God's character (as love) is revealed, and our true humanity (both our nature and destiny) is also disclosed to us. The purpose of this revelation, as Eugene Peterson has said, is not to provide information but *to involve us in this quality of life*

---

[21]Marcus Barth, *The Broken Wall: A Study of the Epistle to the Ephesians* (Chicago: Judson Press, 1959), pp. 39-51.
[22]See Carlyle Marney, *The Recovery of the Person: A Christian Humanism* (New York: Abingdon, 1963), pp. 66-68, 73-85.

described variously as abundant, everlasting and eternal.[23]

What is perhaps most fascinating is the impression we get from the Fourth Gospel that humanity has gone to incredible lengths to avoid the most natural thing in the world. We are like branches of a vine that have tried to grow by cutting ourselves off from the life-giving vine. All God has ever wanted from us is just for us to "rest" in his strength or to "abide" in him, to be nourished by the life that flows from him (Jn 15:1-11), which is what Jesus Christ did. And, of course, in his life of absolute trust in God he judges our lack of trust in our own human flesh (Jn 16:1-15).

The thing that Paul and John drive home is this: we are given our true humanity in Jesus Christ. When we see Jesus Christ, when we observe the quality of life he lived, we see human life as it was meant to be and ourselves as we shall become. As said before, reflection upon the specificity of Jesus' life leads us to say certain things about the inner life of God. This we see in Paul and in the Johannine writings. Before going any further, let's pause to summarize what we have learned so far.

Summary. Through the life of Jesus Christ we have access to genuine knowledge of God. But there is even more here. The life of Jesus Christ also provides us access to genuine knowledge of our humanity. In Christ we discern that the life we are meant to live is a life of trust in God and relationship with others through the power of the Holy Spirit. This life consists in a particular quality of communion.

The Image of God

This brings us back to the idea we alluded to in the opening of this session, the idea that we are created in the image of God (Latin, *imago Dei*). The basic biblical reference for this teaching is Genesis 1:26, which reads, "Then God [Elohim] said, 'Let us make humankind in our image, according to our likeness.'" The plural "let us," as many commentators agree, is probably a reference to the heavenly beings that were believed to compose God's royal court and is a reflection of the religious culture of those who authored this strand of the Genesis narrative. The words *image* and *likeness* are parallel and refer to the same thing, not, of course, to a physical appearance but to what we might call an analogical correspondence

---

[23]Eugene H. Peterson, *Reversed Thunder: The Revelation of John and the Praying Imagination* (San Francisco: Harper & Row, 1988), p. 13.

between God and humanity. The controversies regarding exactly what the image of God is and whether it survives in our humanity have dominated much of Christian theology for centuries. As the editors of the *Oxford Dictionary of the Christian Church* explain:

> Many theories have been advanced to explain in what the *Imago* consists. Several Gk. Fathers, including St. Gregory of Nyssa, the author of the "Spiritual Homilies" attributed to Macarius of Egypt, and St. John of Damascus, identify it with human free-will; others seek it in man's superiority to the rest of creation, or in a quality of soul such as simplicity and immortality, or in his reason. Acc. to St. Augustine, the Image of the Trinity is to be found in the intellectual nature of the soul and its three powers, Memory (the Father), Intellect (the Son) and Will (the Holy Ghost).[24]

During the age of Reformation, Calvin generally followed Luther's idea that the image of God in humanity is not to be identified with any particular faculty or quality, such as reason, but is humanity's ability to be God-related; thus the image of God in humanity was the actual capacity to be in relationship with God. This image was not destroyed in the Fall, Calvin said, but was terribly corrupted and distorted.

Karl Barth, in some respects, follows the Reformers Luther and Calvin. As you might anticipate, Barth does not believe that there is any sort of *natural* correlation between humanity and God by which we, by our own efforts, could work our way upward from humanity to God (a so-called analogy of being, [Latin, *analogia entis*]). But (and this is very important) Barth does perceive what could be called an "analogy of relationship" (Latin, *analogia relationis*) between humanity and God, and he grounds this *analogia relationis* in the belief that humanity is created in God's image.[25]

This is where the discussion of the image of God gets really interesting because Barth's view of this matter is a good deal more radical than one

---

[24]"Imago Dei," in *The Oxford Dictionary of the Christian Church*, ed. F. L. Cross and E. A. Livingstone, 2nd ed. (Oxford: Oxford University Press, 1974), p. 692.

[25]Barth's understanding of analogy of being and analogy of relationship (or analogy of grace) are fascinating. His at times bitter feud with fellow Reformed theologian Emil Brunner was notorious. But the issues over which they fought are vital. See Eberhard Busch, *Karl Barth: His Life from Letters and Autobiographical Texts,* rev. ed. (Philadelphia: Fortress, 1976); and in contrast, see David Cairns's article, "Natural Theology," in *A Handbook of Christian Theology* (New York: Collins, 1979), pp. 249-55. Barth and Brunner aired their differences in a point-counterpoint book, *Natural Theology,* which contains Brunner's essay "Nature and Grace," and Barth's famous reply, "No!" (trans. Peter Frankel [London: Centenary, 1946]).

might imagine. At first sight he simply seems to be harkening back to Augustine, who tried to interpret the image of God in a trinitarian framework. But instead of getting tangled up in the static qualities of rationality and so forth, Barth adopts the much broader and more dynamic and more inclusive framework of relationship. He writes:

> God created man in His own Image, in correspondence with His own being and essence. He created Him in the Image which emerges even in His work as the Creator and Lord of the covenant. Because He is not solitary in Himself, and therefore does not will to be so *ad extra,* it is not good for man to be alone, and God created him in His own Image, as male and female. This is what is emphatically said by Gen. I, and all other explanations of the *imago Dei* suffer from the fact that they do not do justice to this decisive statement. We need not waste words on the dissimilarity in the similarity of the similitude. Quite obviously we do not have here more than an analogy, i.e., similarity in dissimilarity. We merely repeat that there can be no question of an analogy of being, but of relationship. God is in relationship, and so too is the man created by Him. This is the divine likeness. When we view it in this way, the dispute whether it is lost by sin finds a self-evident solution. It is not lost. But more important is the fact that what man is indestructibly as he is man with the fellow-man, he is in hope of the being and action of the One who is his original in this relationship.[26]

Our "likeness" (or what Barth calls the "similitude") with God is our being in relationship, the creaturely reflection of God's own triune being in relationship. Building on Barth's essential insight we can say that the issue of relatedness always concerns a quality of communion that neither renounces nor ignores dissimilarity but that thrives on distinction in union while it also enjoys a commonality (in love) that goes deeper than our individual diversity.

☐ We find this vision in the image of God in Bernard of Clairvaux, who in his sermons on the Song of Songs speaks of God the Lover and God the Beloved, who are joined together in the embrace of divine Love, the Holy Spirit, who is the "mysterious kiss" God also shares with us through the passion of Christ. The Beloved, eternally begotten by the Lover, eternally "of the same essence" as the Lover, stands before the Lover (and is not identical with the Lover), yet is bound to the Lover in love. This is the life

---

[26]Karl Barth, *Church Dogmatics,* 3/2, ed. G. W. Bromiley and T. F. Torrance, trans. G. W. Bromiley (Edinburgh: T & T Clark, 1956-1977) p. 324.

and love that we were created to share.

☐ We find a similar vision of this distinction in union reflected in christo-logical thought that affirms what the classical theologians called the "hypo-static union" of the divine and human natures in Christ—*union without confusion.*

☐ We find this also in the vision of the church that Paul provides, of many diverse and diversely gifted members in one body, bound together by the Holy Spirit, the eternal source of our distinctive gifts and our unity.

☐ And surely we have seen reflected in our own lives the mystery of relat-edness that knows the joy of finding another who is not ourselves, who is free and distinct from us yet who loves us, and with whom we have com-munion. This is the reality of love for which we yearn because this is the pattern of love woven into our humanity, a pattern that reflects the being of God.

St. Patrick's words, "I bind unto myself today, the strong Name of the Trinity," invite us into a startling new vision of the world. The God we wor-ship is not a singular divine entity, a windowless monad, isolated and removed from creation, alone and hidden. *God,* as the Orthodox theolo-gian John Zizioulas has said, *has his being in communion.*[27] The humanity that God has created in his image cannot rest in isolation, indeed, cannot be human in solitariness. This we have seen revealed in Jesus Christ. God in Christ emptied himself, becoming human for the sake of our humanity, showing us the heart, the very inner life, of God, living in trustful depen-dence on the Father through the power of the Spirit. And in so doing the Son shared with humanity his own humanity through the Spirit, obediently living his life of selfless love toward every and all others. This is the reality of interdependence that we are meant to enjoy in Christ through the Spirit.[28]

And—though it may seem odd to say, having gone halfway around the world to get here—G. K. Chesterton said very much the same thing without the benefit of the latest theological investigations into Eastern Orthodoxy or Karl Barth's *Church Dogmatics.* The most basic idea in all

---

[27]John D. Zizioulas, *Being as Communion: Studies in Personhood and the Church* (London: Darton, Longman & Todd, 1985).

[28]Also see Dietrich Bonhoeffer, *Sanctorum Communio: A Theological Study of the Sociology of the Church,* Dietrich Bonhoeffer Works 1, ed. Clifford J. Green, trans. Reinhard Krauss and Nancy Lukens (Minneapolis: Fortress, 1998), especially pp. 34-106.

of Christendom, Chesterton reminds us, is the idea that *God is love*. But it is nonsense to say this without understanding *that God is himself a holy Family, a family bound together by the love that God is*. It is this Trinity of love, this "holy Family," this "beautiful interdependence and intimacy" within the very being of God that is revealed to us in Jesus of Nazareth, the God who became a human to show us what it means to be human.[29]

Summary. We have been created by God, the holy Trinity, to reflect God's own being in relationship. To be fully human, as Christ has shown us in his own person and being, is to live in communion.

The Comprehensive Claim

What we have been saying is that Jesus Christ not only reveals God to us, he also reveals to us our humanity as God intended it to be, as (indeed) it truly is in Jesus Christ in the very heart of God, a humanity that fully reflects the image of the Trinity. Looking to Christ, as Eberhard Jüngel says, we see the person who "relied so totally on God that he could not really be a person without God's existence turned toward him. And because of his total dependence on God he was able, as one who was without pretension in regard to himself, to be completely there for others." Jüngel continues, "His humanity consisted of the freedom to want to be nothing at all for himself. A royal freedom! And the precise opposite of moral exertion!"[30]

We see this in the whole life of Jesus—healing, teaching, liberating—a life that makes a comprehensive claim on us in the name of divine love. This is at the core of Jesus' teaching, as we see in two of the most characteristic stories he told: the parables of the rich young man (Mt 19:16-30; Mk 10:17-31; Lk 18:18-30) and the greatest commandment (Mt 22:34-40; Mk 12:28-34; Lk 10:25-28). In both parables Jesus begins with the traditional law (Torah) of his people and then expands this law by interpreting it in light of the unconditional demand of love.

A rich young man asks Jesus, "Teacher, what good deed must I do to

---

[29]Chesterton, *Everlasting Man*, pp. 261-62.
[30]Eberhard Jüngel, *God as the Mystery of the World: On the Foundation of the Theology of the Crucified One in the Dispute Between Theism and Atheism* (Grand Rapids, Mich.: Eerdmans, 1983), p. 358, in the chapter "The Crucified Jesus Christ as 'Vestige of the Trinity.'"

have eternal life?" And Jesus stops the conversation dead by stating the more fundamental question of authority, as if to say, "Why do you ask *me* this question? Are you simply collecting pious opinions? Only God knows the good, the way of eternal life." Then, with apparently no pause, Jesus presses on, seeming to claim the authority to answer a question only God can answer. And in the process he completely reframes the question asked (because the question had been wrongly put and would have provided an inadequate answer). He provides the answer in the most unexpected way.

Jesus says, "If you wish to enter into life, keep the commandments."

The young man asks, "Which ones?"

Jesus summarizes the commandments, and the young man says that he has obeyed them all.

Ah, so this is a serious inquiry, not just an opinion poll! This young man has obeyed the Torah. He seeks to follow the way of God. Jesus can see by the young man's reply that he is not simply a curiosity seeker. He wants to know.

Mark's account of the story adds the editorial comment at this point that Jesus, looking at the young man, *loved him.*

"What more do I lack?" asked the young man.

Jesus answers, "Only one thing. If you do this you will be complete. Sell all your possessions, and give the money to the poor, and you will have treasure in heaven; then come follow me." When the young man heard this, Mark says, "he was shocked, and he went away grieving, for he had many things."

This story is followed by Jesus' teaching that it is easier for a camel to pass through the eye of a needle than for someone who is rich to enter the kingdom of God. To try to soften Jesus' words to the young man renders his call meaningless. The call to follow Jesus costs all that we are and everything we have because the life Jesus gives is a life without reservation, a life that refuses to withhold the self. The young man was possessed—by his possessions. Jesus was trying to perform an exorcism of sorts. And wherever we see Jesus performing an exorcism in the Gospels, he is teaching the kingdom of God through his actions. The parable, in all three Synoptic Gospels, is placed within the larger context of Jesus' teachings about the kingdom of God, a kingdom (not a place, remember, but the personal reign of God as sovereign Lord over our lives) that must be entered with the spirit of a child (Mt 19:13-14; Mk 10:13-16; Lk 18:15-17) and that reverses the priorities of the world (Mt 19:27-30; Mk 10:28-31; Lk 18:18-30). Then the Gospels tie the entire narrative together by following these teachings with Jesus' private comments about his Passion, that is, his suffering and death (Mt 20:17-19; Mk 10:32-34; Lk 18:31-34). Speaking just to his disciples Jesus talks of his life, his vocation and mission—to be poured out in humiliation and suffering for others—as the paradigmatic parable of the reign of God, the great reversal of fortunes.

In the second story we find Jesus' teaching of the greatest commandment (Mt 22:34-40; Mk 12:28-34; Lk 10:25-28). It is remarkable not in that it provides anything new to the religious tradition of Israel but that it so completely endorses the best rabbinical teachings of Jesus' age and for ages to come. Jesus explains that the greatest commandment is the commandment of love, the comprehensive claim that God makes on our lives to love God with all our being and to love our neighbors as ourselves. "On these two commandments hang all the law and the prophets." This teaching is characteristically rabbinical.[31] Jesus' *pronouncing* this teaching is not remarkable. Jesus' *embodying* this teaching is.

What we find in Jesus, as again Jüngel observes, is a person whose being, whose whole life, consists in a freedom to rely "so totally on God that he could not really be a person without God's existence turned toward him."[32] In other words, what we find in Jesus is the incarnation of the comprehensive claim of divine love, the claim that extends to us because it was accomplished in our humanity. We cannot simply walk away from this rabbi saying that he tells interesting stories or that his teachings offer highly moral foundations for our society. We must either relinquish our claims to ourselves in response to the comprehensive claim his love makes on our humanity, or we must be shocked and offended, and must "go grieving away."

There is in fact always a note of sadness, a consciousness of grief,

---

[31] See Ellis Rivkin, *The Hidden Revolution: The Pharisee's Search for the Kingdom Within* (Nashville: Abingdon, 1978). Certainly Rabbi Akiba, martyred in A.D. 135, sees the twofold law as the essential and comprehensive claim on each person. Jesus is not uttering a novel statement. He is, in fact, referring back to Leviticus 19:18.

[32] Jüngel, *God as the Mystery*, p. 358.

when we find ourselves addressed by the gospel. This is the sword Christ brings that cleaves our hearts in two. In light of Jesus Christ all our attempts at self-justification melt away because the claim of God that we encounter in Christ is more comprehensive than any of the various codes or values or standards we live under and in light of which we justify ourselves. Even as Jesus reveals to us our true humanity, he judges our false humanity, our sin-sickness, our disease, our disgrace and our independence. In light of his humanity we stand accused because at the heart of our being we have turned away from and denied the God on whom we depend for our very being. Denying this God we have shattered the bonds of love that would join us to one another and would reflect the character of God among us. In other words, seeing ourselves in light of Christ, the one whose whole life was an event of self-giving for the sake of the other, we understand the nature of our sin as a refusal to be in communion, as a denial of that social-relatedness that *is* the *image of God*.

Gustavo Gutiérrez, the foremost theologian of liberation, understands this when he says that "sin is not considered as an individual, private, or merely interior reality asserted just enough to necessitate a 'spiritual' redemption which does not challenge the order in which we live." Rather, "sin is regarded as a social, historical fact, the absence of brotherhood and love in relationships among men, and, therefore, an interior, personal fracture."[33]

Summary. That for which we are created is nothing less than the joy and fullness of the most intimate communion with God and one another. The salvation, or liberation, that Christ brings us is fundamentally social because sin is fundamentally social in its corruption of the image of God in us. Our failure is a relational failure, and so our redemption must be the restoration to relatedness. Or to put it another way, God restores us in Christ to the image of God, the essential being in communion, for which we are created.

A Tree Named Adam

Nothing escapes the historical fact of sin—neither society nor laws, nor the

---

[33]Gustavo Gutiérrez, *A Theology of Liberation: History, Politics and Salvation*, ed. and trans. Sister Caridad Inda and John Eagleson (Maryknoll, N.Y.: Orbis, 1973), p. 175.

structures of our groups, nor any aspect of our individual lives, not even our religions. All that we are "misses the mark," "deviates from the right way" or "rebels against" the loving heart and gracious reign of God.

This is the meaning of the classical doctrine of "total depravity." The doctrine does not say that there is no good anywhere in creation (indeed one would have to ignore the fundamental teaching that God's creation is good in order to say such a thing), but, while affirming the essential goodness of creation, we recognize the fact that there is nothing in creation untouched by sin.[34]

Wheat and weeds grow up together in the fields of creation. Even our best acts are laced with bad motives. Even our best intentions are not unmixed. Our life together is shot through and through with the tragically alienating influences of the vanity (emptiness), pride and arrogance, self-worship, gracelessness and independence that annul communion, multiply distrust and undercut our being for the other. We might use a law to justify ourselves. We might try to wiggle through some of the loopholes in our religious codes. But in light of the comprehensive claim of divine love in Jesus Christ, we find ourselves without excuse. Our inability or unwillingness to want and to do what is right (both sins of omission and sins of commission) are symptomatic of the essential orientation of our being against or away from God in self-absorption (sin).[35]

One of the more compelling and one of the most coherent ways to think about the pervasiveness of sin and God's gracious response to sinful humanity is provided in what we might call Christian Platonism, an approach represented to one degree or another by such diverse thinkers as

---

[34]Traditionally this essentially social nature of sin is what the Christian faith is trying to describe with its doctrine of original sin. Certainly this is true in Protestant, evangelical and Reformed traditions. As G. W. Forell explains, "For classical Protestantism, original sin describes the fact that the human being is born in revolt. The revolt against God is not something which he must gradually learn but is the pattern of human nature, because humanity collectively since the dawn of history has been in revolt against God." George Wolfgang Forell, *The Protestant Faith* (Philadelphia: Fortress, 1960), p. 134.

[35]It is against this backdrop of a social conception of sin that Gutierrez writes, "This is why the Christian life is a passover, a transition from sin to grace, from death to life, from injustice to justice, from subhuman to the human. Christ introduces us by the gift of his Spirit into communion with God and with all men. More precisely, it is because he introduces us into this communion, into a continuous search for its fullness, that he conquers sin—which is the negation of love—and all its consequences." Gutiérrez, *Theology of Liberation*, p. 176.

Athanasius,[36] Jonathan Edwards[37] and C. S. Lewis.[38] They tend to think of our humanity almost as a single organism, in this case as a diseased organism; Edwards, in fact, likened humanity to a huge tree stricken with some deadly sickness. The fruit the tree bears, though it should be edible, is bitter and does not nourish; indeed it is sometimes poisonous. We were meant to be towering trees with canopied branches that invite and protect the life of others, but we are hardly more than thorny shrubs. Under the "curse," as we might call it, we become a mere shadow of what we are meant to be.

Humanity, in this view, has its being in solidarity because all humanity is held in existence at every moment in the eternal mind of God. In fact Edwards believed that creation is a sort of material or substantial idea that God holds in God's mind. God thinks, one might say, solid thoughts. If God ever ceased to hold us as an idea in God's mind, we would all vaporize into nonbeing. But God does hold in being all humanity at every particular moment in our time. All humanity—those now living and

---

[36]Athanasius, in *De Incarnatione (On the Incarnation)*, writes, "And as the incorruptible Son of God was united to all men by his body similar to theirs, consequently he endued all men with incorruption by the promise concerning the resurrection. And now no longer does the corruption involved in death hold sway over men because of the Word who dwelt among them through a body one with theirs." He expands upon this idea with his beautiful analogy of the king who enters a city long occupied by rebels, brigands and bandits, and in occupying the city he claims the city as his own. Athanaisus, *Contra Gentes and De Incarnatione*, trans. Robert W. Thomson (Oxford: Clarendon, 1971), pp. 154-59.

[37]Ola Elizabeth Winslow, in her Pulitzer Prize-winning biography, describes Jonathan Edwards's understanding of the pervasiveness of sin, which suggested to me the metaphor of the tree. She writes, "The touchy point in all 'original sin' discussions had long been the relation of Adam's sin to the spiritual state of man since the fall. Why was not each birth a new beginning? By what logic, or more insistently, by what justice, was Adam's sin the sin of all men? Jonathan Edwards accomplished this dubious equation by a theory of the unity of the race, which was his most original contribution to the long standing controversy. The race is one, he argued, by the will of God in its creation. Just as 'a tree, grown great, and a hundred years old, is one plant with the little sprout, that first came out of the ground from whence it grew', so the [human] race, brought into being by the creative act of God, and continuously upheld by that same power, is one through each continuing moment of each man's existence." Winslow, *Jonathan Edwards: 1703-1758* (New York: Collier, 1961), pp. 281-82. For a more technical treatment of Edwards's thought see Michael Jinkins, "The 'Being of Beings': Jonathan Edwards's Understanding of God as Reflected in His Final Treatises," *Scottish Journal of Theology* 46, no. 2 (1993): 161-90. See Edwards's own thought in *Original Sin*, ed. Clyde A. Holbrook (New Haven, Conn.: Yale University Press, 1970), and *Freedom of the Will*, ed. Paul Ramsey (New Haven, Conn.: Yale University Press, 1957).

[38]C. S. Lewis's understanding of human sin and God's gracious response is described in his *Mere Christianity*, both in "What Christians Believe" and "Beyond Personality."

those now dead—are alike held in being in the mind of God. In the divine consciousness all humanity is present as if it were a single vast organism. And this entire multicelled organism is named by the name it has had since it was only a small single-celled growth, the name of *Adam*. God sees this vast organism stretching throughout history. This vast organism is eternally present to the mind of God.

This organism, *this tree named Adam,* was created to joyfully and freely draw its life from God, the ground of its being, as a tree—roots, trunk and branches—is nourished and given life by the earth. But tragically this whole organism, this tree named Adam, has refused to acknowledge and enjoy its essential dependence on God. It has denied the fundamental fact of its being, preferring instead to imagine that it can provide for its own needs.

It is a foolish tree, thinking it can thrive cut off from the ground! The tree stands sick with disease, malnourished, dying in its empty and foolish pride and distrust. This is the picture of our sin painted by Edwards and others. Humanity as a whole is sin-sick, bound together in the solidarity of original sin. Unfortunately Edwards does not have a corresponding vision of the solidarity of grace. But I'd like us to try to complete his thought, harkening back to Athanasius. If we can continue to use the organic analogy, I'd like for us to pull together some of the various strands we have been working with because what we are trying to describe is as large as all creation, from start to finish. And it all comes together when we attempt to understand who we are as human beings created in the image of God.

The tree named Adam is sick unto death. Each branch wants to exist by itself and for itself alone, resenting the life-giving ground on which it depends for nourishment and the branches that surround it and remind it that it does not have its existence in solitude but that it is one among many.

But suppose God grafted a new growth into this old, dying tree. And suppose this new growth had the unique power to send through the whole tree a life-giving and health-restoring sap. Suppose, in fact, that this new growth, because of the consciousness it has of its utter reliance on God and its life for others, had the power to reconnect the tree's root system to the Ground of Being and to change the tree from the inside out so that the tree's old characteristics would be overwhelmed by the characteristics of the new growth. The tree would still bear the scars of its history, but its history would be overwhelmed by a new identity, the identity given to it by the new growth that is grafted in. The old tree had been named Adam, and it was characterized by a sickness so inseparable from its existence that it was called original and total. But now the tree is not the tree it historically was. That which has been grafted into it has overcome its sickness. Christ has united himself to the tree named Adam and has given it a new name, an undeserved name, *his* name, the name of Christ. Through the engrafting of his resurrected life, a life integrated into the communion of the triune God, we are all brought into a new relationship with our ground of being and with one another.

Maybe this image is helpful to you. Maybe it isn't. It certainly relies on a philosophical idealism (which I am not sure I can assent to) that should not be accepted without your critical reflection. There are other ways to describe the problem of sin's persistence in creation, and perhaps we must at the end of the day simply recognize that sin itself is a contradiction of authentic being and existence, an anomaly made possible because of the freedom God has woven into creation. And sin is a fact that, despite its historical tenacity, has no independent existence of its own but is merely a perverse reflection of the good. The point I want to make with this extended analogy, however, is that *our humanity in Jesus Christ is the definitive reality in light of which we are to understand our existence.* This requires us to turn around our thinking on sin and its relationship to our humanity.

Martin Luther, I believe, was right: we are *simul iustus et peccator* (that is, we are always, and at the same time, justified sinners). However, while holding in mind Luther's dictum we must also comprehend that *who we are in Christ* (justified, forgiven, sanctified, reconciled—a new resurrected humanity) *has priority over our identity as sinners.* Our sin, as the author of Colossians says, has been nailed to the cross of Jesus Christ. In Christ we have, in the words of the Apostles' Creed, descended into hell. We have risen from the dead, in Christ. And we stand (to borrow an image from the epistle to the Hebrews) even now in the person of Jesus Christ, our heavenly high priest, in the presence of God the Father Almighty.

The character of this new life to which we are raised *is the self-emptying life for every other in utter reliance on God.* In Christ we discover that this radically new humanity is our true identity. But in discovering our true identity in Jesus Christ, we also discover the nature and extent of our sin. God's claim on us is comprehensive. There are no legal loopholes in Jesus Christ. Christ is the claim of God's love—God's own being in communion,

God's other-centeredness—on our whole lives. Jesus Christ is the comprehensive claim on our lives of the image of God in which we are created. We have rebelled against God's being as communion and against our own essential being in communion. And if this were the whole story, the story would be the supreme tragedy of God's work of creation, and we would all go away shocked in grief. But the Christ who reveals our true identity, and so reveals the nature of our sin, also reveals our destiny in God's work of redemption, our full restoration in Christ through the Spirit to the image of the triune God. This is the good news for which we are created, the good news the apostle refers to when he says:

> Since, then, we have such a hope, we act with great boldness, not like Moses, who put a veil over his face to keep the people of Israel from gazing at the end of the glory which was being set aside. . . . Indeed, to this very day whenever Moses is read a veil lies over their minds; but when one turns to the Lord, the veil is removed. Now the Lord is the Spirit, and where the Spirit of the Lord is, there is freedom. And all of us, with unveiled faces, seeing the glory of the Lord as though reflected in a mirror, are being transformed into the same image from one degree of glory to another, for this comes from the Lord, the Spirit. (2 Cor 3:12-18)

Alleluia. Amen.

Summary. In light of Jesus Christ we cannot escape God in a denial of our true human identity. But neither can we escape God in despair. The promise of our humanity, which we have never kept, has been kept for us in Jesus Christ.

Homework Assignments

1. *The human parable of the God who is love.* Eberhard Jüngel's comments on the life of Christ include the beautiful phrase describing Jesus Christ as "the human parable of the God who is love."

The parables Jesus told were unexpected and unusual stories, often turning upside down the conventional thinking and believing of his audience. They offered the opportunity to make a leap of imagination and faith from one way of perceiving the world to another.

☐ A fellow who works a few minutes is paid the same as the man who works all day long.

☐ A father celebrates the return of his wayward child with a terrific party.

☐ A social outcast emerges as the hero in a story of applied love.

☐ A merchant comes across a gem of such value he sells everything else he owns to buy it.

Each story, and there are many, paints a vivid picture of the kingdom of God, God's reign in the hearts and lives of ordinary people. We might describe the parables as great reversals of our expectations. They are, above all, pictures of grace: God's unmerited favor, God's unconditional acceptance of the undeserving, God's unbounded outpouring of life and love that creates all things out of nothing.

Questions to discuss in small groups: (1) How is it that Jesus is "the human parable of the God who is love"? What does this mean? (2) How does our lecture today relate to the classical teaching of the wonderful exchange?

2. *Jesus Christ, the full disclosure of our humanity.* The preacher and theologian Carlyle Marney once tried to explain to a newspaper reporter his understanding of who Jesus Christ is. He said, "[If] somebody asks me what a quarter horse is, I describe Buck. He's the greatest of the breed I ever saw. . . . He's up there on my place. So when anybody asks me what's a quarter horse like, I say, 'He's like Buck.' If anybody asks me what's a man like . . . I don't describe Napoleon, that poor little, sick fellow. Or Hitler. Or even Winston Churchill, much as I thought he was. . . . I describe Jesus Christ. That's what a man's like. Or there's no incarnation."[39]

One of the key ideas we have introduced in this session is that the New Testament brings us face to face with an amazingly unique affirmation: if you want to see what it means to be human, you don't have to fumble around navel gazing, trying to determine what it means to be human according to your own temperament or feelings, nor do you have to go about from one to another of your peers to find the "perfect person." Here is what God meant by *human:* Jesus of Nazareth, the responsible and real person. Every Adam, from great grandfather Adam to us, looks to *this* human to see what the species is. Questions for group discussion: (1) What might it mean to say that Jesus Christ is the name of our species? (2) What does it mean that God works out of the indicative instead of the imperative? Jesus reveals who we are, not just who we should be.

---

[39]Carlyle Marney, interview with the Charlotte, North Carolina, *News*, December, 24, 1968.

Class 8

The Holy Spirit

RECENTLY, AFTER I HAD SPENT A FRUSTRATING DAY TRYING TO WRITE THIS session on the Holy Spirit, I mentioned to my wife the difficulties I was having. She said that talking about the Holy Spirit reminded her of something she saw at lunchtime at an elementary school where she once taught. The children were given only forks to eat with. No matter what they were given to eat, they could only use forks. So the worst day of the week was always the day when the children were given Jell-O. All the lunchroom ladies would gripe about the mess the children made on Jell-O day. But the teachers understood; you're going to make a mess if you try to eat Jell-O with a fork. Unfortunately the lunchroom ladies at that school never did understand the problem. But we can learn from their mistake.

Today we've got something even more elusive than Jell-O on our theological plates. And we're not even going to try to use forks on this. The church has long understood that this is a meal that requires spoons. And we are going to use the spoons of mystics, poets and prophets to deal with this slippery stuff, and then gradually we will move on to use the fork of constructive theology to pick up the fruit bits that are mixed in.

Learning Ourselves Through the Holy Spirit

Lady Julian of Norwich, the fourteenth-century English anchorite, reflecting on the "shewings of divine love" that God had granted her, speaks of the Holy Spirit. And as she does, she indirectly raises for us a whole host of questions we will deal with today. She writes:

> So it came about that I was able to see with absolute certainty that it was eas-
> ier for us to get to know God than to know our own soul. For our soul is so
> deeply set in God, and so greatly valued, that we cannot come to know it
> until we first know God, its Creator, to whom it is joined. . . . This will teach
> us to look for it [our soul] where in fact it is: in God. And so by the gracious
> guidance of the Holy Spirit we come to know them both together.[1]

Julian's mystical reflections remind us that we are mysteriously estranged from ourselves; we do not really know our own souls. But she does not leave us in an autoagnostic quandary. On the contrary, she points us toward the relationship that opens to us genuine knowledge of ourselves. In this she is very similar to two later Christian thinkers, John Calvin and Henry Scougal.

Calvin, as we have already mentioned, understood that knowledge of ourselves is necessarily connected with knowledge of God. To know who we are and who we are meant to be, we must look to Jesus Christ in faith, which means that the Holy Spirit must awaken us to find our true identity in Christ. This sort of knowledge, as John McNeill says in his comments on Calvin, is never merely "objective knowledge," what we might call head knowledge; rather it is "existential apprehension," a living and experiential knowledge. That is, in our spiritual awakening to who we are *in Christ,* we authentically experience ourselves, or, perhaps like the prodigal son, we "come to ourselves," as it were.[2]

Julian's thought is also similar to that of seventeenth-century theolo-gian Henry Scougal in his devotional masterpiece *The Life of God in the Soul of Man.* James Torrance has said that Scougal's book should be titled *The Life of Man in the Soul of God.* This is, Torrance points out, the real point of Scougal's book. And in this, Scougal is in perfect agreement with Lady Julian and John Calvin. We find our soul when we find, by faith, our soul in the life of God, in the all-encompassing life of divine

---

[1]Julian of Norwich, *Revelations of Divine Love*, trans. Clifton Wolters (London: Penguin, 1966), p. 160.

[2]John T. McNeill, ed., editorial footnotes to *Institutes of the Christian Religion*, by John Calvin, trans. Ford Lewis Battles (Philadelphia: Westminster Press, 1960), pp. 35-36.

love that surrounds and upholds us.[3]

Who we are is hidden in the life of God. This is the idea we have already explored in our discussion of the image of God. And it is only by penetrating into the triune God's eternal life that we discern the shape of our own souls, our true and individual identity. This is what Lady Julian means when she says, "For our soul is so deeply set in God, and so greatly valued, that we cannot come to know it until we first know God, its Creator, to whom it is joined." The discovery of ourselves then is not a matter of our own individual effort or activity. Discovery of our selves is not even introspective. We do not "discover" ourselves *in* our selves. Indeed, *we* don't discover ourselves at all. Rather, *God* "discovers" ourselves for us and to us. Or again as Julian says, "by the gracious guidance of the Holy Spirit we come to know" both God and our own soul.

In his contemplative study, Henri Nouwen draws us into conversation about and with the Holy Spirit through his meditation on Andrej Rublev's fifteenth-century icon of the Trinity (see illustration 8.1). Rublev's icon, Nouwen explains, is, on one level, a painting describing the visit of three angels to Abraham. You may recall the story in Genesis 18: the Lord appeared to Abraham at the oaks of Mamre while Abraham was sitting at the opening to his tent in the heat of the day. The Lord appeared in the form of three angelic messengers. Abraham prepared for them a meal and placed it before them. The angels that day renewed the Lord's promise to Abraham, telling him that although he was nearly a hundred and Sarah over ninety, the Lord would bless them with a son. Through Abraham and Sarah the nations of the world would be blessed. Rublev's icon is a sort of frozen frame image of that moment. But that is not all that is there. For Rublev the icon has another level of meaning.[4]

Rublev interprets the three angelic messengers as the three persons of the holy Trinity. Nouwen leads us through a theological reflection on the meaning of the icon. He observes that each person of the Trinity pictured in the icon holds a staff, signifying that each has the same divine authority.[5]

---

[3]Henry R. Sefton, perhaps the leading authority on Scougal, has written a brief but helpful article on him in *The Encyclopedia of the Reformed Faith*, ed. Donald K. McKim (Louisville, Ky.: Westminster John Knox, 1992), p. 347.

[4]Henri J. M. Nouwen, *Behold the Beauty of the Lord: Praying with Icons* (Notre Dame, Ind.: Ave Maria Press, 1987), p. 23.

[5]Ibid., p. 24.

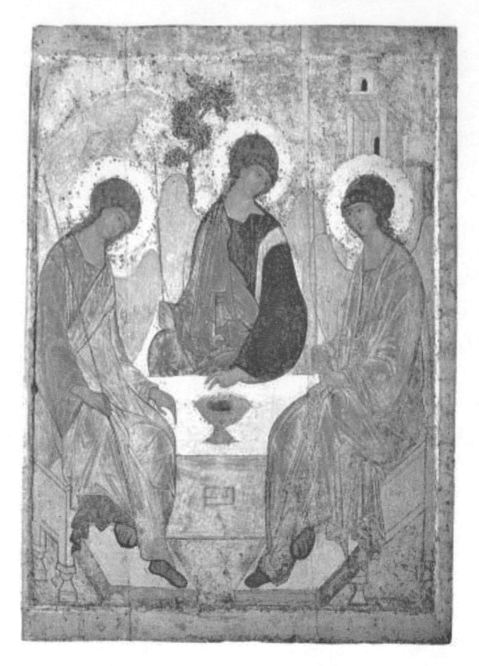

Figure 8.1. "Icon of the Holy Trinity," by Andrej Rublev, Trechikov Gallery, Moscow

The icon describes the whole life of God, both God's inner life, his communion as Father, Son and Spirit, and his life in relation to humanity. The central focus of the icon, the point toward which the observer's gaze is directed, is the meal offered by Abraham to the Lord. It lies in the center of the table in a chalice. In the icon this meal becomes "the sacrificial lamb," writes Nouwen, "chosen by God before the creation of the world." Each person of the Trinity speaks with his hands, showing his relationship to the "sacrificial lamb." The Son, in the center of the icon, points to the lamb with two fingers, "thus indicating his mission to become the sacrificial lamb, human as well as divine, through the Incarnation."[6] Directly to the left of the Son sits the Father, whose hand is raised in a gesture of blessing, indicating that he both blesses and encourages the Son in his mission. The Spirit, sitting to the right of the Son, points to a rectangular opening in the front of the table. The opening in the table signifies the place of the world in this event because it is to the world and for the sake of the world that the Son comes. The table in the icon has become, for the iconographer, a symbol for the high altar. The Spirit, pointing to the opening in the altar, says that "this divine sacrifice is a sacrifice for the salvation of the world."[7] The promise to Abraham (*he shall be blessed to be a blessing* [Gen 12:2]) finds its fulfillment in Christ, who through the Holy Spirit draws all humanity to himself.

Nouwen notes that there is a movement from the Father toward the Son and the Spirit in the icon and that there is a complementary movement of both the Son and the Spirit toward the Father. (Look at the eyes of the three figures. Something is happening; something is being said among them!) In the first movement we see the outpouring of God's love, God's gracious desire to bless the nations of the world, flowing from the heart of the Father, through the Son and the Spirit, and encompassing the whole world. In the second movement—the corresponding and complementary movement—we see the whole world gathered up and brought through the Spirit and the Son to the Father. Looking carefully from one person to another in the icon, we discern a circle of relationships, the central relationship of the Father, Son and the Holy Spirit, and the wider circle of relationship that reaches through the Son and the Holy Spirit, from the heart of

---

[6]Ibid., p. 23.
[7]Ibid., pp. 23-24.

the Father to the whole world. Again we find that the whole world of humanity is included in the life of God in such a way that we can only understand *who we are* by looking at the larger picture of *who God is*. If we step back from the icon and attempt to see not only the many details but the whole structure of the icon, to understand the larger picture of who God is, we see something rather startling. "Gradually," Nouwen says, "a cross is becoming visible, formed by the vertical beam of the tree, the Son, the Lamb and the world, and by the horizontal beam, including the heads of the Father and the Spirit."[8]

The icon, then, consists of two interrelated forms: an inviting, all-inclusive circle of relationships and a cross. The meaning of this is clear, Nouwen says: "There is indeed no circle without a cross, no life eternal without death, no gaining life without losing it, no heavenly kingdom without Calvary. Circle and cross can never be separated. The severe beauty of the three divine angels is not a beauty without suffering." There is here, in the life of God and God's world, what Nouwen calls the "melancholic beauty," what Russian Christians speak of as "their joyful sorrow."[9]

These two contemplative reflections, the first by an English mystic, the second in Nouwen's meditation on a Russian icon, help us gain access to what is perhaps the most difficult area of Christian theology, what is called *pneumatology*, the doctrine of the Holy Spirit.

In these two reflections we taste and see, feel and sense the beauty of God's fierce and gentle Love

☐ who creates and energizes our souls in the image of the creative God

☐ who gives us knowledge of God and of ourselves

☐ who leads us into truth and into authentic relationships with ourselves, others and God

☐ who encircles us and invites us to taste and see the goodness of God and humanity

☐ who is that love of Father and Son who makes possible our reclamation and our return to God and restoration to relationship with others

☐ who is God, God "in procession," the very community of the Trinity, the eternal life of God

Describing God the Spirit is like trying to take a photograph of breath

---

[8]Ibid., p. 25.
[9]Ibid.

escaping from the mouth of a child or the shudder of an earthquake thundering and rending apart the land; it's like trying to understand the warmth of a candle, the terror of an all-consuming fire, the intoxicating aroma of a lover's scent. On one hand, we cannot see this Spirit. We can only sense intuitively God's presence and God's effects. On the other hand, we can hear the eruption, the stormy blast of God, the pneumatic shock waves of the rending divine. We are not equipped to comprehend the fullness of the Spirit. This is the region where theology as a science is stretched to its limits to keep up with theology as faith, and both must resort more and more to theology as poetry even to approach haltingly a hint of an approximation of a description of who God the Spirit is.

This brings me to the threshold, however, of the first and the most important thing I must say about the Spirit of God: we believe that the Holy Spirit is not a *what* but a *who*. Everything else is merely a footnote to this great confessional fact. When we speak of the Spirit of God, we are speaking of Some*one*, not some*thing*. Not even if we write *thing* with a capital T.

When we speak of God as Spirit, we are speaking of the essential mystery of God as God, God's very Godness in contrast to everything God creates. Jesus, in his conversation with the Samaritan woman, says that "God is spirit, and those who worship him must worship in spirit and truth" (Jn 4:24).

The word *Spirit* in this sense is like a flashing theological signal light to tell us that we have come up against a boundary over which we cannot cross by our own feeble power. We do not have access to God except as God gives us that access, because God is well beyond the boundaries of creaturely perception. To worship (to serve and adore, to believe in and trust) the God who is Spirit, we must be given access through the Spirit of God. Knowledge of God, through whatever intermediate means (listening to the reading or the proclamation of Scripture, answering the needs of others through prayer or in reflection on God's creation), is always given through the Spirit because God is Spirit, and our means of access to God must correspond to God's being.

This is what makes nonsense of the conventional distinction between "special revelation" and "general revelation," as though certain things about God could be known "generally," that is by common natural observation, while other things about God could only be known by God's "special" revelation through Jesus Christ. Revelation, if it really is revelation of God, is always "special." We shall return again to this subject at the end of our session, when we discuss faith as the gift of the Holy Spirit.

There is thus a sense in which we speak of God the holy Trinity as Spirit. But there is also another sense in which we speak of God the Spirit when we speak of the third person of the Trinity, as God in one eternal "mode" or "way of Being" (as Reformed theologian Karl Barth says) or one "way of subsisting" (as Roman Catholic theologian Karl Rahner says). We speak of God the Spirit, or the Holy Spirit, when we speak of God *in procession.*

But we find ourselves speaking (and I feel very conscious of it just now) as though we are walking around on eggshells, uncertain of where to place our feet next or how hard to step, afraid that with every clumsy step we take in our theological clodhoppers, we shall crush a thousand distinctions and qualifications that must be made. Perhaps nowhere else do we feel like such theological bulls in the china shop as we do here in the doctrine of the Holy Spirit.

It's an extraordinary paradox, isn't it, that God as God meets us most *immanently and intimately* while being most *indefinable and inscrutable.* God is closer to us, Lady Julian says, than we are to our own souls. But when we attempt to speak of the God who is closer to us than we are to our own souls, God as Holy Spirit, we find ourselves groping about, rummaging through a bag of metaphors, symbols and images, like children rummaging through a toy box, picking up first this toy and then another, finding that none of them is really what we are looking for.

F. W. Dillistone writes:

Doves, flames, seven-fold gifts which no one has ever classified intelligibly, gifts bestowed by episcopal hands—what sort of teaching does our Church give to interpret this medley of symbols? If we are honest, would not most of us have to confess that we are precisely in the position of those twelve whom St. Paul found at Ephesus (Acts 19:1-12), who did not so much as know if there was any Holy Ghost? And in consequence all this glorious knowledge that the whole creative process is the scene of His energy, that every least impulse towards fullness of life is linked up at every level with His majestic effort, that in us all, wherever men and women are loving and joyous and peaceful and brave, He is manifested, and that all our aspirations towards a truer brotherhood, a nobler community of mankind are acknowledgments of His leading—all this finds no place in the worship and witness of our Church.[10]

Indeed, the nature of the Spirit makes it difficult to get a clear picture of who the Holy Spirit is. The Spirit never points to the Spirit. Always the Spirit points to another, always away from the Spirit. The Spirit is consistently self-effacing, as someone has said. The Spirit is the self-emptying act of God. And yet the Spirit is so personally God in God's self-emptying that the Spirit is not simply an action but is a divine person. But how do you visualize, comprehend, understand such a person?[11]

The Spirit is always in relationship. As Karl Barth says, the Spirit is "the common element, or, better, the fellowship, the act of communion, of the Father and the Son." We are struggling here to grasp the ungraspable. The Spirit is, personally, the divine relationship, God's relatability, the very "act" of communion who as *the act of God* is never simply an "act" among other acts in the general category of "action" but is actually God acting. Barth continues, "He is the act in which the Father is the Father of the Son, or the Speaker of the Word and the Son is the Son of the Father or the Word of the Speaker." The Spirit is, Barth explains, (following the lead of Augustine *De Trinitate* 15.27.50), "the *amor,* the *caritas,* the mutual *donum* between the Father and the Son. . . . He is the love in which God . . . as the Father loves the Son and as the Son loves the Father . . . He is the 'result' of their common 'breathing.'"[12]

The God whose very life is communion shares this living communion and communal life, *which is the Holy Spirit,* with humanity. Or as Emil Brunner explains, "The Holy Spirit is the spirit of fellowship, bringing individuals out of their isolation, making 'one body' of them. . . . As the fire is to be known by its brightness and warmth, so the Spirit of God is to be known by the fellowship it produces. And as fire kindles fire . . . so life

---

[10]F. W. Dillistone, *The Holy Spirit in the Life of Today* (London: Canterbury Press, 1946), pp. 17-18.

[11]Here perhaps more than any other place we feel incapable of finding an appropriate personal pronoun to use when speaking of God. And yet here more than perhaps any other place we must refer deliberately to the Spirit personally, either as "him" or "her" but never as "it." In this, the old style of "holy Ghost," though inadequate in so many other ways, was definitely preferable to an impersonalized "spirit" as merely a sort of generic metaphysical force.

[12]Karl Barth, *Church Dogmatics* 1/1, ed. G. W. Bromiley and T. F. Torrance, trans. G. W. Bromiley (Edinburgh: T & T Clark, 1936), p. 470.

kindled by the Holy Spirit must spread and ignite all with its burning."[13]

The Spirit, St. Bernard says in a sermon on the Song of Songs, is the mutual "kiss" of the divine Lover and the Beloved, "the kiss" Christ also shared with his disciples when he "breathed on them."[14] But how does one describe a kiss, a breath of air? Specifically, how does one describe a kiss or a breath of air that is not simply an embrace but God?

The danger is always present in our theological discussions of reducing the mysterious Spirit of God to something "pale and shapeless, like an unmade bed," as Frederick Buechner so vividly put it.[15] The very idea of spirit baffles all attempts at formal analysis. Yet, just as surely, the Spirit who is God demands analysis; that is, the Spirit compels us in our careful theological engagement of God in a dialogue of discovery. God demands of us a response that is not simply prerational or subrational but that involves us fully as persons, including our intellectual capacities. After all, the Spirit of God in the Old Testament is the Spirit of wisdom, and in the New Testament the Holy Spirit is the Spirit of truth.

As soon as I say this, however, I am struck by the awareness that whatever rational response we make, our response cannot be *merely* rational and remain true to the subject of the Holy Spirit because God's kind of wisdom and truth is a way of being in relationship, what we might call "being truthed." So our analysis or study of God's Spirit must be a living, relational, faith-full analysis, an existential analysis, the analysis of divine Love by lovers of the divine.[16]

To engage in this analysis of divine Love, we are cast again into an investigation of God's dealings with humanity. The Holy Spirit draws us into relationship with Jesus Christ, whose whole life (poured out for others) was lived in complete and trustful reliance upon God the Father through the power of this same Spirit. This Spirit who meets us and draws us to participate by faith in Christ's faithful reliance on the Father, is the Spirit who is the eternal bond of life and love between the Father and the

---

[13]Emil Brunner, *Our Faith* (New York: Scribners, 1962), p. 89.

[14]Bernard of Clairvaux, Sermon Eight on "The Song of Songs," in *Selected Works*, trans. G. R. Evans (New York: Paulist, 1987), p. 236.

[15]Frederick Buechner, *Wishful Thinking: A Theological ABC* (New York: Harper & Row, 1973), p. 90.

[16]See Augustine of Hippo "On the Trinity" 8.8, in Augustine, *On the Holy Trinity, Doctrinal Treatises, Moral Treatises,* Nicene and Post-Nicene Fathers, ed. Philip Schaff (Grand Rapids, Mich.: Eerdmans, 1980), 3.122.

Son. Our investigation into who this Spirit is, then, must also be a participation in the love and life the Spirit is.

A Wind, a Fire, a Power Divine

The Old Testament (through a variety of sources) speaks of the Spirit as *ruach,* the Lord's invisible and transcendent, though strangely immanent, power. The Hebrew word *ruach,* which we translate Spirit, basically means "wind" or "breath." It may seem at first glance that there is little commonality between the fierce and unpredictable breath of YHWH, the Lord of the Hebrews, blowing through the desert canyons of ancient Palestine and the divine Spirit, the *hagion pneuma* (Greek), the *Spiritum Sanctum* (Latin), affirmed in the Symbol of Constantinople, which says, "[We believe in] the Holy Spirit, the Lord and Giver of life, who proceeds from the Father (and the Son), who together with the Father and the Son is worshiped and glorified, who has spoken through the prophets." But on closer examination we can see that these are the same Spirit.

The Spirit is none other than the Lord rushing through the formless void, creating out of nothing all that is. The mysterious, brooding wind of God swept over the face of the inchoate deep, we are told in Genesis 1:2, bringing order out of primordial chaos. The Spirit is the creative power of God, through whom God speaks the creative Word. We learn throughout the Old Testament that the Spirit is that creative power by which God continually animates all things, without which all creation would fall into nonexistence. As Minear says, "In Hebrew consciousness, man lives within the orbit of God's immediate action, from moment to moment, under the direct control of the divine Hand. God is the Creator who acts in every situation, whether in nature or history."[17]

The psalmist says of the Lord, "When thou lettest thy breath go forth they shall be made" (Ps 104:30 Coverdale). And another psalm parallels the activity of Word and Spirit in creation, saying that it was "by the Word of the LORD the heavens were made and all their host by the breath of his mouth" (Ps 33:6). Indeed we see here a linkage between the Spirit and Word that we find often in the Old Testament and that carries into the New.

---

[17]P. S. Minear, *Eyes of Faith* (Philadelphia: Westminster Press, 1946), p. 149, with reference to A. Guillaume, *Prophecy and Divination* (London: Hodder & Stoughton, 1938), both cited in George Johnston's excellent general article, "Spirit," in *A Theological Wordbook of the Bible,* ed. Alan Richardson (New York: Macmillan, 1950), p. 233.

The breath *(rûaḥ)* of God and the Word *(dābār)* of God cannot be divorced from one another; they are distinct but essentially related aspects of the same divine reality. God *breathes* forth the *Word*. Both *rûaḥ* and *dābār* are active in creation.

The Spirit was especially understood as that power by which God influenced people to accomplish great deeds of courage and strength, even deeds of artistic value (as with Joshua in Deut 34, or Samson in Judg 14 and Bezalel and Oholiab in Ex 36). The Spirit bestows the gifts of wisdom and discernment upon humanity. Joshua was described in Deuteronomy 34:9 as "full of the spirit of wisdom." Wisdom speaks in Proverbs 1:23 (KJV) saying, "Turn you at my reproof. Behold, I will pour out my spirit upon you. I will make known my words unto you."

And of course the Spirit discloses God's presence with the people of Israel through prophecy. Here again we see the Spirit and the Word closely associated. At first, in the earliest sources, we find prophecy as a rather bizarre, ecstatic utterance that comes upon certain "holy" people. For instance:

> After that you shall come to Gibeath-elohim, at the place where the Philistine garrison is; there, as you come to the town, you will meet a band of prophets coming down from the shrine with harp, tambourine, flute, and lyre playing in front of them; they will be in a prophetic frenzy. Then the spirit of the LORD will possess you, and you will be in a prophetic frenzy along with them and be turned into a different person. Now when these signs meet you, do whatever you see fit to do, for God is with you. (1 Sam 10:5-7).

Elijah, we are told, "was wrapped in a tempest." Hardly a more vivid picture of the prophet can be imagined than this; the prophet lives in the eye of a hurricane of God's Spirit; the prophet stands clothed in the gale force wind of the Lord. Elisha was "filled" with the breath of the Lord, so much so that when he spoke, he breathed God's Word. Of course, we receive from the prince of the prophets, Isaiah, the greatest statement of the relationship between the Spirit and the Word, the statement that Jesus quoted at the beginning of his own ministry:

> The spirit of the Lord GOD is upon me,
>   because the LORD has anointed me;
> he has sent me to bring good news to the oppressed,
>   to bind up the brokenhearted,

to proclaim liberty to the captives,
   and release to the prisoners;
to proclaim the year of the LORD's favor,
   and the day of vengeance of our God;
   to comfort all who mourn;
to provide for those who mourn in Zion—
   to give them a garland instead of ashes,
the oil of gladness instead of mourning,
   the mantle of praise instead of a faint spirit. (Is 61:1-3)

From the eighth century B.C. onward we see the fullest development of Hebrew pneumatology (the theological understanding of the Spirit). Micah, preaching during this era rich in prophecy, speaks of himself as "filled with power, with the spirit of the LORD, and with justice and might, to declare to Jacob his transgression and to Israel his sin" (Micah 3:8).

Above all,

> the Spirit was to be the possession of the Coming Davidic King (Is. 11.2), and of the Servant of the Lord (Is. 42.1); and in the future Messianic Age there would be an unprecedented extension of the Spirit's activities and power (Jer. 31.31ff.; Ezek. 36.26f.).[18]

Indeed the earliest Christians were quick to understand the outpouring of the Holy Spirit on the church as a fulfillment of the prophet Joel's message: "Then afterward I will pour out my spirit on all flesh." In the "great" and "terrible" day of the Lord, sons and daughters shall prophesy, old men shall dream dreams, young men shall see visions (Joel 2:28-29; cf. Acts 2:17-21).

Running throughout the Old Testament there is a dual representation of the Spirit of the Lord that seems to be drawn together in the later prophets: the idea that the Spirit is the universal creative force of God and the corresponding view that the Spirit is at work particularly through the covenanted community. As we see in the Psalms, the Spirit from which we cannot flee (in Ps 139:7-12, because the Spirit is present everywhere we go) is the Spirit that empowers us for moral purity and holiness (in Ps 51:10-17, because he is the source and standard for life in Israel, the community of the covenant). The Spirit of the Lord who directs our

---

[18]"Holy Spirit," in *Oxford Dictionary of the Christian Church,* ed. F. L. Cross and E. A. Livingstone, 2nd ed. (Oxford: Oxford University Press, 1977), p. 660.

common moral and religious life is the all-pervading Spirit, whose dominion is creation. We are aware that in the Old Testament that the Spirit is something "wholly other" than the world of creatures. But we do not yet discern a full-fledged, personal, divine Spirit.

The Spiritual Humanity of Jesus Christ

As we turn to the New Testament, we sense a shift from the awesome though vague "numinous" of the Spirit to the personal, active Spirit

☐ through whom Jesus is conceived

☐ who descends upon Jesus at his baptism

☐ who supports him in his wilderness experience of temptation

☐ and who is the source of his remarkable life of faithful reliance on God the Father

Jesus was the true person of faith, the genuinely and fully pneumatic or spiritual human being. His entire life was characterized by the self-effacing humility of the Spirit, always pointing away from himself and toward God the Father, always refusing to grasp power for himself but simply resting with childlike trust in his heavenly Father, the source of life. The whole life of Jesus might be interpreted as an exposition of the familiar passage in Zechariah (4:6): "This is the word of the LORD . . . not by might, nor by power, but by my spirit, says the LORD of hosts." All that Jesus did, *he did resting in the power of the Spirit* rather than in his own creaturely resources.

Jesus was, in this sense, virtually transparent, a clear window through which others could see the "almighty love" of God, to borrow von Balthasar's phrase. His whole life was carried out resting in the Spirit, as though consciously floating on the breath of God, as though he had kicked out all the props of self-interested, self-absorbed, self-centered support that characterize conventional creaturely existence, the self-justification and self-glorification we so commonly rely on for security and equilibrium. Here was a person whose strength was God's Spirit, an invisible and unshakable force that gave Christ the freedom to be powerless, the strength to be humble, the authentic human being in community with others, living purely for the sake of the other.

This Spirit is the life force that Jesus shared with his followers, breathing on them, kissing them, as St. Bernard said, with the eternal embrace of God the Lover and the Beloved. And so his followers learned, "The Spirit is the Lord," even as "Jesus is Lord." The Spirit is the force by which God's

Word is spoken. The Spirit and Christ share the same character, the same life and love, the same power of eternal self-emptying that we see in the Father so that now when we speak of the Holy Spirit, the Spirit of God, the Spirit of Christ or the Spirit of the Father, we are speaking of one and the same divine person, the same personal reality of God's own act of self-emptying love.[19] And it is this same Spirit by whom Jesus Christ lived that is shared with us through faith. This is the *paraclete,* the adviser, the one who stands beside us as Christ's advocate with us and our advocate in relation to the world, whom Christ sends to us from God the Father so that we may discover and share in his love and bear witness to him in the world (Jn 14:18-31; 15:26).

It is only when we come to the doctrine of the Holy Spirit that so many of the various threads of Christian doctrine come together. Karl Barth, as we have noted, said that the Holy Spirit is the act of God's communion. We have already said that we are created as humanity in the image of God's communion. And now we discover that through Christ we are drawn by the Spirit into a genuine participation in this communion, this image of God, which is our true identity and destiny. We have spoken of the Word of God as God's creative power, the Word made flesh through whom God has revealed God's character. Now we see that God's Word is spoken through God's Spirit and that God's Spirit bears witness to God's Word. As Irenaeus observed long ago, the Word and the Spirit are the two hands of God. God has always been at work in creation with the hands of Word and Spirit, making, molding, shaping, holding, sustaining, liberating, judging and recreating.[20]

The Lord Is the Spirit

The witness of the Christian church is that God meets us as Lord in this world. The God who is transcendent is transcendently immanent. God, the Source of all being, flows out into all that God creates. And the very act of divine outpouring is not a created thing but is God the Spirit.

One of the earliest major controversies in the church revolved around this issue. It was a controversy that paralleled the Arian dispute in Christol-

---

[19]Basil the Great, *On the Holy Spirit,* trans. David Anderson (Crestwood, N.Y.: St. Vladimir's Seminary Press, 1997), pp. 34-42.

[20]Irenaeus, *Against Heresies,* ed. Alexander Roberts and James Donaldson, The Ante-Nicene Fathers (Grand Rapids, Mich.: Eerdmans, 1981), 1:487-92.

ogy. As you will remember, the Arians believed that God the Creator is God in the full sense, uncreated and immutable deity, but that the Son of God is a creature, the highest and greatest creature of all, perhaps even a semidivine creature (as long as you defined divine as a derivative quality), but a creature of the Creator nonetheless. In the wake of the Arian heresy, also during the fourth century, while the details of the Nicene confession were still being hammered out, another theological option was raised. A group called the Macedonians or Pneumatomachians ("opponents of the Spirit") disagreed with the Arians in that they believed that both the Father and the Son are fully God, but they refused to say that the Spirit is also God. They said, instead, that the Spirit is a godlike creation, or created phenomenon, subordinate in being both to the divine Father and the divine Son.

It was to this group that the Cappodocian fathers, especially Basil the Great of Caesarea, responded.[21] And it was to clarify this very point that the more elaborate and carefully worded statement on the Holy Spirit (which was quoted earlier in this session) was added to the Nicene-Constantinopolitan Creed. However, in attempting to solve this one problem, another was raised.

The champions of orthodoxy and catholicity in the ancient church wanted to insure that the Holy Spirit not be thought of as some kind of inferior semidivine creature or force. Thus they strongly affirmed that it is proper and pious to speak of the *homoousion* of the Spirit of God, that is, that the Holy Spirit is "of the same essential being" as the Father and the Son.[22]

---

[21]Indeed, Basil says that those who reject the divinity of the Spirit threaten the very integrity of their Christian faith and witness. "What makes us Christians?" he writes. " 'Our faith,' everyone would answer. How are we saved? Obviously through the regenerating grace of baptism. How else could we be? We are confirmed in our understanding that salvation comes through Father, Son and Holy Spirit. Shall we cast away the standard of teaching we received? This would surely be grounds for great sorrow; if we now reject what we accepted at baptism, we will be found to be further away from our salvation than when we first believed. We would be no different from someone who died without baptism, or who had been baptized with an unacceptable form. We made this profession when we first entered the Church; we were delivered from idols and came before the living God. Whoever does not hold fast to this confession as his sure foundation at all times, to the end of his life, makes himself a stranger to God's promises." Basil the Great, *On the Holy Spirit*, pp. 46-47.

[22]Kelly provides a valuable historical-theological survey of the development of the doctrine of the *homoousion* of the Spirit, noting particularly the contributions of Athanasius and the

On this the church was able finally to come to agreement. But here's the point where they became stuck, in a little phrase put in parenthesis in the version of the Nicene Creed used so often in Protestant churches because the Eastern church and the Western church could not come to agreement on it: "the Holy Spirit . . . who proceeds from the Father *(and the Son)."* This small parenthetical phrase precipitated what has come to be called the *filioque controversy,* a theological split that long and fundamentally separated the world of Eastern Orthodox Christianity from the Latin West (and the various communions of Western Christianity, generally including Protestant churches).

The word *filioque* simply means "and the Son." The phrase did not actually appear in the earliest version of the Nicene-Constantinopolitan Creed (which dates from 381). It was not added until the Third Council of Toledo in 589. Two hundred years later it was defended by Paulinus of Aquileia at the Synod of Friuli, and from around 800 it found its way into the eucharistic liturgy that was used throughout the empire of the Franks. The phrase grew in popularity in Western Europe (and only there), though it wasn't uniformly adopted as an official standard in the Western church until some time around the year 1000. The doctrine of the *filioque* has stood for centuries as the principal doctrinal sticking point between the Eastern and the Western churches because the Eastern church has tenaciously resisted the statement that the Holy Spirit proceeds both from the Father and the Son.

☐ The Eastern church has maintained that the Holy Spirit eternally processes from the Father in much the same way that the Word eternally originates from the Father.

☐ The Western church, just as vigorously, has said that while the Word eternally originates in the Father, the Holy Spirit eternally processes from the Father and the Son.

So in the Eastern church the Trinity can be represented with a diagram something like this:

Cappadocians, and the relationship between the controversy over the person of the Spirit and the doctrine of the Trinity. See J. N. D. Kelly, *Early Christian Doctrines,* rev. ed. (London: A & C Black, 1977), pp. 252-71. Also see Gregory of Nazianzus, "The Fifth Theological Oration—On the Spirit," in *Christology of the Later Fathers,* ed. Edward R. Hardy (Philadelphia: Westminster Press, 1954), pp. 194-214.

Father—> Spirit—> Son

While in the West the Trinity is generally represented using a triangular diagram:

Father

Són_____Spirit

This profound disagreement over the procession of the Holy Spirit has divided Eastern from Western Christianity for centuries. Unfortunately the controversy has also tended to overshadow the more significant theological issue that the persons of the Trinity co-inhere in the eternal life of divine love, that the Father and Son are bound together in a joyful mutual surrender of the one to the other, which is "very God," the self-giving God, God the Spirit.[23]

Encouraging developments, however, have occurred in recent years. Indeed, over the past three decades significant strides have been made in reconciliation and agreement between Eastern and Western churches. In March of 1991 a "Joint Statement of the Official Dialogue Between the Orthodox Church and the World Alliance of Reformed Churches" was issued in Geneva. The paper announced the success of a dialogue between leaders and theologians representing churches of the Reformed tradition and the Greek Orthodox Church. Between 1979 and 1983 a series of meetings were held in which participants tried, as Thomas F. Torrance has said, "to cut behind the differences between Orthodox and Reformed Churches, in the East and in the West, in such a way as to provide a basis that is both evangelical and catholic for the witness of the Church in the world today."[24] Other consultations were held in Russia in 1990 and in Geneva in 1991.[25]

---

[23]In my view one of the most helpful attempts to comprehend the problem and to construct a meaningful dialogue between the two theological positions was proposed in T. F. Torrance, *Theology in Reconciliation* (London: Geoffrey Chapman, 1975).

[24]Thomas F. Torrance, *Trinitarian Perspectives: Toward Doctrinal Agreement* (Edinburgh: T & T Clark, 1994), p. 110. Also see Thomas F. Torrance, ed., *Theological Dialogue Between Orthodox and Reformed Churches* (Edinburgh: Scottish Academic Press, 1985); Thomas F. Torrance, ed., *Theological Dialogue Between Orthodox and Reformed Church,* vol. 2 (Edinburgh: Scottish Academic Press, 1993); and Thomas F. Torrance, *The Christian Doctrine of God, One Being Three Persons* (Edinburgh: T & T Clark, 1996).

[25]Torrance, *Trinitarian Perspectives,* p. 111.

After centuries of broken fellowship between Eastern and Western churches, and after years of debate and reflection by leaders of these communions, the participants in these landmark dialogues reached a consensus on the doctrine of the Trinity.

The breakthrough is not merely diplomatic, it is theological. As T. F. Torrance writes:

> Clearly more thought must be and will be given to this, but, as I understand it, the fact that the One Being of God the Father belongs fully to the Son and the Spirit as well as to the Father tells us that the Holy Spirit proceeds ultimately from the Triune Being of the Godhead. Does this not imply that the Holy Spirit proceeds from out of the mutual relations within the One Being of the Holy Trinity in which the Father indwells the Spirit and is himself indwelt by the Spirit? This approach is reinforced by the truth that, since God *is* Spirit, "Spirit" cannot be restricted to the Person of the Holy Spirit but applies to the whole Being of God to which the Father and the Son with the Holy Spirit belong in their eternal Communion with one another.[26]

The consequences of this new ecumenical consensus are breathtaking. Torrance adds, "It breaks through the traditional formalisations within which East and West have been divided. . . . It transcends the rift between" the teachings of these Eastern and Western churches over the procession of the Holy Spirit. Torrance concludes, "The procession of the Spirit is to be thought of not in any partitive way but only in a holistic way, as procession from the completely mutual relations within the one indivisible Being of the Lord God who is Trinity in Unity and Unity in Trinity."[27]

Other voices have entered into and extended these conversations as theologians from Roman Catholic and Orthodox churches also attempt to reach a consensus on this ancient dispute. One particularly beautiful contribution is that of Thomas Weinandy who attempts to express the profound reality of God's inner life (remember the perichoretic doctrine we discussed earlier?) by emphasizing the spirit of mutuality and the spirit of love shared by the Father, Son and Holy Spirit, and the indwelling of one person of the Trinity by the others. He writes, "The Father begets the Son in or by the Holy Spirit. The Son is begotten by the Father in the Spirit and thus simultaneously proceeds from the Father as the one in whom the Son is begotten. The Son, being begotten in the Spirit, simultaneously loves the

---

[26]Ibid., p. 113.
[27]Ibid.

Father in the same Spirit by which he himself is begotten (is Loved). . . . The Holy Spirit, in proceeding from the Father as the one in whom the Father begets the Son, conforms the Father to be Father for the Son and conforms the Son to be Son for (of) the Father."[28]

Weinandy attempts in this statement to take us beyond our conventional time-bound conceptions of relationship by emphasizing the word *simultaneous*. T. F. Torrance addresses a similar issue by saying that in the inner life of God the holy Trinity "there is no 'before' or 'after.'" Rather: "The Holy Spirit dwells in and flows from the inner being and life and light of the Holy Trinity, where he shares fully in the reciprocal knowing and communing of the Father and the Son. It is as such that he comes into the midst . . . of us, proceeding from the Father, receiving from the Son, revealing God to us and making us partake in him of God's knowing of himself."[29]

Clearly the centuries-old and bitterly divisive *filioque* controversy pales in significance in contrast to the stunning recent developments in the ecumenical dialogues on the Trinity, reminding us of the confession of the nascent church: "Beloved, let us love one another, because love is from God; everyone who loves is born of God and knows God. Whoever does not love does not know God, for God is love. God's love was revealed among us in this way: God sent his only Son into the world so that we might live through him. In this is love, not that we loved God but that he loved us and sent his Son to be the atoning sacrifice for our sins. Beloved, since God loved us so much, we also ought to love one another. No one has ever seen God; if we love one another, God lives in us, and his love is perfected in us" (1 Jn 4:7-12). Indeed, the ancient rift between East and West stands ironically and tragically as a symbol of the way theological discourse—even theological discourse about the Holy Spirit, who is the essential love, life and community of God as holy Trinity—can disintegrate into spiteful and divisive prattle and mutual castigation that breeds distrust and disrupts community.

We can learn from the doctrine of the Holy Spirit that it is only in community that we become all we are meant to be because we were created

---

[28]Thomas G. Weinandy, *The Father's Spirit of Sonship: Reconceiving the Trinity* (Edinburgh: T & T Clark, 1995), p. 17.
[29]Thomas F. Torrance, *The Trinitarian Faith* (Edinburgh: T & T Clark, 1988), p. 222.

for communion by the God whose very being is in communion, and that it is only in giving ourselves away that we become truly human because we were created for giving by the giving God. We can learn of mutuality and hospitality, openness and grace from the God who eternally empties himself into another and who in divine self-emptying is forever filled with the life and love who is God. We can learn to place service above self because we have witnessed the life of Jesus Christ, who in the power of the Holy Spirit came not to be served but to serve and to give his life as a ransom for others. For too long the study of the God who is love became yet another occasion to promote misunderstanding and hatred. As someone has observed, the greatest sins are inevitably perversions of the highest goods; as it is in ethics, so also in theology. But perhaps we have learned something here at long last.

The Giving God

The Reformers, in their discussions of the Holy Spirit, emphasize that it is God who gives us the ability to trust Christ, the ability to live the new quality of life (eternal life) that Christ offers us. Luther, in his explanation of the third article of the Apostles' Creed, says:

> I believe that I cannot by my own reason *(Vernunft)* or strength *(Kraft)* believe in Jesus Christ, my Lord, or come to Him; but the Holy Ghost has called me *(berufen)* by the Gospel, enlightened me with His gifts, sanctified and kept me in the true faith; even as He calls, gathers, enlightens, and sanctifies the whole Christian Church on earth, and keeps it with Jesus Christ in the one true faith; in which Christian Church He daily and richly forgives all sins to me and all believers, and will at the Last Day raise up me and all the dead, and give unto me and all believers in Christ eternal life. This is most certainly true.[30]

The Holy Spirit is, as we have seen, not only *Spiritus Creator,* but also *Spiritus Re-creator* (that is, active in Christ's mission of redemption) and *Spiritus Transcreator* (that is, active in and through the church for the sake of the whole world). The Spirit breathes through the Bible, speaking the Word of God to us in the moment of hearing. The Spirit also breathes, as it were, through us, creating in us faith so we can hear the Word of God and learn to rest in and trust God. The Spirit, breathing through us, draws us

---

[30]Martin Luther, *Small Catechism* (St. Louis: Concordia, 1943).

together into community. The Spirit unites us to the Christ who has united himself to our common humanity in the incarnation. The Spirit indeed makes it possible for us to enjoy the forgiveness of Christ (justification) and to grow in our understanding and living out of Christ's justification of us (sanctification).

This is what Calvin means when he says that "the Holy Spirit is the bond by which Christ effectually unites us to himself."[31] "Christ," Calvin writes, "came endowed with the Holy Spirit in a special way: that is, to separate us from the world and to gather us into the hope of the eternal inheritance. Hence he is called the 'Spirit of sanctification' because he not only quickens and nourishes us by a general power that is visible both in the human race and in the rest of the living creatures, but he is also the root and seed of heavenly life in us."[32]

The sixteenth-century Protestant Reformers understood the Spirit of God in a way that draws together two lines of thought in the Old Testament: (1) the Spirit as the universally present power and creative force of God (e.g., "the earth was a formless void and darkness covered the face of the deep, while a wind [breath, spirit] from God swept over the face of the waters" [Gen 1:2]; "By his wind [again breath, spirit] the heavens were made fair; his hand pierced the fleeing serpent" [Job 26:13]), and (2) the Spirit as the power behind morality and holiness in Israel, the covenanted community (e.g., "For the palace will be forsaken, . . . until a spirit from on high is poured out on us, and the wilderness becomes a fruitful field. . . . Then justice will dwell in the wilderness" [Is 32:14-20]; and, of course, "The spirit of the Lord GOD is upon me, because the LORD has anointed me; he has sent me to bring good news to the oppressed, to bind up the brokenhearted, to proclaim liberty to the captives, and release to the prisoners; to proclaim the year of the LORD's favor, and the day of the vengeance of our God; to comfort all who mourn" [Is 61:1-2; cf. Lk 4:18-19]).

The Reformers take these thoughts and allow them to resonate, expand and deepen even further by interpreting them in light of the New Testament witness. The Spirit who breathed the Word in creation, and by whom Jesus Christ breathed the power of God, breathes into us now the transforming power of Christ, creating among us the community of faith in Jesus

---

[31]Calvin *Institutes* 3.1.1.
[32]Ibid., 3.1.2.

Christ, the body of whom Christ is the head, the communion of the new covenant sealed in the blood of Christ, restoring us to God's creative intention for full humanity and sending us forth as disciples gifted with the Spirit of Christ (read Acts 1—5, Rom 12—15 and especially 1 Cor 11—14 with these reflections in mind). Thus Calvin writes, "For by the inspiration of his power he so breathes the divine life into us that we are no longer actuated by ourselves, but are ruled by his action and prompting."[33] The Spirit enlightens us; that is, the Spirit gives us faith to discern the divine reality that surrounds us, helping us to perceive what is really there. The giving of faith, Calvin says, "is the principal work of the Holy Spirit." The Spirit, he continues, "may rightly be called the key that unlocks for us the treasures of the Kingdom of Heaven; and his illumination, the keenness of our insight."[34]

The teachings of the Reformers on the Holy Spirit represent an extension of their firm belief in *sola gratiae* (grace alone). Not even our faith is our own. Were Christ not to draw us by the Spirit, we would not return to the Father's house. Were the Spirit not to open our eyes, we would search the Scriptures in vain, if at all. Faith is a miracle, a gift from the God who gives himself away for the sake of others. The Spirit, through whom the Word is breathed, creates within us a hearing for the Word, and hearing the Word through the power of the Spirit we are given the ability to entrust our lives to the God on whom our lives depend.

This is the means by which God has chosen to share with us the life Jesus lived in the power of the Spirit, his life of trust and communion, a life given away freely for the sake of others. Indeed, it is by the power of the Spirit, Calvin tells us, that we are delivered from "the death-dealing blindness" *(mors caecitatis)* with which the world is afflicted and are "given eyes to see Christ."[35] This is a special kind of sight, a faith-sight, an ability to see who we truly are (already) in Christ. The Spirit enables us "to see Christ" because the Spirit, in fact, unites us to Christ so that his life flows into us and becomes our own.

This is in part what Lady Julian of Norwich was getting at in the passage quoted at the beginning of these lectures when she said that we see our-

---

[33]Ibid., 3.1.3.
[34]Ibid., 3.1.4.
[35]John Calvin, *Commentary on the Gospel of St. John,* ed. David W. Torrance and Thomas F. Torrance, trans. T. H. L. Parker (Grand Rapids, Mich.: Eerdmans, 1959), 5:84.

selves for who we truly are *only when we see ourselves in God*. It is only
through the gift of faith, given us by the Holy Spirit, that we gain this
extraordinary quality of insight, this "life-giving" power to see what is really
there in Christ, which runs counter to the "death-dealing blindness" of the
world.[36]

We are given this vision of our true identity in Jesus Christ by the Holy
Spirit in and through and for the sake of our life together. Thus we have
come full circle: the Spirit who is the breath of God's own inner fellowship
shares with us the fullness of God's life, the life God gives us in Christ, as
we live together in the Spirit. We must confess, as soon as we confess our
faith in the Holy Spirit, our faith in his gift to us, the holy catholic church.
And this we'll discuss next time.

Summary. The Holy Spirit is "God in procession," God sharing God—
the divine Lover in loving self-giving to the divine Beloved, the divine
Beloved in loving surrender to the divine Lover. The God who is Love does
not reserve himself but flows outward, creating out of nothing all that
exists and freely embracing all creation. By the power of the Spirit, Christ
came into the world and lived the divine life of unreserved love, and now
Christ shares with us this same life through the same Spirit. The call to discipleship, the call to follow Christ, is the call to enjoy the life and love of
Jesus Christ in our human reliance upon God the Father through the power
of the Holy Spirit.

Homework Assignments

1. Look again at the icon by Andrew Rublev (p. 186). What else do you see?

On one side of a sheet of paper write "Observations," on the other side
write "Questions." Begin with observations. What more do you see in the
picture? Look both at the details and at the picture as a whole. What things
do you notice that raise further questions?

If possible you may want to get a copy of Henri Nouwen's book *Behold
the Beauty of the Lord: Praying with Icons* in order to investigate the icon
more closely. With Nouwen's help you may be able to test your observations and perhaps extend your questions further.

With a reproduction of the icon before you, allow your heart and mind

---

[36]John Calvin, *Commentary on II Corinthians*, ed. David W. Torrance and Thomas F. Torrance,
   trans. T. A. Smail (Grand Rapids, Mich.: Eerdmans, 1964), 10:49-50.

to center prayerfully into contemplation on God. The icon acts as a picture reminder, a kind of devotional text, a means to focus your prayers on the God who cannot be pictured. The purpose of the icon is to help us explore spiritually who God is revealed to be in Jesus Christ. The tradition of icons is similar to our tradition of stained glass images. The image directs our attention beyond the image to what the church fathers called the "imageless image of God," Jesus Christ.

In the icon we see the holy Trinity represented in an inviting way, literally *inviting* us to the table at which we remember the once for all sacrifice of the Son of God. We see the Father's house represented, the house being both "father Abraham's" (Abraham is often called a father of faith) and the house of God the Father, the eternal source of all being. Allow yourself ample time for silent prayer and reflection on the God who draws us in Jesus Christ through the power of the Spirit to the side of our heavenly Father and who sends us from his "dwelling place" into the world as children of God. Going "into the world" has special significance in the symbolism of this icon. The world is symbolized by the rectangular opening in the table. The world is contained in the sacramental table and thus is contained in the sacrifice of Jesus Christ, the lamb of God. In other words, there is no world outside of this sacrifice. And our entry into the world—and our proper relationship to this world—is through Jesus Christ.

2. *The common spirit.* Karl Barth once said that the entire theology of Friedrich Schleiermacher was done from the perspective of the Holy Spirit. Whether or not this judgment is accurate, it is true that Schleiermacher's writings on the Spirit are extremely perceptive. His focus is always on the experience of the Christian in community, which means he is looking at the place where the Spirit is seen as most active. Schleiermacher writes:

> The expression "Holy Spirit" must be understood to mean the vital unity of the Christian fellowship as a moral personality; and this, since everything strictly legal has already been excluded, we might denote by the phrase, its *common spirit.* . . . If there were no common spirit, the Christian Church would be no true common or corporate life; yet this is what it has professed to be from the beginning as regards the divine Spirit dwelling in it, and this is how it has been accepted in the self-consciousness of every effective member. This will for the Kingdom of God is the vital unity *of* the whole, and its

common spirit in each individual; in virtue of its inwardness, it is in the whole an absolutely powerful Godconsciousness, and thus the being of God therein, but conditioned by the being *of* God in Christ.[37]

Obviously there's enough in this brief passage to occupy our attention for a very long time, but what I'd like to draw our attention to is this single, very powerful idea of "the common spirit." And I'd like to do this through a very simple exercise. It will be especially helpful if you are doing this exercise in a group; otherwise you'll have to use your imagination a bit more.

The Holy Spirit is the very breath of God, and like the breath of every living creature (again, thinking *analogically* of similarity in dissimilarity), the Spirit of God may be thought of as exhaled and inhaled. If you are in a group, turn your chairs so that everyone in the group is facing one another. Now close your eyes and as a group inhale slowly, taking the breath down deep inside of you, then slowly exhale. Do this several times.

In the quiet of this moment, reflect on the common breath of your group. You all share the same breath because it has passed into your bodies and out of your bodies, supplying you with life-giving oxygen, then the breath has moved on, supplying the needs of another, though you also continue to be nourished with the life-giving breath of the other. The breath is "yours" in that it has passed through you, but it is not yours in the sense of a possession. The breath you breathe is "theirs" again, but not in a possessive sense. The breath has shared life with you, but you cannot keep it captive. In fact, to try to hold on to it (to hold your breath) invites disaster. You will faint! Neither can you only exhale all the time. You must take breath in and let breath out. There is a rhythm to breathing that is necessary for life to be maintained.

I mentioned that the breath is not the possession of a single member of the group because it is shared by everyone. But the breath isn't simply a possession of the group either. It is larger than the group and "other" than the group. And it demands the freedom to move beyond this group, beyond this room. What is necessary to the life and health of a single person is necessary to the life and health of a particular group. The breath

---

[37]Friedrich Schleiermacher, *The Christian Faith*, ed. H. R. Macintosh, trans. James S. Stewart (Edinburgh: T & T Clark, 1928), pp. 535-36.

must move "as it wills." If the room is closed to outside ventilation, the air will lose its life-giving quality (too much carbon dioxide, too little oxygen), and the group will die together even if the members of the groups were sharing air freely among themselves.

Now reflect further on this analogy yourself. This will be especially interesting if you are doing this exercise in a group. What more can we say about the "common spirit"?

Further Reading

Let me suggest a couple of good general books that offer helpful discussions on the subject of the Holy Spirit:

Green, Michael. *I Believe in the Holy Spirit.* Grand Rapids, Mich.: Eerdmans, 1975.

Migliore, Daniel L. *Faith Seeking Understanding: An Introduction to Christian Theology.* Grand Rapids, Mich.: Eerdmans, 1991. (See chap. 9, in particular).

Class 9

The Holy Catholic Church

"Almighty God,
Who hast poured upon us the new light of thine Incarnate Word.
Grant that the same light enkindled in our hearts
may shine forth in our lives,
through Jesus Christ our Lord."

MASS OF CHRISTMAS AT DAWN, SARUM RITE

As has been the practice throughout this series of lectures, let us begin our theological reflection, this time on the church, by asking the question of *who*. In this case the question may sound a little odd, however, because we will ask, Who is the church? Only after we have asked this question will we turn to the secondary question, What must the church do? In other words, the indicative precedes and gives rise to the imperative. This is nowhere more true than in ecclesiology (the doctrine of the church).

A Confessional Starting Point

Some time around 1561 Heinrich Bullinger, one of the most important (though least remembered) Swiss Reformers, wrote a confession of faith. It was a very personal confession. Theologian Jack Rogers explains that it was written after Bullinger survived the plague of 1561. We can pretty safely assume that part of the reason Bullinger wrote the confession was his gratitude to God for delivering him from "deadly pestilence." Rogers tells us that Bullinger's confession was also meant to be a sort of swan song, the final theological legacy he wished to leave to the people of Zurich, among whom he had served as pastor and leader for nearly fifty years.

Bullinger, in fact, originally attached the confession to his will as a bequest. (It was meant to be literally a part of his last will and testament to the Reformed Church of Zurich.) In 1566 Reformed Christians in the some-times troubled city of Heidelberg asked his assistance in clarifying the basic issues of Christian belief, so for their benefit he had his confession published and sent to them.[1]

The confession provides one of the most insightful confessional statements on the character of the Christian church to emerge in the Reformation period. I want us to hear a considerable portion of this creed.

(THE CHURCH HAS ALWAYS EXISTED AND IT WILL ALWAYS EXIST) Forasmuch as God from the beginning would have men to be saved, and to come to the knowledge of the truth (I Tim. ii. 4), therefore it is necessary that there always should have been, and should be at this day, and to the end of the world, a Church—

(WHAT IS THE CHURCH?) that is, a company of the faithful called and gathered out of the world; a communion (I say) of all saints, that is, of them who truly know and rightly worship and serve the true God, in Jesus Christ the Savior, by the word and Holy Spirit, and who by faith are partakers of all those good graces which are freely offered through Christ. (Citizens of One Commonwealth.) These are all citizens of the one and the same city, living under the one Lord, under the same laws, and in the same fellowship of all good things; for the apostle calls them "fellow citizens with the saints and members of the household of God" (Eph. ii.19), terming the faithful upon earth saints (I Cor. iv.1), who are sanctified by the blood of the Son of God. Of these is that article of our Creed wholly to be understood, "I believe in the holy Catholic Church, the communion of saints."

(ONLY ONE CHURCH IN ALL TIMES) And, seeing that there is always but "one God," there is one mediator between God and men, the man Christ Jesus (I Tim. ii.5); and one Shepherd of the whole flock, one Head of this body, and, to conclude, one Spirit, one salvation, one faith, one Testament or Covenant,—it follows necessarily that there is but one Church. *(CHURCH "CATHOLIC")* which we therefore call CATHOLIC because it is universal, spread abroad through all the parts and quarters of the world, and reaching unto all times, and is not limited within the compass of time or place. . . . And they that are such in the Church of God have all but one faith and one spirit; and therefore they worship but one God, and him alone they serve in spirit and in truth, loving him with all their hearts and with all their strength, praying unto him alone through Jesus Christ, the only Mediator and Intercessor; and they do not seek life or justice but only in Christ and by faith in him;

---

[1]Jack Rogers, *Presbyterian Creeds: A Guide to the Book of Confessions* (Philadelphia: Westminster Press, 1985), p. 119.

because they acknowledge Christ the only head and foundation of the Church, and, being surely founded on him, do daily repair themselves by repentance, and do with patience bear the cross laid upon them; besides, by unfeigned love joining themselves to all the members of Christ, do thereby declare themselves to be the disciples of Christ, by continuing in the bond of peace and holy unity.[2]

In this wonderfully full and theologically rich statement we are confronted with the living reality of the church, a reality much larger and more diverse than we often assume and yet that is sharply and clearly focused on the crucified Jesus Christ who provides the identity, the meaning and the mission of this church, which God has called through the watery grave and midwife of baptism. In order to understand what Bullinger's confession has to say to us, there's some theological unwrapping we need to do. We'll start where we left off at the end of the last session.

The Community Created by the Holy Spirit

I ended the previous lecture by saying that the Holy Spirit creates community among us as a reflection of the communal life of the holy Trinity. What we discern first in our examination of the church, therefore, is the extraordinary teaching that God has always been creating this community of faith and worship among us. The doctrine of the church reminds us that God's original intention and ultimate design is to call us out of isolation into communion.

This is, at least in part, what the Second Helvetic Confession is saying when it says that "the Church has always existed . . . because God from the beginning would have men to be saved, and to come to the knowledge of the truth." This is also what the venerable old "Scots Confession" teaches. It reads:

As we believe in one God, Father, Son, and Holy Spirit, so we firmly believe that from the beginning there has been, now is, and to the end of the world shall be one Kirk [Church], that is to say, one company and multitude of men chosen by God, who rightly worship and embrace him by true faith in Christ Jesus, who is the only Head of the Kirk, even as it is the body and spouse of Christ Jesus. This Kirk is catholic, that is, universal, because it contains the chosen of all ages, of all realms, nations, and tongues, be they the Jews or be they of the Gentiles, who have communion and society with God the Father,

---

[2]John Leith, ed., *Creeds of the Churches*, 3rd ed. (Atlanta: John Knox Press, 1982), pp. 141-42.

and with his Son, Christ Jesus, through the sanctification of the Holy Spirit.[3]

John Leith, commenting on this confession, says, "God created human beings to live in fellowship with himself."[4] And it is this fellowship that the creeds are speaking about when they teach that the church has been from the very beginning wherever people were drawn together to worship the Lord God and to love one another. In other words, the teaching of the church's catholicity, or the universality of the church, is a firm rejection of all cultic or sectarian expressions of religion that attempt to restrict God to a single territory, time or race. This is certainly true of the "church" of Israel, which God called out from among the nations of the world, with which God covenanted unconditionally, and which is finally and fully embodied in Jesus Christ. God's mission to Israel was not an end in itself but was a mission through the people of Israel to and for the sake of the whole world.

Karl Barth, in his lectures on the Scots Confession, echoes this creed when he says that the church consists of all those people "gathered together by the Holy Spirit, the Israel of *all* those who have become debtors to [the Lord], and who have been freed by Him, the *one Holy* Church of Jews and Gentiles." Barth continues:

> Despite the differences in natural languages, it is united by the common language of the Holy Spirit, who speaks of the great acts of God. Despite the differences between the living and the dead, it is united by the common benefit which we may yet receive, while those who are dead have already received it once and for all. . . . And this people is sanctified despite the fact that it is a disobedient people, as is unmistakably clear in the light of its origin in the Cross of Christ. It is sanctified through Him who makes the ungodly righteous, through the election and calling of its Lord and Head, through its being free in faith to assent to its salvation.[5]

The biblical scholar Claus Westermann underscores this fact in his observations on the structure and organization of the Pentateuch, the first five

---

[3]"The Scots Confession," in *The Book of Confessions* (Louisville, Ky.: The Office of the General Assembly of the Presbyterian Church, U.S.A.). The Scots Confession dates from 1560 and was authored under the direction of John Knox. It was the first Reformed confession in the English language.

[4]John Leith, *The Church: A Believing Fellowship* (Atlanta: John Knox Press, 1981), p. 2.

[5]Karl Barth, *The Knowledge of God and the Service of God According to the Teaching of the Reformation*, The Gifford Lectures for 1937 and 1938, trans. J. L. M. Haire and Ian Henderson (London: Hodder & Stoughton, 1938), pp. 151-52.

books of the Hebrew Scriptures. He explains that the story of God's dealings with the Hebrew people, from the legends concerning the birth of this
people in the patriarchal narratives (the stories of the Abraham, Isaac and
Jacob) to the story of the deliverance of this people and their establishment
through the Torah, *is set within a larger, universal framework.* "Everything
that happens," he writes, "between Israel and its God, everything that happens between an individual and God stands in this broader context." God
is dealing with the whole world, the whole of creation, the whole of
humanity. This is the large context of God's work of redemption. Whatever
God does in the history of Israel, whatever God does in the life of an individual, God does for the sake of the world that God creates and nurtures,
and for the sake of a humanity that God has called out of nonbeing and
isolation into joyful community.[6]

This idea corresponds to Calvin's understanding of the "childhood of the
Church in the Old Covenant."[7] The faith that women and men have always
had in God, when it has been genuine faith in God, has always been God's
gift through Christ, though Christ may not yet have appeared in the flesh.
The Spirit has been at work among humanity from the beginning, calling
people out of isolation and chaos into communion with God, into worship,
service and the neighborhood of others. The Spirit has particularly been at
work among and through the Hebrew people, leading them through God's
promises regarding their nation to "a higher promise," the promise of the
Messiah himself.

If we can comprehend the fullness of God's universal "calling forth" of
humanity into communion, we can understand and appreciate the meaning
of a teaching that, if it is discussed in a narrower sectarian context, is
merely divisive and chauvinistic. This is, of course, the ancient teaching
that "there is no salvation outside the church" *(Extra ecclesiam nulla salus).*
As a statement of God's universal purpose to call all human beings into
redemptive communion with him and with others, this is simply a statement of fact. Salvation is itself the integration of persons into communion
with God and other persons, and, as such, this integration of persons in
communion is the fulfillment of God's original intention and ultimate pur-

---

[6]Claus Westermann, *What Does the Old Testament Say About God?* ed. Friedemann W. Golka
(Atlanta: John Knox Press, 1979), p. 39.
[7]See John Calvin *Institutes of the Christian Religion* 2.11.2, ed. John T. McNeill, trans. Ford
Lewis Battles (Philadelphia: Westminster Press, 1960).

pose for all humanity. Wherever redemptive community of faith in God is called into being, it is the result of God's Word and Spirit, which are never restricted to our cultural or sectarian expressions.

Isolation, biblically speaking, corresponds to chaos and destruction, the ultimate disintegration of persons, from which God seeks to save humanity by sharing with us a genuine participation in the communion of the triune God in whose image we are created. God draws us to participate in this saving communion by integrating us into the human community of faith in the crucified Christ.

The origin of our confession of the catholicity (universality) of the church then is not primarily the story of Pentecost, when the Spirit of God called into being Christian communities from among the nations of the world, as important as that story is to the identity and vital mission of the church. The miracle of Pentecost demonstrates the astonishing diversity of Christian community that has its concrete historical and cultural reality in peoples as numerous as grains of sand on a beach, each speaking their own tongues (a metaphor for their historical and cultural diversity) yet hearing and understanding in their own tongues the joyful good news of the gospel of Jesus Christ.

The *origin* of our confession of the catholicity of the church lies in the creation of humanity in the communal image of God, and God's calling forth of persons to participate in that communion, which reflects his eternal being in communion. This is the communion we encounter by faith in Christ, whose whole life was a human outpouring of the triune God's communal life in and through the power of the Spirit. The church of Jesus Christ, as the historic Reformed confessions (that is the Second Helvetic and the Scots confessions) affirm, does not hold an exclusive right to the designation "community of faith" or "church," though we Christians believe that the church of Jesus Christ does uniquely understand the open secret that every genuine human community exists more or less (for weal or woe, and sometimes sinfully and perversely) as a reflection of God's eternal being, which is finally and fully revealed in Jesus Christ. This then is the glory of the church, the "testimony" or "witness" it bears to the good news of the Christ in whom we are given to share the redemptive knowledge of God and ourselves.

Summary. We bear witness to the catholicity of the church, which means we announce the good news that God is at work and has always

been at work throughout the world re-creating a humanity in the image of
the God who has his very being in communion as Father, Son and Holy
Spirit.

Blessed to Be a Blessing

What we see in the people of Israel and in the church of Jesus Christ is the
unfolding of the promise God made to Abram and his descendants: "I will
bless you . . . and in you all the families of the earth shall be blessed" (see
Gen 12). God chose to work through a people on the margins of history to
accomplish his purpose of drawing humanity into redemptive communion.

We have heard from the beginning of this session an idea repeated over
and over in different ways, the idea that God calls people forth to live
together by faith in God. The idea is grounded in the history of Israel and
is given expression in the Septuagint's[8] use of the word *ecclesia*. This word
was used to describe those who are assembled together or are called
together, especially those who are "within the covenant" as opposed to
"the stranger in your midst" (Deut 23:3; Neh 13:1). R. H. Fuller explains that
the Septuagint actually translates two Hebrew words with the single Greek
word, *ekklēsia*. The Hebrew words are *'edâ* and *qāhāl*. *Edâ*, the older
word, retains the root meaning "to appoint." And so the *ecclesia* is "a company assembled together by appointment." *Qāhāl*, a later word, carries the
root meaning "to call." It originally meant "the assembling together of the
community for counsel, or the mustering of men of military age for war."[9]
The Greek word *ekklēsia*, used to render both of these terms, was adopted
by the early Christian communities as their self-designation. They understood themselves to be the people of God, appointed by God, God's royal
priesthood, *called out* of the world and *called into* the communion of faith
by, in and through Christ Jesus.

The significance of the Word of God (as the One by whom they were
called) and the Spirit (as the One through whom they were called) was not
lost on these earliest members of the Christian church. God called them

---

[8]The Septuagint (represented often by the abbreviation LXX, the Roman numeral for 70) was
the ancient translation of the Hebrew Scriptures into Greek. It is called the Septuagint ("the
seventy") because of the legend that it was translated by 70 scholars. The Septuagint, which
was translated c. 285-246 B.C., was the Old Testament of the early Greek-speaking church
and is frequently quoted in the New Testament.

[9]R. H. Fuller, "Church," in *A Theological Wordbook of the Bible*, ed. Alan Richardson (New
York: Macmillan, 1950), p. 46.

together. They did not call themselves into community. Indeed, this much should be clear from the assortment of disciples Jesus called to follow him during his earthly ministry. The original disciples were not people who were likely to band together on their own initiative or to agree mutually to associate together because they found one another's company to be congenial. They were, quite simply, brought together into community by the action of "an other," the Christ who called them.

Our own English word *church* derives ultimately from another Greek word, a word originally applied to the building in which the people of God met for worship. The word *kyriakon* means "that which belongs to the Lord." In common usage today, it carries the double meaning quite well, pointing both to the church building and to the church assembly or congregation, both of which "belong to the Lord." It is here that we see the force of the indicative in relation to the doctrine of the church.

Summary. The church is first and foremost that community called out from among those who live in the prison of isolation and asunderedness, in chaos and disintegration. The church is called into saving communion with God and other persons. God works throughout creation to accomplish this redemptive mission. But this mission is never achieved among us without faith, without trusting ourselves to God and to one another.

Members of One Body

At the heart of our identity as the church of Jesus Christ lies the reality of our spiritual union with Christ. By the power of the Holy Spirit we no longer have our existence in isolation, in the self-absorbed insanity of the individual turned in upon itself. The Spirit of God has drawn us into union with Christ and with one another in the church, the "body of Christ." And as members of the body of Christ we are introduced to a fullness of life (life as communion) that is so extraordinary in power that our previous existence (in alienation from God and others) appears to us but a kind of death. Calvin expresses this truth when he says that "there is no other life of the soul than that which is breathed into us by Christ; so that we begin to live only when we are engrafted into Him, and enjoy a common life with Him." This is the "secret union," as Calvin calls it, which "belongs truly to the members" of Christ's body.[10]

---

[10]John Calvin, *Commentary on Galatians, Ephesians, Philippians, and Colossians,* ed. David W. Torrance and Thomas F. Torrance, trans. T. H. L. Parker (Grand Rapids, Mich.: Eerdmans, 1965), p. 142.

We who in our sin-shattered humanity were alienated from God, from ourselves and from other persons—existing under the tyranny of anxiety, dread and fear; dominated by resentment, envy, jealousy, and the lust for dominion and revenge—have been united to Christ Jesus by the power of the Holy Spirit. We are united by the Spirit with the same Christ who overcame humanity's alienation from God and from our humanity in his incarnation. And so in union with Christ we are brought to life, called out of that whole way of existence that refused faithful reliance on God, and loving interdependence with other persons. In union with Christ we discover that what we once considered our "partiality" or "incompleteness" is actually our special giftedness. In isolation we were incomplete, unable to be everything (to ourselves or others) that we needed and wanted to be. But in union with Christ, through the Holy Spirit, and in communion with other members of the body of Christ, we discover that our particular and singular individuality is complemented by that of others, and that specifically in those ways in which we felt fragmented, we now know ourselves to be whole, in relationship to Christ and with others.

☐ We had known ourselves to be morally impotent because we were unable to accomplish the moral life for which we were created. Now we discover that the essence of the moral life consists not of our punctilious observation of moral codes and legal statutes, as important as these laws are to our life together, but in simple childlike trust in God, in the surrender of ourselves to God and in the commandment to be "neighbor" to those around us.

☐ We had found ourselves to be woefully incomplete, unable to be all things to all people, unable to keep the promise of our humanity. Now we discover that the essence of our human life consists not in being all things in and of ourselves but in being in relationship, in enjoying the giftedness of others and in exercising our own gifts in the reciprocal communion of our uniqueness, under the guidance of the Spirit of God.

Ironically, it seems that God uses our sense of incompleteness and restlessness to draw us into community with God and others so that we might be given the wholeness we need. This is at the heart of Augustine's beautiful and familiar prayer at the opening of his *Confessions:* "You stir man to take pleasure in praising you, because you have made us for yourself, and our heart is restless until it rests in you."[11] This is what the seventeenth-cen-

---

[11]Augustine *Confessions* 3, trans. Henry Chadwick (Oxford: Oxford University Press, 1992).

tury poet and pastor George Herbert was expressing in his poem "The Pulley," in which we find God creating humanity and giving humanity many gifts, *except* the ultimate gift of rest, the sense of being at peace in oneself. Humanity, Herbert tells us, is kept in "repining restlessness" by God. Herbert has God the Creator say of humanity:

> Let him be rich and weary, that at least,
> If goodness lead him not, yet weariness
> May toss him to my breast.[12]

Someone like an Augustine or a George Herbert, writing from within the life of the Christian community (though their own particular Christian communities are different in so many ways), sees something perhaps not so apparent from the outside of such a community of faith: our deficits, our incompleteness and our restless longing for complement, for mutuality and completeness are all gifts from the hands of the God who is Love, the God who has his very being in communion. And the awareness of our own lack draws us into the fellowship where we are made whole in relation to the God who is the ground of our being (being-in-communion) and through the web of relationships with others who seek their wholeness in God and in relation to one another.

The concept of the church as the body of Christ, which lies behind everything that we are saying, derives from the apostle Paul, who wrote, "For as in one body we have many members, and not all the members have the same function, so we, who are many, are one body in Christ, and individually we are members one of another. We have gifts that differ according to the grace given to us" (Rom 12:4-6). Ephesians 4—5 says much the same thing as does Colossians (Col 1:18), where we are told that Christ is the head of the body, in whom we share as members. The most detailed discussion of Paul's understanding of the church appears in 1 Corinthians 12:12-27. Writing to the divided and troubled Corinthian church, Paul says that the body of Christ is an organic whole in which we share through the Holy Spirit.

Now, notice what Paul doesn't say! Paul doesn't say that the church is a machine made up of many parts or units, like a chariot, that all work together to do a job. The church, by contrast, is a living organism that shares the same life, the life of Christ. We are living members of this one

---

[12]George Herbert, *The Country Parson, The Temple*, ed. John N. Wall Jr. (New York: Paulist, 1981), p. 285.

body. Indeed, Paul so completely identifies the church with Christ that he actually calls the body by the name of Christ and says (in the words of John Calvin) that it is "not until He [Christ] has us as one with Himself" that Christ is "complete in all His parts," or that Christ wishes "to be regarded as whole!"[13]

Summary. What we are saying is that we only discover our wholeness as the body of Christ through our being in communion with others in and through Jesus Christ. Our restlessness and sense of incompleteness draws us into the body of Christ. Or, to be more exact, the Holy Spirit uses our restlessness and sense of incompleteness to draw us into this communion, through which we find our wholeness. We discover in Paul's writings that Christ, as von Balthasar has said, "wishes to do nothing apart from his brothers and sisters." Even though God is not incomplete, God wishes to do what God does with us and through us, so that we can share in the fullness of God's love and life.[14]

This highly communal conception of the Christian church stands against the two most popular ecclesiastical myths of our time, the interconnected myths of *solitary religion* and *voluntary religion*.

The Myth of Solitary Religion

We live in the time and the land of the rugged individualist. We might in fact say that we live in the time and land of the rugged isolationist. I'm not using "rugged isolationist" in the sense of international politics (at least not necessarily) but to describe a kind of personal self-regard. To us, especially those of us in North America, the rugged individual is the person who "does for himself": the lonely cowboy astride his horse, the heroic inventor guided by the genius of his singular vision, the romantic prophet of high principles (a type of secular monk or hermit) standing his ground against the onslaught of cynicism or social ills, the brave industrialist or the business entrepreneur courageously risking his reputation and fortune for the sake of fame and greater fortunes still. All of these are personal images that appeal to most of us.

---

[13]Calvin, *Commentary on Galatians, Ephesians, Philippians, and Colossians*, p. 138.
[14]Note Hans Urs von Balthasar's rich discussion of this idea in *Prayer* (San Francisco: Ignatius, 1968), pp. 177-97.

There is, of course, great strength in each of these expressions of self-reliance. And this should not be minimized. But there is also great danger in these images.

Alexis de Tocqueville, the astute French observer of American culture whose remarkable study *Democracy in America* was published (in two parts) in 1835 and 1840, perceived the threat of alienation in the American religious psyche, a threat that derived directly from our reverence for individualism and our tendency toward isolation. He wrote: "Each man is forever thrown back on himself alone, and there is danger that he may be shut up in the solitude of his own heart."[15]

That's a striking phrase isn't it?

The danger of being shut up in the solitude of our own hearts is a phrase that could serve as the motto for much of the religious life of our time.

Robert Bellah and his colleagues suggest in their sociological study of religious attitudes in America, *Habits of the Heart,* that the radical individualism of our country could conceivably produce "220 million American religions, one for each of us." We could, they explain, become a nation of individuals *shut up in the solitude of our own hearts.* To make their point they describe the case of a young woman named Sheila Larson who subscribes, she says, to a religious faith she named after herself, "Sheilaism." She says, "I believe in God. I'm not a religious fanatic. I can't remember the last time I went to church. My faith has carried me a long way. It's Sheilaism. Just my own little voice."[16]

Most people would not go as far as Sheila does (at least not in their frankness), but the result is pretty much the same. How often do we hear people say that they "just can't stand to go to church because of all the hypocrites." "Much better to worship God by myself," some say, "where I can concentrate on God and listen to his voice alone, than to pray in a room cluttered with disagreeable old sinners." Of course, the problem with

---

[15]Alexis de Tocqueville, cited in Robert N. Bellah et al., *Habits of the Heart: Individualism and Commitment in American Life* (Berkeley: University of California Press, 1985), p. 37.

[16]Ibid., p. 221. In a recent series of lectures Ellis Nelson describes Sheila Larson's religious faith as a primitive religious faith, the self-centered faith of an infant. C. Ellis Nelson, "Childish Religion," an audio recording of the Jones lectures, Austin Presbyterian Theological Seminary, January 2000.

this way of thinking is that it fails to see that *when we are left to worship by ourselves, what we usually worship is ourselves.* Solitary religion tends toward idolatry, the worship of false gods made in our own image. The great scandal of the church according to Christian faith is not that it is full of hypocrites and sinners but that God actually reveals himself in the midst of and through the lives of these hypocrites and sinners. This parallels what Karl Barth referred to as the scandalous "secularity of the gospel." In reality it is not despite but precisely *in the irreducible otherness of community* that God reveals himself.

God works through Christian community as "the great iconoclast,"[17] using the contrasting personalities, stereotypes and peculiarities; local customs, mythologies and histories; cultural viewpoints and interests of others in the larger community of faith to break through and break down our most cherished stereotypes and mythologies, our images of ourselves and our false images of God. God frequently uses the rituals of others to relativize our own. God often uses the unholy foolishness of others to call our own into question. God even uses the interpretations and conceptions of God held by others to call into question and correct our own interpretations and conceptions that, left to themselves, become idolatrous. And often we see that our theological reflections are greatly improved when hammered out on the anvil of someone else's theological perspective. This is why—as we have known for years in the field of practical theology—those churches in communication with a larger community of churches are healthiest in themselves.

Summary. The solitary worshiper tends to breed idolatry, the uncritical worship of the self, while the worshiper in communion is not left to herself but must continually examine her own life in light of the faith experience of others.

The Myth of Voluntary Religion

Voluntary religion is pretty much solitary religion exercised in groups. It is

---

[17]The idea of God as "the great iconoclast" comes from C. S. Lewis, *A Grief Observed* (New York: Seabury, 1961), p. 52. The full passage is worthy of quotation: "My idea of God is not a divine idea. It has to be shattered time after time. He shatters it Himself. He is the great iconoclast. Could we not almost say that this shattering is one of the marks of His presence? The Incarnation is the supreme example; it leaves all previous ideas of the Messiah in ruins. And most are 'offended' by the iconoclasm; and blessed are those who are not. But the same thing happens in our private prayers. All reality is iconoclastic."

the religion of choice (literally) for most people today in Western society, that is, in Western Europe and North America. It owes its formal development, at least in part, to the seventeenth-century British philosopher John Locke, the founder of what we call empiricism. Locke, in his famous essay "Letter Concerning Toleration," provided the classic statement of voluntary religion. He described the church as "a voluntary society of men, joining themselves of their own accord to the public worshiping of God."[18]

Locke's concept of the church as a religious society of like-minded individuals has become so common in many circles, especially in the United States, that it is virtually accepted as self-evident. In voluntary religion the individual tries to find other individuals who share tolerably similar private conceptions of God. And having found others who share the similar private religious views, a religious society is founded (a "church") to which these individuals voluntarily commit themselves until their ideas change or they find that the ideas of others have become so greatly at variance with their own that they must move on to another religious society.

Solitary religion goes hand in hand with voluntary religion. As Karl Barth says in his commentary on Calvin's catechism, both solitary and voluntary religion misunderstand the nature of the church. In Barth's view the church is virtually the opposite of a voluntary religious society:

> Imagine citizens called by the trumpet and rushing from everywhere. They are present, they form a company, the company of the faithful, of those who, called by God's faithfulness, have responded with their faithfulness. It is God who has convoked them. It is important to note that the Church is not formed by a human gathering of people who would have the same opinions, but by a divine convocation that constitutes into a corps individuals until then scattered at the mercy of their opinions. The nineteenth century was certainly in error, when it understood the Church as a "religious society."[19]

C. S. Lewis, in a remarkable letter to a friend, critiques the idea of the voluntary church, what he calls "a human society united by their natural affinities." To the contrary, Lewis explains, the church of Jesus Christ is "the

---

[18]John Locke, "Letter Concerning Toleration," in *On Politics and Education* (New York: Walter J. Black, 1947), pp. 27-28.

[19]Karl Barth, *The Faith of the Church: A Commentary on The Apostles' Creed According to Calvin's Catechism*, ed. Jean-Louis Leuba, trans. Gabriel Vahanian (New York: Living Age Books, 1958), p. 136.

Body of Christ in which all members however different . . . must share the common life, complementing and helping one another precisely by their differences."[20]

This takes us back, by another route, to Paul's metaphor of the body of Christ. If we take seriously the view that the church is the body of Christ, then we must take seriously both the otherness of the various members of the body and the union with one another that does not reside in the members but is the gift given by Christ, the head of the body. Indeed, the members are so different from each other, often in their beliefs and behaviors, that they may not appear to one another to belong to the same body. An eye seems to bear little similarity or affinity with a big toe; a kidney is a very different sort of organ from an ear, with very different functions and roles. And yet eyes, ears, fingers, toes and kidneys are all needed for the life and health of the whole body. Their belonging to the body, in other words, does not depend on their similarity, perspective, role or function. In the instance of the church this is even truer than in the case of a physical body because it is through the irreducible otherness of contrasting members that we are frequently shown the reality of Jesus Christ among us. And our differences as members are only magnified when we reflect on the extraordinary complexity and diversity of Christian communities throughout history and throughout the world today. Whatever our unity is as Christians, it does not reside in us but in the One to whom we belong. And whatever this unity means, we cannot confuse unity with unanimity, or identity with that which is merely identical. We belong to the God whose being is in communion, whose life is mutuality.[21]

Summary. The members of the body of Christ do not experience unity by virtue of similarity with one another; this much should be clear to us. Our oneness is the gift of the Head to whom we are united by the power

---

[20]C. S. Lewis, *Letters of C. S. Lewis*, ed. W. H. Lewis (New York: Harcourt Brace Jovanovich, 1966), p. 224.

[21]See David Rhoads, *The Challenge of Diversity: The Witness of Paul and the Gospel* (Minneapolis: Fortress, 1996); Stanley Hauerwas, *In Good Company: The Church as Polis* (Notre Dame, Ind.: University of Notre Dame Press, 1995); Michael Jinkins, *The Church Faces Death: Ecclesiology in a Postmodern Context* (New York: Oxford University Press, 1999); Lesslie Newbigin, *The Gospel in a Pluralist Society* (Grand Rapids, Mich.: Eerdmans, 1989); and Shirley C. Guthrie Jr., *Diversity in Faith—Unity in Christ: Orthodoxy, Liberalism, Pietism, and Beyond* (Philadelphia: Westminster Press, 1986). These books offer concrete ways of thinking about the plurality within church and society.

of the Holy Spirit. Neither our faith nor our ideas, nor our actions make us one. Jesus Christ alone makes us one, and only in Christ are we united. This has important implications for a genuine communion in the presence of an ever-growing pluralism. We can stop looking for the ground of unity in each other or in joint committees on various subjects. We will find that our unity is given to us in Christ alone.

The Specificity of the Church

Until now we have been discussing the identity of the church in rather general terms. But the life of the church carries on day in and day out in the most specific and concrete situations among women and men and children in actual congregations of believers, in worshiping communities. This is where we understand and experience the life of the church. As John Leith in fact says, "Nowhere else is the church so visible to us as in the life and worship of a local congregation."[22]

Certainly the congregation is the church as most of us know it, in all its contradictions, in the inconsistencies and brokenness of human fellowship, yet with all the promise and possibilities and potential for greatness that God gives it. In fact, if we don't love the church we experience "warts and all," we don't love the church that God loves, because there is no other. "The Church," as Carlyle Marney once said, "is a womb where God's kind of persons happen, are made, are called forth."[23] The church is that place where human beings are grown into the spitting image of Christ. And it is a messy, frequently unpleasant and often painful business, this growing of humans. Clarence Jordan, the founder of the Koinonia Community, got at this same idea when he said that the "job of the Church" is "to become the womb of God through which [God] can bring his child into the world."[24]

The recurring analogy of childbirth is not just coincidental. The development of people in the church is a lot like the organized chaos of a delivery room and the painful experience of birth. The church doesn't "happen" in theory. The church happens in fact, in those concrete congregations where people are born into the fullness of human life, are pulled into the relation-

---

[22]Leith, *Church*, p. 22.

[23]Carlyle Marney, *Priests to Each Other* (Valley Forge, Penn.: Judson Press, 1974), p. 20.

[24]Clarence Jordan, cited in *The Substance of Faith*, ed. Dallas Lee (New York: Association, 1972), p. 21.

ality of life in Christ—sometimes kicking and screaming—with a mixture of
incredible pain and unutterable joy. To love the church is also to love the
process by which God has chosen to recover among us God's own triune
image as Father, Son and Holy Spirit, the image of eternal communion.
Marney, expanding on this idea, described three dimensions of the
church's life through which we become what we are meant to be: *koinonia, diakonia* and *leiturgia.*

Koinonia. "Life in the church is *koinonia* (fellowship)," Marney writes.
"This is what we mean when we speak of persons as means of grace. We
mean that we meet God in each other."[25] The heart of *koinonia* is the relationship of persons with one another, persons seeking the other for the
sake of the other's highest good and finding in the other the meaning of
our own personhood. In this, our life together reflects the self-emptying
life, the *kenosis,* of God revealed in Jesus Christ. It is only in the abandon-
ment of the self in such a relationship that we paradoxically find ourselves.[26] But this is not all.

Also essential to the *koinonia* of human persons in the Christian community of faith is the appropriation of grace, the communication to one
another of unconditional forgiveness in the name of Christ. The freedom
we have to grow with one another in the community of faith is possible
only because we are extended grace by this Other, Christ. We know this
grace concretely in the face of the others with whom we share community—and even those beyond the margins of our community—who pro-
phetically become "Christ" to us. Persons have the freedom to unfold,
develop and grow because they are nurtured by others in *koinonia,* the fellowship of the grace of God in Jesus Christ. As Marney says, *"We are priests
to each other.* I do not priest me. I priest you and vice versa. On this the
community of witness takes its rise. Without it no church exists at all."[27]

In the context of *koinonia,* the fellowship of grace, we are empowered
to break out of the isolation and disintegration that are deadly to the
human life called forth by the Spirit of God, because in *koinonia,* as priests
to one another, we are able to confess our sin to one another and receive
from each other forgiveness in the name of Jesus. This environment of

---

[25]Marney, *Priests to Each Other,* p. 20.
[26]See Reuel L. Howe's handling of this idea in *The Miracle of Dialogue* (New York: Seabury
Press, 1963).
[27]Marney, *Priests to Each Other,* p. 22.

grace is a reflection in our human communities of the *perichoresis* of the holy Trinity, which we discussed earlier. And it is in confession to one another that, as Dietrich Bonhoeffer has explained, "the break-through of the Cross" occurs.[28]

Isolated in my own sin I may have spun a web of pride, *superbia* (the root of all sins), in which I demand the right to live under my own law; to coddle my own hatreds, envies and lusts; to envision my own private future; and to craft my own private death. I want to be a god unto myself. But in confession, in the presence of you, my priest and companion, I must submit to the most profound humiliation because I must see myself in light of the Christ who renounced himself for the sake of others. In the eyes of a forgiving brother or sister, I see myself in need of forgiveness, forgiven in the shadow of the cross.[29]

Koinonia is never a cozy club for pious denial. It is the joint venture of a surgical team committed to the health and wholeness of one another.

Diakonia. "There is also in the church," Marney says, "the life of *diakonia,* the service of obedient" persons.[30] To borrow a phrase from the Christian philosopher Elton Trueblood, the church is "the company of the committed."[31] Because we belong to the Lord who came to serve *(kuriakon)*, we also are servants of others. In other words, the concrete shape our discipleship to Jesus Christ takes is the discipline of service in and for the sake of the world.

T. F. Torrance explains, *"Diakonia* is pure service fulfilled in accordance with the requirements of an external Authority, that of the Lord, yet *diakonia* is intrinsically related to that Authority through its content of love."[32] The church is a community of "deacons" who through their service to one another and to the world express the love that has laid claim to their lives in Christ.

"We are to be to others," as George MacLeod, founder of the Iona Com-

---

[28]Dietrich Bonhoeffer, *Life Together/Prayerbook of the Bible,* Dietrich Bonhoeffer Works, ed. Geffrey B. Kelly, trans. Daniel W. Bloesch and James H. Burtness (Minneapolis: Fortress, 1996), 5:111.

[29]Ibid., pp. 111-18.

[30]Marney, *Priests to Each Other,* p. 20.

[31]Elton Trueblood, *The Company of the Committed* (New York: Harper, 1961).

[32]T. F. Torrance, "Service in Jesus Christ," in *Service in Christ: Essays Presented to Karl Barth on his 80th Birthday,* ed. James I. McCord and T. H. L. Parker (Grand Rapids, Mich.: Eerdmans, 1966), p. 2.

munity, once said, "what Christ has become for us." This is the heart of the
church's life of service, to set up Christ's cross in the middle of the market-
place of humanity.[33]

Thus our life together in the church includes both the *ministerium Verbi
divini* (the service of the divine Word) and the *magisterium* (the teaching
office of the church). Indeed, these must be understood as two sides of the
same coin. We submit ourselves to the living authority of the Word of God
who by the power of the Spirit leads us into the way of life, the life of ser-
vanthood in the likeness of Christ whose eternal life is faithful obedience to
God the Father. We want to bear the Word of God and to proclaim the
Word of God; we trust ourselves to the Word to be used as God wills.[34] We
live under the Word of God, "captive to the Word," as Luther said, as servants of the Word.

In turn, the church as a living communion of believers stretching back
through history perpetuates its dialogue with and concerning the Word,
who has spoken to each successive generation of the church in ways
appropriate to the time and place of each, and who has been heard and
obeyed within our creaturely limitations. We seek to enter into this living
dialogue to hear the teaching voice of the church through the voices of its
teachers. This *magisterium* (teaching office of the church) is that proper
function of the combined (and at times contradictory) voices of the
church's doctors and saints to whom we submit ourselves for instruction in
the awareness that our own individual perspectives are frail, sinful and
inadequate, and desperately in need of correction.

Leiturgia. Marney finally draws the total life of the church under a single
title—*leiturgia* (liturgy), the life of worship. He writes:

> All these [people], then, who are aware of sin and need, fulfillment, and the
> need to praise; those who are aware of self and selves; those who are veter-
> ans of meeting with God—these come into the church. This church is the
> communion of the saints, the fellowship of believers, the way, the body of
> Christ, the communion of the Holy Spirit and his work; it finds its common
> experience, locale, conviction, effect, result, and its reason for being in the
> life, teaching, death, resurrection, and coming of Christ Jesus, unique Son of
> God and Savior of the world.[35]

---

[33]George MacLeod, *Only One Way Left* (Glasgow: Iona Community, 1956), p. 35.
[34]Karl Barth, *Evangelical Theology* (Garden City, N.Y.: Doubleday, 1964), pp. 34-36.
[35]Marney, *Priests to Each Other,* pp. 20-21.

Worship is the total life of the church through which the community of faith says Amen (So be it!) through the power of the Holy Spirit to the God and Father of our Lord Jesus Christ. This is what the Westminster Confession is pointing toward when it says that the chief end of humanity is to "glorify God and enjoy him forever."

Worship in its fullest sense should never be understood simply as a ceremony of ritual, symbols, words and music that happens once a week on Sunday mornings at eleven o'clock. "In all of life we have our dealings with God," as Calvin said.[36] And so our whole lives are meant to be that fitting sacrifice and reasonable service that we present to God in Jesus Christ.

The church, however, recognizes the fact that we do not glorify and enjoy God in all of life, that we do not offer God that service of worship we want and need to offer. We have already seen that the church extends the fellowship (koinonia) of Christ's forgiveness and so participates in the grace of Christ, and the church extends the service (diakonia) of the servant Lord and so participates in the obedience of Christ. Now we see also that the church worships God inasmuch as it participates in the perfect worship (leiturgia) that Christ offers to God on our behalf. Christ is, as the epistle to the Hebrews describes him, the Leitourgos, our true worship leader, "a high priest . . . who is seated at the right hand of the throne of the Majesty in the heavens, a minister in the sanctuary and the true tent of the Lord" (Heb 8:1-2). It is through the worship of Christ, our worship leader, that we "come boldly to the throne of grace, that we may obtain mercy and find grace to help in time of need" (Heb 4:16). It is only in Christ that we share in the fullness of our liturgical or worship life.[37]

"Jesus comes," James Torrance writes, "as our Brother Man, to be our great High Priest, that He might carry on His loving heart the joys, the sorrows, the prayers, the conflicts of all His creatures, that He might reconcile all things to God, that He might intercede for all nations as our eternal Mediator and Advocate, that He might stand in for us in the presence of His Father." As head of all things, "He makes us His Body, and calls us to be a royal priesthood . . . that we might be identified with Him and participate

---

[36] See John T. McNeill's introduction to John Calvin, *On God and Political Duty*, rev. ed. (New York: Bobbs-Merrill, 1956), pp. vii-xxv for an excellent reflection on Calvin's thought.

[37] For fuller development of this idea see Michael Jinkins, "The God Who Worships: When the God We Worship Becomes the Worshiping God," *Reformed Liturgy & Music* 32, no. 2 (1998): 72-77.

with Him in His great priestly work and ministry of intercession, that our prayers on earth might be the echo of His prayers in heaven."[38]

Summary: Our entire life together as members of the church can be interpreted as a kind of participation in the life of Jesus Christ through the power of the Spirit. Our fellowship *(koinonia)* is a participation in the eternal communion of the Father, Son and Spirit, in which we share through Christ. Our service *(diakonia)* to others is an extension of the life and service of this fellowship we have been drawn into. Our worship *(leiturgia)* becomes our sharing in the Yes that Jesus Christ has spoken and continues to speak in our flesh to God on our behalf.

The Church and the Kingdom of God

One of the most helpful statements concerning the church and its ministry in the world was produced in 1982 by the Commission on Faith and Order of the World Council of Churches. We'll close our session today by walking through this statement's section "Baptism, Eucharist and Ministry," which deals with the church's ministry. As we have seen already, the call "to become Gods people" is addressed by God to "the whole of humanity." This is the call that meets us in the midst of a broken world. And because it is a call to live "in communion with God through Jesus Christ in the Holy Spirit," it is also a call to share, through the Holy Spirit, the quality of life Christ lived.[39]

God makes an unconditional and sovereign claim on us through the church in the actuality of our lives among others. And in our life among other people we see beyond the horizon of earthly vision to a purpose and a meaning that God reveals in Christ.

The church, as this statement of faith says, bases its life together "on Christ's victory over the powers of evil and death, accomplished once for all." The life in community to which God calls us is a life of "praise to God" and "service" to our "neighbors," a life of "freedom, mutual forgiveness and love." We have the freedom to live this life of praise and service because we are an eschatological community, that is, a community pulled into the future by the victorious power of Christ over evil and death. Through Christ

---

[38]James B. Torrance, "The Place of Jesus Christ in Worship," in *Theological Foundations for Ministry*, ed. Ray S. Anderson (Edinburgh: T & T Clark, 1979), pp. 348-49.

[39]"Baptism, Eucharist and Ministry," in *Creeds of the Churches*, ed. John Leith, 3rd ed. (Atlanta: John Knox Press, 1982), p. 631.

our hearts and minds are directed toward the consummation (the fulfillment) of the kingdom of God, "where Christ's victory will become manifest
and all things made new." It is this singular vision of God's purpose for the
world that energizes our life together.[40]

The church therefore, again as the statement says, is empowered by the
Holy Spirit to preach and prefigure the kingdom of God on earth. In a variety of specific historical, cultural, social and political contexts in which the
church finds itself, it is responsible to bear witness to the kingdom of God
because Christ Jesus, the head of the church, is also head of all creation.
Everything that we do in worship and service we do in the name of Christ
(the Lord of creation) in the power of the Spirit (who is the Lord). This
worship and service must take concrete form in specific situations, in obedience to Christ. "The members of Christ's body are to struggle," the confession says, "with the oppressed towards that freedom and dignity
promised with the coming of the Kingdom."[41]

This is the vision of God's kingdom, established in obedience to Christ in
the power of the Spirit, which guides our ministry together. Because we recognize that "the Holy Spirit bestows on the community diverse and complementary gifts" for the upbuilding of the whole body and "the service of the
world to which the Church is sent," the church's ministry must be guided by
the question "How, according to the will of God and under the guidance of
the Holy Spirit, is the life of the Church to be understood and ordered, so
that the Gospel may be spread and the community built up in love?"[42]

What we see in these passages is the rather startling idea that the church
is not simply a garden-variety religious organization. The church is an out-
post of the kingdom of God on earth, through which God works wonders
of redemption and liberation. As Jürgen Moltmann has said, the existence
of the church represents a radically new quality of life (in every age). To be
the church is to grasp the fact that "where Jesus is, there is life. There is
abundant life, vigorous life, loved life, eternal life. There is life-before-death."
And this passionate quality of life is shared life.[43]

---

[40]Ibid., p. 632.
[41]Ibid., pp. 632-33.
[42]Ibid., p. 633.
[43]Jürgen Moltmann, A Passion for Life: A Messianic Lifestyle (Philadelphia: Fortress, 1978), p.
    33. Also see José Miguez Bonino, Room to Be People (Philadelphia: Fortress, 1979), which
    also asks the question "Is there life before death?"

To quote another contemporary confession, the recently adopted "Brief Statement of Faith" of the Presbyterian Church (U.S.A.), to live as the church means:

> In a broken and fearful world
> the Spirit gives us courage
> to pray without ceasing,
> to witness among all people to Christ as Lord and Savior,
> to unmask idolatries in Church and culture,
> to bear the voices of peoples long silenced,
> and to work with others for justice, freedom and peace.[44]

Summary. As I said at the beginning of this discussion, our intention has been to answer the primary question of who we are in order to answer the secondary question of what we must do. This we have done. And as we have seen, because we are the people we are, made in the image of the tri-une God, our life together must take on a particular shape, the shape of Jesus Christ in whose life, death and resurrection God revealed to us God's own being in communion, in the image of whom we live together by the power of the Holy Spirit.

Karl Barth once observed that "the existence of the true Church is not an end in itself." The church exists for the sake of the world.[45] This is the teaching that we need to recover. Too much of the time, as Joseph Sittler has said, we Christians "walk through the world holding our noses, as it were, as if God's creation somehow smelled bad and we ought not get too close to it." But this is neither why we were created nor why we are graciously called together into the body of Christ. Sittler concludes, and I shall also, by reminding us that "God made the whole world, and meant it—all of it—to be loved."[46] This is our mission as the church—to love the world into the kingdom of God.

Homework Assignments

Your final paper is due at the end of the course. This paper will be a little different from the first one. This time you will do a critical book review

---

[44]"Brief Statement of Faith," *The Constitution of the Presbyterian Church (U.S.A.): Part I: Book of Confessions* (Louisville, Ky.: The Office of the General Assembly, 1996), p. 276.

[45]Karl Barth, *Church Dogmatics* 4/2, ed. G. W. Bromiley and T. F. Torrance, trans. G. W. Bromiley (Edinburgh: T & T Clark, 1936), pp. 619-21.

[46]Joseph Sittler, *Gravity and Grace: Reflections and Provocations*, ed. Linda-Marie Delloff (Minneapolis: Augsburg, 1986), p. 83.

(2,000 words or so) on one of the following books. (A critical review means an analytical-reflective review, not necessarily a negative one.) Every one of these books is worth reading, so you can't go wrong.

Barth, Karl. *Evangelical Theology.* Translated by Grover Foley. Garden City, N.Y.: Anchor Books, 1964.

Bonhoeffer, Dietrich. *Discipleship.* Edited by John D. Godsey and Geffrey B. Kelly. Translated by Reinhard Kraus and Barbara Green. Minneapolis: Fortress, 2000.

Campbell, Will D. *Brother to a Dragonfly.* New York: Seabury, 1977.

Chesterton, G. K. *Orthdoxy.* The Collected Works of G. K. Chesterton 1. Edited by David Dooley. San Francisco: Ignatius, 1986.

Gutiérrez, Gustavo. *A Theology of Liberation: History, Politics and Salvation.* Edited and translated by Sister Caridad Inda and John Eagleson. Maryknoll, N.Y.: Orbis, 1973.

Johnson, Elizabeth A. *She Who Is: The Mystery of God in Feminist Theological Discourse.* New York: Crossroad, 1994.

LaCugna, Catherine Mowry. *God for Us: The Trinity and Christian Life.* San Francisco: HarperSanFrancisco, 1991.

Moltmann, Jürgen. *The Crucified God.* Translated by R. A. Wilson and John Bowden. New York: Harper & Row, 1974.

Von Balthasar, Hans Urs. *Prayer.* Translated by Graham Harrison. San Francisco: Ignatius, 1986.

Here's what you need to do.

1. Read the book carefully, taking notes on what you read. One of my teachers in seminary once said that if you are given the choice between (a) reading one book and taking notes on it, or (b) of reading three books without taking notes, *always choose to read the one book and take notes on it.* You will better understand what you read, work it more deeply into your own thinking and better retain it if you take notes on it. I've found it helpful over the years (when I'm reading a book I have bought) to index the book as I read it, just making a quick jot of important or interesting ideas on the blank pages at the end of the book.

2. Write a critical (analytical) review. You may want to read a few article-length book reviews to get a feel for how this is done. *The Scottish Journal of Theology, Theology Today* and other major theological journals carry article-length book reviews. Some of the general magazines (e.g., *The Econo-*

mist) and the book review publications available at newsstands will sometimes have larger book reviews too. In getting ready for this assignment you will want to avoid the short reviews. They don't allow enough space to develop both summary and critical analysis.

3. In your written review of the book:

☐ Summarize the book, noting its most important ideas.

☐ Provide a critical reflection on the book, noting its strengths and weaknesses, as well as the points on which you agree and disagree. Make sure you provide, at this level, a careful analysis of the book's major ideas.

☐ Then give room for your own dialogue with secondary sources (what other important theologians may have said regarding this book *or* what other Christian thinkers may have said touching on the same subject).

Suggestions: If you are doing this course with others, make enough copies of your report to exchange with all members of the class so you can benefit from each other's work. It might be a good idea for each member of the group to read a different book, but (on the other hand) you may all want to explore the same resource and discuss it in depth as a group.

If you are doing this course alone, write the book report in full, reflect on it and then *do not* throw it away. Save your book report and return to it in six months or a year to read it again. Watch how you have grown.

I would suggest that you at some time read all of these books. Wrestling with giants strengthens our theological muscles and can become a habit-forming exercise.

Class 10

The Forgiveness of Sins

"I will arise, and go to my Father,
and will say unto him,
Father, I have sinned against heaven, and before thee,
and am no more worthy to be called thy son."

SENTENCES AT MORNING AND EVENING PRAYER,
BOOK OF COMMON PRAYER

*I*N A PAPER THAT C. S. LEWIS WROTE IN 1947 ON THE SUBJECT OF FORGIVENESS, he puzzled over the inclusion of the phrase "the forgiveness of sins" in the Apostles' Creed. "At first sight," he says, "it seems hardly worth putting in. 'If one is a Christian,' I thought, 'of course one believes in the forgiveness of sins. It goes without saying.'" This was only "at first sight." "But," he continues, "the people who compiled the Creed apparently thought that this was a part of our belief which we needed to be reminded of every time we went to church." Lewis winds through pages of labyrinthine reflections until he comes out with a theological statement that is pure gold. He writes, "To be a Christian means to forgive the inexcusable, because God has forgiven the inexcusable in you."[1]

The Environment of Forgiveness
The very inexcusability of sin lends to forgiveness its essential quality, that gratuitous freedom deriving from the being of the God who has shown us who he is in Jesus Christ. As Paul says, "God proves his love for us in that while we still were sinners Christ died for us" (Rom 5:8). Certainly this is at

---

[1]C. S. Lewis, *Fern-seed and Elephants* (London: Collins, 1975), p. 43.

the heart of Christ's own words. Jesus instructs us to pray for the forgiveness of our sins in the same breath as we are reminded to forgive those who have sinned against us (Mt 6:12). And he goes on to say that when we forgive others for their sins against us, we also shall be forgiven by God; but if we do not forgive, we shall not be forgiven (Mt 6:14-15). He tells us that it is not by loving our friends but by loving our enemies, those who deliberately offend and hurt us, that we share in God's completeness (Mt 5:38-48). He draws together God's forgiveness and our response of grateful love of God to say that the more God has forgiven us, the more we shall love God (Lk 7:40-50). He insists that forgiveness has no limitations; it must be not only unconditional but endless (Mt 18:21-35). And he tells us that it is only in a context of the forgiveness of others that an authentic worship of God is possible (Mt 5:23).

It is as though forgiveness forms a sort of environment, an atmosphere of grace, in which Christian faith can live and breathe and thrive. Those who live and move in this atmosphere breathe forgiveness. They exhale the forgiveness of others and inhale God's forgiveness of themselves (remember our analogy of respiration when we spoke of the life of the Holy Spirit among us). This is, at least in part, what Frederick Buechner has in mind when he writes:

> To forgive somebody is to say one way or another, "You have done something unspeakable, and by all rights I should call it quits between us. Both my pride and my principles . . . demand no less. However, although I make no guarantees that I will be able to forget what you've done and though we may both carry the scars for life, I refuse to let it stand between us." . . .
>
> To accept forgiveness means to admit that you've done something unspeakable that needs to be forgiven, and thus both parties must swallow the same thing: their pride.[2]

Let's reflect on what is being said here: to live in the environment of forgiveness, to inhale and to exhale the grace of God, means that we have to "swallow our pride." It works both ways: (1) To forgive sin, we must put aside our pride, any claim to dignity that would make it impossible to extend fellowship to the people who have wronged us. (2) To accept for-

---

[2]Frederick Buechner, *Wishful Thinking: A Theological ABC* (New York: Harper & Row, 1973), pp. 28-29.

giveness, we must also set aside our pride, and any claim to the false dignity that would insist that we have done nothing wrong.

The Christian faith teaches that forgiveness is the basis for relationship—indeed the *only* basis for relationship—in this fallen world because only in the context of forgiveness can we get over the hurdle of our mutual hurtfulness and the insularity of our pride and self-interest. Forgiveness involves an unconditional acceptance of others despite what they have done, and recognition that God's acceptance of us is just as unconditional and does not depend on what we have done. In both cases pride is excluded.

At the heart of this insight lies one of the Reformation's guiding principles, *sola gratia* (grace alone). As a friend once told me, *There's nothing you can do to make God love you any less. And there's nothing you can do to make God love you any more.* God's love and God's grace, both of which are concretely expressed in God's forgiveness, are unconditional and unlimited; they don't depend on us at all. God demonstrates the quality and the power of God's own unconditional love and grace in this fact, that even while we rebelled against God (as sinners) in self-absorbed independence, Christ died for us.

As I have said before, it is supremely in the event of the cross that we see the true character of God's self-emptying love. It is in pouring himself out for the sake of others *(kenosis)* that we see God's glorification *(plerosis)*. In the same way, it is in our *kenosis* that we share in the *plerosis*, the fullness, of God's life, the mind and spirit and full humanity of Christ, in Christ's life abundant and life eternal.

St. Benedict, in his *Rule,* a guide to the communal life of the monastery, makes this point when he says that we glorify God when we put the interests of others before our own. Indeed, it may not be too much to say that we best demonstrate the character of God when we do that which is most apparently *not* in our own interests.[3]

The forgiveness of sin strikes at the heart of our personal self-interest and security, in which we take such *pride.* As von Balthasar says, the forgiveness of sins goes beyond merely the "remission of punishment" (which is conceivable) to an "erasing of all guilt" (which is totally inconceivable).[4]

The strings of control we wish to hold on others are cut if we willingly

---

[3]A good edition of Benedict's *Rule* is found in Owen Chadwick, ed., *Western Asceticism* (Philadelphia: Westminster Press, 1958).

[4]Hans Urs von Balthasar, *Credo: Meditations on the Apostles' Creed,* trans. David Kipp (New York: Crossroad, 1990), p. 89.

lay aside their guilt. The position of moral ascendancy, which is the highest position conceivable in worldly communions, is relativized by the act of forgiveness. We relinquish our moral ascendancy in the act of forgiveness. When we forgive someone, we are saying that we stand side by side with them as sinners under the mandate of the God who forgives us all. It is impossible to forgive the sin of another without declaring our solidarity with the other in our sin. Entering into such an environment of forgiveness involves recognition of our utter dependence on God.

In other words, although *we* may be able to make it through this eye of the needle, *our pride cannot.* We are always, to borrow the familiar image from D. T. Niles, a community of beggars seeking the bread of grace.[5] Indeed, as Christians this is the only positive claim we can make—that we are forgiven—and because we are forgiven, we have become forgivers.

The *Verbum visibile* of Forgiveness

The sheer graciousness of forgiveness confronts us with a thorny problem, however. Certainly Paul was dealing with this problem when he asked the rhetorical question, "What then shall we say? Should we continue in sin that grace may abound?" "*Mē genoito!*" Paul answers. Literally, "May such a thing never be!" The spirit of Paul's response is better captured in the phrase "God forbid!" (Rom 6:1-2). The unconditionality of forgiveness is the free decision of God. And as such it does not provide the excuse for licentiousness but the opportunity for gratitude.[6]

This is why Martin Luther was able, on the one hand, to affirm the utter freedom of God's grace, as when he tells Philip Melanchthon:

> If you are a preacher of grace, then preach grace that is true and not fictitious; if grace is true, you must bear true and not fictitious sin. God does not save fictitious sinners. Be a sinner and sin boldly . . . but have faith and rejoice in Christ more boldly still, for he is the victor over sin, death and the world.[7]

---

[5]Niles's famous definition of evangelism is often wrongly quoted. He said that evangelism is "one beggar asking another where to find bread." See Clyde E. Fant and William M. Pinson, eds., *20 Centuries of Great Preaching* (Waco, Tex.: Word, 1971), 12:175.

[6]The issue I raise here, that of antinomianism, I have dealt with more comprehensively in the article "The Devil's Theology: Theological Reflection on James Hogg's *The Private Memoirs and Confessions of a Justified Sinner* (1824)," *Evangelical Quarterly* 62, no. 2 (April 1990): 157-74.

[7]Martin Luther, in a letter to Melanchthon, dated August 1, 1521, in *Martin Luther: Documents in Modern History,* ed. E. G. Rupp and Benjamin Drewery (London: Edward Arnold, 1978), p. 73.

On the other hand, Luther insisted just as vigorously that we must not take God's forgiveness of us for granted, nor presumptuously treat it as an excuse for immoral license. Luther also writes:

> God forgives sins merely out of grace for Christ's sake; but we must not abuse the grace of God. God has given signs and tokens enough, that our sins be forgiven; namely, the preaching of the gospel, baptism, the Lord's Supper, and the Holy Ghost in our hearts.[8]

Forgiveness occurs, as Luther clearly understood, neither in isolation nor as the arbitrary or inadvertent result of an automated pardon machine. Forgiveness is the free act of God, and it occurs in the context of community with God and with other forgiven people. Which leads us to say that forgiveness not only rests in God's unconditional acceptance of us despite what we have done, forgiveness also places us under an unconditional obligation to live in light of the character of the God who forgives us. This is what Luther is driving at when he connects our response to God's forgiveness with "the preaching of the gospel, baptism, the Lord's Supper, and the Holy Ghost in our hearts."

Through the Word and sacraments, the witness of the Holy Spirit confronts us with forgiveness that is real (not fictitious), real enough to forgive us all our real sins and real enough to demand of us a real response. For such is the nature of God's forgiveness.[9]

As we are drawn ever deeper into genuine community, we sense our complete dependence on God; we become more profoundly aware that we are a body dependent for our very life on Christ, the head. And "the dependence of the body on the Head means the confession that the people of God are sinful, and he only is holy. But it also means inevitably the demand that they at least get up and start moving, set out on the way that leaves their sinfulness behind and moves toward his holiness."[10]

Living in the environment of forgiveness, then, means at least four things:

1. We live in a community that has both vertical and horizontal dimensions of grace and that these dimensions are interconnected (in other words, they form a cross).

---

[8]Martin Luther, *Table Talk* 218, ed. Thomas S. Kepler (Grand Rapids, Mich.: Baker, 1952).

[9]John Leith provides a helpful discussion of forgiveness in *The Reformed Imperative* (Philadelphia: Westminster Press, 1988), pp. 57-61.

[10]Shirley Guthrie Jr., *Christian Doctrine* (Richmond, Va.: Covenant Life Curriculum, 1968), p. 360.

2. We accept the fact of our guilt and therefore that the reality of God's forgiveness of us is completely undeserved.

3. We extend forgiveness unconditionally to those who have wronged us as a concrete and visible participation in God's character.

4. We participate in this community of grace as forgiven sinners among forgiven sinners; we allow ourselves to remain open to the God who yearns for us to share more fully in the life of Jesus Christ and who promises to give us, through the power of the Holy Spirit, the eternal life he wishes us to enjoy.

This is why Shirley Guthrie mentions the sacrament of the Lord's Supper in the context of the conflict between our desire for holiness and our failure to be holy.

> That is what the Lord's Supper is all about. On the one hand it is a way of reminding us constantly that we do not live from our own strength. We have to be fed, nourished, given new life over and over again. But on the other hand the Lord's Supper means that we are fed, nourished and given new life—not just so that we may flex our spiritual muscles for everyone to admire, but so that we can get to work growing up "in every way into him who is the head, into Christ" (Eph 4:15).[11]

John Calvin's understanding of the Lord's Supper is at the heart of Guthrie's thought. Rather than arguing over "transubstantiation" or "consubstantiation," as the battle over the Eucharist was defined in the sixteenth century, Calvin reflected on the meaning of the Lord's Supper by focusing on the dynamics of the Christian life. He didn't ask, *how* the bread and wine become the body and blood of Christ. This was not Calvin's concern. His concern was from whom do we derive our life as Christians? The Lord's Supper, for Calvin, communicates the living reality of our union with Christ, and when we share in this Supper, we feast on the Christ who nourishes us by faith.[12]

Each time we receive the Lord's Supper we affirm this basic article of faith: we do not have the resources to sustain our life as Christians; what we need to live is given us by the sovereign act of God. Indeed the three names for this sacrament each provide us with a glimpse into its meaning:

☐ *the Lord's Supper,* in which we feed by faith on the Lord himself and are

---

[11]Ibid.

[12]See T. H. L. Parker's excellent discussion of Calvin's view of the sacraments in his study: *John Calvin* (Tring, U.K.: Lion, 1975), pp. 49-57. Also see Calvin *Institutes* 9.14-19.

nourished through the power of the Holy Spirit

☐ *holy Communion,* which reminds us that we grow up into the likeness of Christ only in fellowship with the triune God and with one another as the Spirit works through us

☐ the *Eucharist,* literally, the "thanksgiving," by which we express our gratitude to God for giving us new life in Christ and through which we offer ourselves (as "a living sacrifice") to God in our heavenly high priest, Jesus Christ, through the Holy Spirit

We cannot stop here, however. We must go on to say that the sacrament of *holy baptism* also proclaims this good news, that before we can utter a single word of our acceptance of God, God already has accepted us unconditionally, has drawn us into communion with himself and with the community of faith, where we shall be nurtured by him through the Word and the Spirit. It is imperative that adults and infants be seen both as recipients of this sacrament and (as is pictured in the sacrament) as recipients of God's active claim on their lives, not as instigators of some active claim on God through the sacrament. In other words, infant and adult baptism do not paint two separate and complementary pictures of discipleship; they both paint the same picture because, however old we may be at our baptism, we always come to God "as children," making no claims about the efficacy of our faithfulness, nor laying any claim on God. The sacrament of baptism is the act of the community of faith by which it speaks God's unconditional acceptance of us prior to anything we may do or say, an acceptance that draws persons out of the prison of solitude into the fellowship of the covenant God has made with us.

Both sacraments, the Lord's Supper and holy baptism, are, in the wonderful phrase of Augustine, *verbum visibile* (that is, "visible word"). The sacraments stand together, shoulder to shoulder, announcing the reality of the grace of God through which we are accepted without condition and by which we are laid under the unconditional obligation to be to others what Christ has been to us.

The church, in the concrete reality of accepting God's forgiveness and in extending forgiveness to others, announces the good news that God "will really be victorious in the world despite all sin and darkness and will really prevail by bringing about the completion of the world in the form of salvation rather than judgment."[13]

---

[13]Karl Rahner, *Meditations on the Sacraments* (New York: Seabury, 1977), p. xv.

The sacraments communicate among us a genuine participation in Jesus Christ, the Word of God, preeminently the *verbum visibile,* who himself is God's announcement of grace. Thus we remember that our sacramental response is dependent on God's prior act toward us and is only possible because Jesus Christ himself is the sacramental act of God on our behalf, this act in which God demonstrates his loving forgiveness of us and by which God calls us into the community of forgiven sinners.

The Ethics of *Perichoresis*

As I mentioned earlier, the sheer graciousness of forgiveness, its unconditionality and limitlessness, confronts us with a grave problem, the problem of immoral license. And we would be remiss if we did not deal with this more fully. It is the problem that Dietrich Bonhoeffer confronted in his extraordinary testament *Discipleship,* also known as *The Cost of Discipleship.* While recognizing the unconditionality of grace, Bonhoeffer insists that we must sharply differentiate between "costly grace" and "cheap grace."

Bonhoeffer writes:

> Cheap grace is the mortal enemy of our church. Our struggle today is for costly grace.
>
> Cheap grace means grace as bargain basement goods, cut-rate forgiveness, cut-rate comfort, cut-rate sacrament; grace as the church's inexhaustible pantry, from which it is poured out without hesitation or limit. It is grace without a price, without costs. It is said that the essence of grace is that the bill for it is paid in advance for all time. Everything can be had for free, courtesy of that paid bill. The price paid is infinitely great and, therefore, the possibilities of taking advantage of and wasting grace are also infinitely great. What would grace be, if it were not cheap grace?
>
> Cheap grace means grace as doctrine, as principle, as system. It means forgiveness of sins as a general truth; it means God's love as merely a Christian idea of God. Those who affirm it have already had their sins forgiven. The church that indulges in this doctrine of grace thereby confers such grace upon itself. The world finds in this church a cheap cover-up for its sins, for which it shows no remorse and from which it has even less desire to free itself. Cheap grace is, thus, denial of God's living world, denial of the incarnation of the word of God.[14]

---

[14]Dietrich Bonhoeffer, *Discipleship,* ed. John D. Godsey and Geffrey B. Kelly, trans. Reinhard Kraus and Barbara Green (Minneapolis: Fortress, 2000).

The alternative to this cheap imitation of God's grace is "costly grace."
Bonhoeffer writes:

> Costly grace is the hidden treasure in the field, for the sake of which people
> go and sell with joy everything they have. It is the costly pearl, for whose
> price the merchant sells all that he has; it is Christ's sovereignty, for the sake
> of which you tear out an eye if it causes you to stumble. It is the call of Jesus
> Christ which causes a disciple to leave his nets and follow him.

> Costly grace is the Gospel which must be sought again and again, the gift
> which has to be asked for, the door at which one has to knock again and
> again.

> It is costly, because it calls to discipleship; it is grace, because it calls us to
> follow Jesus Christ. It is costly, because it cost people their lives; it is grace,
> because it gives them their lives. It is costly, because it condemns sins; it is
> grace, because it justifies the sinner. Above all, grace is costly, because it was
> costly to God, because it costs God the life of God's son—"you were bought
> with a price"—and because the life of God's son was not too costly for God
> to give for our lives. God did, indeed, give him up for us. Costly grace is the
> incarnation of God.[15]

I'd like to read this wonderful book to you in its entirety. Once I start
reading from it, I hardly know where to stop. It is simply one of the most
profound and true representations of the Christian faith ever written. (In
the end Bonhoeffer paid the "cost of discipleship" with his own life.)

What Bonhoeffer describes so vividly in his discussion of cheap grace is
the Christianity of convenience that is very much a part of contemporary
society, what the writer Flannery O'Connor wryly described as "the Church
of Jesus Christ without Christ crucified."[16] This is the false church to which
one may belong voluntarily (like a club) without bothering to commit one's
life to Christ. This is the false church in which we rest content to be saved,
as Jonathan Edwards once observed, *in* our sins but not *from* our sins.

Certainly this is the misconception of grace common in many religious
circles today. But this is not grace. God's grace does not simply deliver
us from some penalties and consequences of our sin while leaving us in
our sin. Rather, God seeks to deliver us from sin itself. This is the goal of
God's forgiveness—to open for us a new life in which sin does not have
dominion or control over us. As George MacDonald explains in one of

---

[15]Ibid.
[16]See Flannery O'Connor, *Wise Blood* (New York: Noonday, 1977).

his "Unspoken Sermons," God's love and justice are not opposed but are
two sides of the same divine reality, the reality of God's gracious and
forgiving character. MacDonald writes, "God is, in His own righteousness, bound to destroy sin. . . . I trust that He is destroying sin in me."
Jesus, MacDonald continues, points to this purpose in God's heart, to
"save His people from their sin."[17] Indeed, as MacDonald's contemporary
John McLeod Campbell said, it is the love of God that desires us to love,
the justice of God that will not rest until we become just.[18]

This, of course, is another way of talking about what Bonhoeffer
described as costly grace. This "costly grace," he explains, "comes to us as
a gracious call to follow Christ, it comes as a word of forgiveness to the
fearful spirit and the broken heart . . . [and] it forces people under the yoke
of following Jesus Christ."[19]

What we quickly discern from Bonhoeffer is that grace wouldn't be
grace at all if it left us in our sin, in our self-centered alienation, independence and disintegration. Grace is only grace if it seeks to draw us into
communion with God and with others in that life which shares God's own
self-emptying love.

This leads us to understand that the life God desires us to live is the
quality of life we see in Jesus Christ, the "passionate" life, as Moltmann
described it, the life freely poured out for the sake of others, abandoning
any self-filling security, trusting instead to be filled by God, the eternal
source. This life, which is by definition *life in community,* reflects the inner
life of God, the perichoretic life of the Father, Son and Holy Spirit, the
mutual penetration of divine persons in self-abandonment and mutual participation. It is this life of *perichoresis,* or coinherence, which forms the
center of our ethics because it is also this life eternal that provides the
meaning of our justification and our sanctification.

Social responsibility, mutual nurture, the life of community—these are
not disjointed "items" that can or should be appended to our theological
reflection. These are the essential elements of that life that has been at the

---

[17]George MacDonald, *Creation in Christ*, ed. Rolland Hein (Wheaton, Ill.: Harold Shaw, 1976),
    pp. 69, 76. Also see Gary W. Deddo and Catherine A. Deddo, eds., *George MacDonald: A
    Devotional Guide to His Writings* (Edinburgh: St. Andrew Press, 1996).
[18]J. M. Campbell, *The Nature of the Atonement* (Grand Rapids, Mich.: Eerdmans, 1996), pp.
    146-50.
[19]Bonhoeffer, *Discipleship.*

center of our reflection from the very beginning of this study. The shape of our life together is determined by the character of the triune God. This is the inescapable fact of an adequate doctrine of God, as a reflection on the One whose life is divine communion, in the image of whom we are created.

Our social responsibility cannot be separated from our salvation, a fact that will have serious implications for any adequate statements concerning evangelism *and* ethics. To be *in Christ* is to lose ourselves for the sake of others, but only in losing ourselves do we gain ourselves. The life we are meant to live consists in this quality of self-loss, self-abandonment, for the sake of the other. Our salvation is not something separate from or in addition to our participation in the communion of the triune God but is itself our sharing in this life of complete reliance on God and social mutuality. For this purpose we believe we have been created.

In light of these remarks we can understand the unconditional obligation of grace as a liberation from isolation and alienation, and as a liberation for integration into the community of faith and for grateful service in God's world. We can also, in light of these remarks, make sense of (and critique) some of the rather mechanistic discussions we hear about repentance, forgiveness and salvation.

Someone may say, for instance, that we must repent before we can be forgiven by God. But in fact, our repentance is nothing less than our returning (that's what *repent* means) from alienation to God, a returning that Christ accomplishes for us in the incarnation (in solidarity with all humanity) and in which we now participate through the Holy Spirit, the Spirit who united us in Christ in the community of faith. This repentance is possible only because God in his infinite grace has already forgiven us. Our salvation is nothing less than our restoration to full communion with God and others, communion that is identical with repentance, which is given to us as a gift, again in Christ.

Thus such questions as "If God has forgiven me, why should I *have* to repent?" fall apart into the nonsense they are. We are dealing with the reality of personal grace, not with mere theoretical abstractions. As I mentioned in our last class, we need a recovery of these real, personal dimensions of Christian theology. We are not talking about a divine What, some metaphysical machinery; we are talking about the divine Who, the divine Lover, who desires to have and to hold us, who wants to breathe into us his life and to embrace us in his love.

To say, "I don't have to repent because God has already forgiven me," is like saying "Because my lover has forgiven me, there's no need for us to be loving."

To say, "I don't have to live a moral life because God has forgiven me," is like saying "Because my beloved loves me and desires me, I don't have to be with her."

There is always a possibility that we can reject the divine Lover's love and life, but we should never be under the illusion that this possibility is more than a tragic folly. Rejecting our divine Lover, spurning God's love and life, is possible, but it is insanity. And it is hard to understand why anyone would.

Perhaps the most astonishing fact in all of this is that God desires to express divine love and life through the reality of this rather dubious bunch of forgiven sinners we call the church. And that indeed is a miracle of grace. It is easy enough to accept the fact that the "holiness" of the church does not belong to its members but, as Barth says, "is conferred upon them as a matter of the fact that God has chosen them . . . in order to reveal himself in them."[20] What is simply incredible is that God has chosen them for this purpose.

We might well imagine that we could rendezvous privately with the divine Lover in some secluded spot. But it is almost impossible to believe that the divine Lover whose "lips are like a crimson thread" and "breasts are like two fawns" (Song 4:1-5) is wooing us through a cantankerous old deacon named Buster and a contentious bunch of church members whose idea of divine romance consists of two hymns and a sermonette. And for this I have no answer except to say that what is impossible for human beings is possible with God—and maybe that is why God does things the way God does them.

Summary. Forgiveness is the concrete actualization of the Christian faith. It is here that we see clearly the character of the God who is revealed in Jesus Christ. God forgives us without condition, prior to any response we may or may not make. We show (or do not show) the character of God in

---

[20]Karl Barth, *The Faith of the Church: A Commentary on The Apostles' Creed According to Calvin's Catechism*, ed. Jean-Louis Leuba, trans. Gabriel Vahanian (New York: Living Age Books, 1958), p. 138.

our own lives by forgiving others. The call to the community of faith in Christ (i.e., the church) is the call to become a forgiven forgiver. As Christians we have no other positive claim to make.

Homework Assignment

This is your last homework assignment, and you may want to consider it your final examination as well. Your final assignment is to map the Apostles' Creed. You can use crayons, felt-tip markers, finger-paints or whatever else. You can cut out magazine pictures or paste, glue, cut, color and draw. However you do it, your task is to communicate the essential tenets of the Christian faith and the ways in which they connect. You can include interpretative statements of your own and all the symbolism you like. Creativity and original thinking will be rewarded. You can make the map as large as you like. Some students have made very good maps on a single sheet of paper, others have mapped the creed on a banner large enough to hang in a church's sanctuary.

Have fun!

Remember: Following the next session, you turn in your final paper, the critical book review.

Class 11

The Resurrection
of the Body &
the Life Everlasting

*"Almighty God,
who hast brought again from the dead our Lord Jesus,
the glorious Prince of salvation:
Grant us power, we beseech thee, to rise with him to newness of life,
that we may overcome the world with the victory of faith,
and have part at last in the resurrection of the just. Amen."*

BOOK OF COMMON PRAYER, ALTERED

*T*HE CHRISTIAN FAITH IS LIKE A LONG ROPE PULLED TIGHT. IN ONE DIRECTION the rope stretches out behind us, disappearing into the distant past. The rope is anchored in that direction at the point at which the God who created all things, including time, became a human being in our time, lived, suffered, died and was raised again from the dead. The rope runs straight and true from that distant anchor planted long ago in our history, into the dim future, our future, which we are told is ultimately gathered into God's eternal present, the "eternal now," to borrow Paul Tillich's phrase.[1]

A Teleological Vision

We have our standing in the belly of this beast called "time." We exist. We walk. We talk. We dream. We hope. We survey our present and savor our past with that combination of pleasure and regret that seems peculiar to

---

[1]Paul Tillich, *The Eternal Now* (New York: Scribner's, 1963).

our humanity. We are aware, sometimes distinctly aware, at other times only vaguely, that our lives are shot through with eternal significance that transcends anything in this creaturely realm. We sense the beauty and truth of the verse of the nineteenth-century poet and priest Gerard Manley Hopkins:

> The world is charged with the grandeur of God.
> It will flame out, like shining from shook foil;
> It gathers to a greatness, like the ooze of oil
> Crushed.[2]

Our identity, Paul tells us, is hidden with God in Christ. We exist in the present eschatologically (i.e., as persons who live toward "the last things").[3] Thus our identity in Jesus Christ (who stands at the right hand of God the Father) pulls us inexorably into the future, God's future on our behalf. Yet our destination, in a sense, lies as much behind us as before us. The meaning of our lives derives from our purpose, and our purpose is tied like a rope round the waist of the God who strides knee-deep through our history like a giant walking through the waves that break on the seashore. And when God strides out into the deep water stained blue like blood on its return journey to the heart, and when God disappears from view into the vastness of the ocean of time and space, and swims out past the horizon of possibility beyond the range of our vision, we still have hold of this rope anchored in the past and stretching out into the future, touching at every point on the same eternal moment in the life of God.

The Christian faith is, in other words, teleological (i.e., a faith oriented toward "the end" or "purpose" for which God created us).[4] It stretches like this rope pulled toward a goal. This goal lends meaning to everything humanity has ever experienced and all that we have to say about the rela-

---

[2]Gerard Manley Hopkins, "God's Grandeur," in *Poems and Prose,* ed. G. H. Gardner (London: Penguin, 1963), p. 27.

[3]Eschatology refers to our study of "last things" (Greek, *eschatos,* "last"); generally eschatology deals with the full and final establishment of the kingdom of God and the end of human history, the second coming of Christ and the final judgment. See A. T. Hanson's article "Eschatology" in *The Westminster Dictionary of Christian Theology,* ed. Alan Richardson and John Bowden, rev. ed. (Philadelphia: Westminster Press, 1983), pp. 183-86.

[4]Teleology refers to our study or reflection or attempts to explain and understand the world in which we live based on its purpose and design (Greek, *telos,* "end"). I referred earlier in the course, you may remember, to teleologically rich theologies such as that of Thomas Aquinas.

tionship between God and humanity. It is the character of God's purpose
that defines who we are, because this purpose shares its character with the
God who is revealed in Jesus Christ.

Martin Luther King Jr. once said, "The end of life is not to be happy, nor to
achieve pleasure and avoid pain, but to do the will of God come what may."[5]
This is my point: from the word *go,* the Christians sought to understand God's
purpose for creation and God's will for each and all of us. When I open the
pages of Thomas Aquinas's *Summa Theologica,* I am struck by how forcefully
and subtly Aquinas describes this teleological vision, this profound concern to
understand our purpose in the mind and heart of God. God is "the beginning
of things, and their last end," Aquinas tells us.[6] In order to understand *why we
are here,* we must understand *who placed us here;* we must understand the
character of the One who made us for his own purposes.

We believe, audaciously, that purpose is given by God to all creation
and that everything that exists is created by God for his own loving purpose. This is the fundamental teaching of the Christian faith. Purpose, we
believe, is not a private affair. Human purpose is not merely a matter of
opinion. We do not create our own purposes *ex nihilo* (out of nothing). We
discover our purpose, the purpose for which God created us. In an age
such as ours, which exists, as Lesslie Newbigin has said, in a sort of teleological vacuum, this is not only disconcerting and strange news, it is
supremely good news.[7]

"Of ourselves," Emil Brunner once said, "we know only that all things
die! What our eyes see and experience daily is that there is nothing perfect.
When we look about on this great universe we shudder."[8] In our age, perhaps more than in any prior age, we are tempted to allow ourselves to be
swallowed up in a sense of our own smallness and meaninglessness, and
to conclude that because we are so small, we are also insignificant, that we
are only carbon-based planetary parasites infesting the surface of this
globe, hedged in by birth and death.

"Is there any meaning to it all?" we ask.

---

[5]Martin Luther King Jr., cited in Gayraud S. Wilmore, *Last Things First* (Philadelphia: Westminster Press, 1982), p. 101.

[6]Thomas Aquinas *Summa Theologica* Q.2, trans. Fathers of the English Dominican Province
(New York: Benzinger Brothers, 1948).

[7]Lesslie Newbigin deals with this crucial issue throughout his book *Foolishness to the Greeks:
The Gospel and Western Culture* (London: SPCK, 1986).

[8]Emil Brunner, *Our Faith* (New York: Scribners, 1962), p. 151.

Many voices answer, "No! There is no meaning, except perhaps the meaning we wish to assign to life." But, Brunner reminds us, "The Word of God, the Creator of all these suns and races" says, "Yes! You mean something! You mean something to God!" We have meaning, Brunner says, because we belong to the God who created us and because the God who created us loves what he has made. Beyond this life of contingency and transience "is another life, that longs to break forth" on us. "It has broken forth once in Jesus Christ, the Risen Lord, and it will break forth for us all in the Resurrection. This other life is *Eternal* life."[9] It is the quality of this eternal life, which has broken in upon our existence in Jesus Christ, that both judges our shattered existence and gives it meaning, that both reveals our human frailties and points beyond our frailties to God's purpose to make us like Christ.

It is precisely here that we come to one of the most fascinating insights in Karl Barth's thought, that we see most fully our humanity not in the suffering man Jesus Christ, not even in his crucifixion, but in the risen Christ. The resurrected Christ reveals to us the human life that is life fully *from* and *with* and *after the manner of* God, that is, *eternal* life. This risen Christ meets us in judgment because the quality of his risen life judges us dead and calls us to new life.[10]

In the risen Christ we glimpse God's purpose for us, the end and goal of our humanity, and as such the meaning of our existence. In the presence of this risen Christ, in whom we see our *new* humanity, we shed our *old* humanity, the old life of despair, sin and death. As Barth says, this time in his lectures on the Heidelberg Catechism, our old self "dies from joy at the new self!"[11] And so, as the Heidelberg Catechism explains, we receive "comfort" when we anticipate Christ's judgment of the quick and the dead. The catechism says:

Q. What comfort is it to you that Christ shall come again to judge the quick and the dead?

A. That in all afflictions and persecution, with uplifted head, I may wait for the Judge from Heaven who has already offered Himself to the judgment

---

[9]Ibid.

[10]Karl Barth, *Church Dogmatics* 4/3, ed. G. W. Bromiley and T. F. Torrance, trans. G. W. Bromiley (Edinburgh: T & T Clark, 1936), pp. 310-12.

[11]Karl Barth, *Learning Jesus Christ Through the Heidelberg Catechism*, trans. Shirley C. Guthrie Jr. (Grand Rapids, Mich.: Eerdmans, 1964), p. 132.

of God for me, and has taken away from me all curse.[12]

The human life that we presently live, we live in expectation of that life which is ours already in Christ Jesus. His life is the human life for which we are intended, the resurrected life, eternal life, the life that exists on the very breath of God. Or as Barth again says in the exposition of his theological anthropology, to be a human being is to be in "true and absolute Counterpart" to God, that is, in relationship—the creature in loving and joyful reliance on God.[13]

It is this life in "true and absolute Counterpart" (in relationship) that is revealed and shared with humanity in Jesus Christ. This life in relationship is the creaturely reflection of the inner life of the triune God, the Son in loving reliance on the Father, receiving from and returning to the Father that love and eternal life that is the Holy Spirit. It is this same love and eternal life, this life of communion, which meets us in the risen Christ. And by the power of the Holy Spirit we taste this life even before death.

The Resurrection of the Body

So it is that our identity and destiny are grounded in the being of God, in the inner life of God as Father, Son and Holy Spirit, the life that is revealed to us in Jesus Christ, who poured out his life on behalf of others in utter dependence on God and who now calls us into communion, into the life of personal integration that liberates us from alienation and independence.

When, therefore, we speak of our future hope, we are speaking neither of absorption into an undifferentiated "All" (a drop of spirit diffused into a vast metaphysical ocean of Spirit) nor of a solitary, private redemption of the individual, separate from and unrelated to others (there appear to be no private rooms in our Father's house).

Our destiny is linked inextricably with our identity, and our identity is not separable from our bodily, historical existence. The future redemption that we anticipate is redemption as human beings, not redemption from human being; it is resurrection of the body, not liberation of the spirit from

---

[12]Heidelberg Catechism, question 52, the translation used here is from Thomas F. Torrance, *The School of Faith* (London: James Clarke, 1959), p. 78.

[13]Barth, *Church Dogmatics* 3/2, p. 135. Look at the entire section "Real Man." And for a fine treatment of the resurrection and the relationship of Christ to creaturely time, also see in this volume the section titled "Jesus, Lord of Time," pp. 437-511.

a fleshly prison house; it is salvation from alienation and assunderedness to a way of being that is inconceivable to us as we now are yet that is revealed to us in the risen Christ who took our "fleshly" humanity into the very heart of God.

I remember a conversation my daughter, Jessica, had with me a few years ago about heaven. Jessica was nine years old at the time and a very good and original theologian. Jessica enjoys good food, and she was wondering what sorts of things we might eat in heaven. I told her that I am not really sure that we will eat food in heaven. Our nourishment, I told her, will be derived (I suspect) in some other way, though I'm sure we shall be nourished there by the God on whom we depend for our very being. I mentioned that after his resurrection, Jesus was a body, though a different kind of body than we, a spiritual body, a body that bore the scars of his suffering, that was able to be touched and was able to consume food. But, I said, I'm not sure that the food was necessary to his risen life in the way that food is necessary to our present existence.

She listened as I rambled on for a while.

Then she furrowed her brow a little, frowned and shook her head, and said, "So we probably aren't going to eat food in heaven?"

I answered, "Well, no. I don't think so."

Then she sighed and said, "OK. But it's going to take a couple of weeks to get used to."

The nature of our resurrected bodies is difficult to get a handle on. It may take even more than a couple of weeks to get used to.

The apostle Paul struggled with this, and so have many of the greatest Christian minds through the centuries, often coming up with widely (and sometimes wildly) divergent ideas. But on the essential point we have some agreement: When we are raised from the dead, we will be raised bodily, which means that our resurrection will be analogous to our creation and that our resurrection will be into that life of communion for which we were originally created.[14]

---

[14]One of the most important works on the nature of the resurrection is Tertullian's *On the Resurrection of the Flesh*. This is a must read. Tertullian wants us to understand that our resurrection from the dead is a miraculous event in which our fleshliness, our embodiedness, is brought into relationship with God. Our flesh is not immune to God but will be raised incorruptible.

The First Fruit of Resurrection

Christ's resurrection is, as Paul says, the first fruit of those who die, "for since death came through a human being, the resurrection of the dead has come through a human being; for as all die in Adam, so all will be made alive in Christ" (1 Cor 15:20-21).

The resurrection may be described, then, as having three theological dimensions. It is

☐ *teleological* (the purpose of human existence)

☐ *eschatological* (the end of human existence)

☐ *communal* (the ultimate reconciliation of human existence)

We have touched already on the teleological nature of the resurrection of the body but have only mentioned the communal aspect of resurrection. It is important that we deal more fully with this matter.

The resurrection of the body is not an event in isolation but an event in community. Paul says, "As *all* die in Adam, so *all* will be made alive in Christ" (review Romans 5). This needs to be stressed, especially in our time when the significance of the Christian community is so often obscured in the headlong pursuit of the individual. Gustaf Aulén said, near the close of his systematic theology, "The Christian hope is altogether a corporate hope. Since Christian faith exists only as participation in the body of Christ the church, the Christian hope is a hope of the ultimate perfection of the church in the kingdom of glory."[15]

We will return to this point again. It is absolutely essential to understand, yet it is virtually forgotten: *Our hope of resurrection is the hope of wholeness for persons in communion.* There is no wholeness of persons outside of communion. We will be raised to the true humanity for which we were originally intended, the humanity created in the image and likeness of the triune God. As I have already said, this image and likeness of God is nothing less than our being in communion, which is the creaturely reflection of God's own eternal being in communion. It is to this quality of life, this reconciliation of persons in community, that we are raised in Christ Jesus. But there must be a corresponding transformation of persons in order for this community to become reality. This also is included in the Christian teaching of resurrection.

This was brought home to me several years ago in a conversation with

---

[15]Gustaf Aulén, *The Faith of the Christian Church* (Philadelphia: Fortress, 1960), p. 391.

some friends. While we lived in Scotland, we became close to another American couple. The husband, Gary, whom I mentioned in the introductory chapter, was also working on his Ph.D. in theology. His wife, Cathy, was active in the parish church in Banchory, just west of Aberdeen. Cathy was involved in a Bible study with several women in her church. The study group was not exactly harmonious; there were some severe personality conflicts. One day a leader in the group got all caught up in the excitement of the moment toward the end of the lesson she was teaching, and she said, "Just think, when we get to heaven we'll be able to be together all the time!" Cathy, always a very level-headed person, said, "Yeah, and isn't it wonderful that we'll be so transformed that we'll be able to enjoy it."

That is the miracle!

The resurrection of the body is resurrection to community. And because it is resurrection to community, it is also resurrection to transformation. Which means that the resurrection is *eschatological,* bringing us finally to the culmination of creation and redemption. It is its eschatological nature that is perhaps most apparent to us when we speak of resurrection, and that is why I have chosen to speak of it last. The resurrection calls into the question the whole human endeavor.

You may remember a point Lesslie Newbigin made, *that the resurrection of Christ is not the reversal of a failure, but the proclamation of a victory.*[16] The Christian teaching of the resurrection of the dead in Christ announces God's redemptive goal for all humanity, a goal that decisively counters the ways and means of the world, all the worldly powers, principalities and authorities whose might and force rest on their ability to enforce their will on pain of death.

The faith we have in God to raise us up on the last day is the faith we have that God's ways are higher than humanity's ways and that all the subordinate powers that try to usurp the place of God will finally be subdued, that even the mighty power of death will be relativized by the power of God to re-create us from the dust of the earth. The resurrection of the body is the proclamation of God's creative and re-creative power over all inauthentic claims to power. The apostle Paul says that Christ is the first fruits of the resurrection, after whom comes "the end, when he [Christ] hands over

---

[16]Lesslie Newbigin, *Foolishness to the Greeks,* p. 127.

the kingdom of God the Father, after he has destroyed every ruler and
every authority and power. For he must reign until he has put all his enemies under his feet. The last enemy to be destroyed is death" (1 Cor
15:23-26). Irenaeus says that when Christ summed up or recapitulated in
himself the whole human race from the beginning to the end, he also
summed up humanity's death. Christ, in his incarnation, took into himself
the whole tragic scenario of our false humanity, including our God forsak-
enness, our alienation, our death, and brought all this humanity into the
very being of God, the life of the Trinity, where God healed our humanity
of its inauthenticity, alienation and sickness unto death. *This* we have seen
earlier in our lectures.

We must now say that Jesus Christ brought our death into himself, into
the life of the Trinity, so that now we might be raised to newness of life,
eternal life, genuine participation in the very life of God. This risen life,
this eschatological reality, has broken in upon us in the resurrection of
Christ, an event grounded in our time, yet revealing the character of
God's time, an event whose effects were subject to empirical observation,
yet whose cause is utterly transcendent.[17] The future as Not Yet! has broken into and relativized and decisively judged our present as the divine
Even Now!

Peregrini et hospites super terram

"Peregrini et hospites super terram," reads the Vulgate translation of
Hebrews 11:13. The New Revised Standard Version translates the same
phrase as "strangers and foreigners on the earth." But the Vulgate here is
better; at least it is more vivid. This is who we are, pilgrims, trekking,
homeless aliens, exiles for the sake of Christ.[18]

The phrase from Hebrews, as it is translated in the Vulgate, brings to
mind the medieval *peregrinatio,* the long and purposeful missionary wan-
derings of the ancient Celtic Christian missionaries pacing to and fro over
the face of the earth, challenging the northern seas in coracles (tiny round
boats of wickerwork and hides), traversing fields and mountains, knocking
on doors armed only with grace and knowledge, often welcome but never

---

[17]A good treatment of the temporal-eternal significance of resurrection is provided in George
Eldon Ladd, *I Believe in the Resurrection of Jesus* (Grand Rapids, Mich.: Eerdmans, 1975).
[18]John Baillie draws his masterful survey of the subject to a close by reflecting on this phrase
from the Vulgate. Baillie, *And the Life Everlasting* (New York: Scribner's, 1933), p. 335.

truly belonging. These paradigmatic (and peripatetic) pilgrims sought "a better country, that is, an heavenly one" (Heb 11:16).[19]

We also are pilgrims and strangers. As theologian John Baillie wrote:

> While taking every possible delight in the lovely things of earth and immersing ourselves deeply in its manifold interests and allurements, while giving up our hearts without let or stint to earthly loves and attachments, and while using every earthly power we possess in the loyal service of our earthly citizenship, let us yet keep it ever in mind that we are "men of the road," *viatores, peregrini,* who have here no continuing city.[20]

Or as George Whitefield, the eighteenth-century evangelist, writes, "Everything I meet with seems to carry this voice with it—'Go thou and preach the Gospel; be a pilgrim on earth; have no party or certain dwelling place.'"[21] Whitefield, himself a vagabond preacher, even prayed, "Lord Jesus, help me to do or suffer thy will. When thou seest me in danger of *nestling*—in pity—in tender pity—put a *thorn* in my nest to prevent me from it."[22]

This theme seems to have been on the mind of von Balthasar in the days just before his death. He closed his *Credo* with the beautiful reflection "And Life Everlasting. Amen." The editor of the *Credo* says that the book reaches its high point in this section. And he is right. The editor writes:

> The words acquire a tone that sweeps one along and arouses enthusiasm, as if spoken by someone who sees his passage into this eternal life as a prospect immediately before him and, in his irrepressible joy, would like to infect those many others, who drag themselves through this present life and yearn for nothing more than "eternal peace," with his youthfully forward-pressing hunger for living.[23]

Von Balthasar himself says, "For anyone who is permitted to step out of his or her narrow and finalized life, and into this life of God's, it seems as if

---

[19]Christopher Bamford and William Parker Marsh provide a resource on the Celtic pilgrim in their anthology, *Celtic Christianity: Ecology and Holiness* (Hudson, N.Y.: Lindisfarne, 1982).

[20]Baillie, *Life Everlasting*, p. 337.

[21]George Whitefield, cited in William James, *The Varieties of Religious Experience: A Study in Human Nature*, The Gifford Lectures 1901-1902 (New York: Modern Library Edition, 1994), p. 349.

[22]Ibid.

[23]Medard Kehl, introduction to Hans Urs von Balthasar, *Credo: Meditations on the Apostles' Creed*, trans. David Kipp (New York: Crossroad, 1990), pp. 15-16.

vast spaces are opened up before one, taking one's breath away." The life of God, the life eternal, is everlasting. It is the absolute miracle of life flowing forever from the heart of God, boundlessly unfolding, out of the sheer grace of God, the utter freedom of God's love, *gratis*. The love of God, which is the very life of God as Trinity, is life beyond all depths, life the depths of which "cannot be plumbed," life that is entered through the narrow portals of death, but life that swallows up death and defeats it.[24]

Summary. We believe that the Christ who united himself to us and took our humanity into the very inner life of the triune God longs to share life eternal with us. As much as we may love this present life, we long also for the life everlasting. But according to the teaching of the Christian faith, the life everlasting is not a static life. Rather we believe it to be dynamic life, if not in process certainly unfolding into the eternal stretches of God's eternity. And so the "eternal rest" for which we long is not an arrival at a destination point but is a childlike, trustful reliance, *resting* in the God whose original purpose for us is fulfilled in our sharing in his own life in communion. This is the witness of the Christian faith, that this miraculous life on earth is only the first leg of an ever more miraculous adventure. And so the emphasis in the phrase *everlasting life* should be as much on life as on everlasting. Our hope is not for survival in a shadow land beyond the grave; we hope for the fullness of life, shared life, breathed from the nostrils of God, the holy Trinity.

Amen

On the evening of December 9, 1968, the aged Karl Barth was working on a lecture, his last lecture, and one he never gave. Only a few days earlier he had said, "The last word which I have to say as a theologian and also as a politician is not a term like 'grace,' but a name, 'Jesus Christ.' He *is* grace, and he is the last, beyond the world and the church and even theology."[25]

Barth had been thinking a lot about death in those days, his friends said, and about life after death. But on that night in December he continued to work. The phone rang as he sat writing at his desk. He stopped writing in

---

[24]Von Balthasar, *Credo*, pp. 102-3.
[25]Eberhard Busch, *Karl Barth: His Life from Letters and Autobiographical Texts,* rev. ed. (Philadelphia: Fortress, 1976), p. 496.

midsentence and answered the phone. It was his old friend Eduard Thurneysen. They talked a while, and after the conversation Barth did not return to his lecture. He left it for another day.

He died that night, and his lecture ended in midsentence. But the thought is complete. It reads, " 'God is not a God of the dead but of the living.' In him they all live."[26] These were to be the last words we received from the pen of one of the most prolific Christian theologians in history.

For Barth, in the context of his last lecture, his statement means that in endeavoring to do our theological work, we must listen to the voices of those who have gone before; we must continue to listen and to learn. Those who have gone before us into death are alive unto God. They and we belong to the same body of Christ. This body, as Calvin reminds us, which Christ has begun to perfect even in this life, with its diversity of gifts among many members, Christ will increase by degrees (Calvin says) and will bring to completion in heaven.[27]

This is at least in part what Paul means when he says to the church at Rome, "Not one of us lives for himself, and no one dies for himself, for if we live, we live for the Lord, or if we die, we die for the Lord; therefore whether we live or die, we belong to the Lord. For to this end Christ died and lived again, that He might be the Lord both of the dead and of the living. . . . For it is written, 'As I live, says the Lord, every knee shall bow to me, and every tongue shall give praise to God' " (Rom 14:7-11).

Eugene Peterson, in his reflective commentary on the book of Revelation, says that *amen* is the last word in worship. "It is the worshiping affirmation to the God who affirms us."[28] It is appropriate, then, that *amen* should be the last word in theology as well because theology ultimately is an act of worship. Of course, as we've already seen, we hardly know how to utter this affirmation, this amen to God, in worship, in morality and public ethics or in theological endeavors. At the heart of the Christian message is the astonishing belief that God himself does for us what we need to do but cannot. To be more precise, God in Christ is the all-encompassing

---

[26]Ibid., p. 498.
[27]John Calvin *Institutes of the Christian Religion* 3.25.10, ed. John T. McNeill, trans. Ford Lewis Battles (Philadelphia: Westminster Press, 1960).
[28]Eugene H. Peterson, *Reversed Thunder: The Revelation of John and the Praying Imagination* (San Francisco: Harper & Row, 1988), p. 68.

"Amen," our own joyful affirmation and response to God, an affirmation spoken with human lips by the Word of God himself. Because it is our humanity that speaks this affirmation and because this affirmation is spoken by the power of the same Spirit who now works within us, we also share in Christ's amen to God. So we shall continue to do, until *every tongue shall confess that Jesus Christ is Lord to the glory of God the Father.* Amen.

Bibliography

Allison, Dale. *Jesus of Nazareth: Millenarian Prophet*. Minneapolis: Fortress, 1998.

Alternative Service Book 1980. Oxford: Oxford University Press, 1984.

Althaus, Paul. *The Theology of Martin Luther*. Translated by Robert C. Schultz. Philadelphia: Fortress, 1966.

Aquinas, Thomas. *Summa Contra Gentiles*. Translated by Anton C. Pegis. Notre Dame, Ind.: University of Notre Dame Press, 1975.

―――. *Summa Theologiae*. Translated by Fathers of the English Dominican Province. New York: Benziger, 1948.

Athanasius. *Contra Gentes and De Incarnatione*. Edited by and translated by Robert W. Thomson. Oxford: Clarendon, 1971.

Augustine of Hippo. *Confessions*. Translated by Henry Chadwick. Oxford: Oxford University Press, 1991.

―――. *On the Holy Trinity, Doctrinal Treatises, Moral Treatises*. Edited by Philip Schaff. Nicene and Post-Nicene Fathers 3. Reprint. Grand Rapids, Mich.: Eerdmans, 1980.

Aulén, Gustaf. *Christus Victor: An Historical Study of the Three Main Types of the Idea of the Atonement*. Translated by A. G. Herbert. New York: Macmillan, 1969.

―――. *The Faith of the Christian Church*. Translated by Eric H. Wahlstrom. Philadelphia: Fortress, 1960.

Baillie, Donald E. *God Was in Christ: An Essay on Incarnation and Atonement*. New York: Charles Scribner's Sons, 1948.

Baillie, John. *And the Life Everlasting*. New York: Charles Scribner's Sons, 1933.

Bainton, Roland. *Here I Stand: A Life of Martin Luther*. Nashville: Abingdon, 1950.

Balthasar, Hans Urs von. *Credo: Meditations on the Apostles' Creed*. Introduction by Medard Kehl. Translated by David Kipp. New York: Crossroad, 1990.

―――. *Prayer*. Translated by Graham Harrison. San Francisco: Ignatius, 1986.

Bamford, Christopher and William Parker Marsh, eds. *Celtic Christianity: Ecology and Holiness*. Hudson, N.Y.: Lindisfarne, 1982.

Barth, Karl. "Christ and Adam: Man and Humanity in Romans 5." Translated by Thomas A. Smail. *Scottish Journal of Theology* Occasional Papers 5. Edinburgh: Oliver & Boyd, 1956, 1963.

―――. *Church Dogmatics*. Edited by G. W. Bromiley and Thomas F. Torrance. Translated by G. W. Bromiley. 14 vols. Edinburgh: T & T Clark, 1956-1977.

―――. *Deliverance to the Captives*. New York: Harper & Row, 1961.

―――. *Dogmatics in Outline*. Translated by G. T. Thomson. New York: Harper & Row, Harper Torchbook, 1959.

―――. *The Epistle to the Romans*. Edwyn C. Hoskyns. London: Oxford University Press, 1933.

―――. *Evangelical Theology*. Translated by Grover Foley. Garden City, N.Y.: Anchor, 1964.

―――. *The Faith of the Church: A Commentary on the Apostles' Creed According to Calvin's Catechism*. Edited by Jean-Louis Leuba. Translated by Gabriel Vahanian. New York: Meridian, 1958.

―――. *The Göttingen Dogmatics: Instruction in the Christian Religion*. Edited by Hannelotte Reiffen. Translated by Geoffrey W. Bromiley. Grand Rapids, Mich.: Eerdmans, 1991.

————. *The Knowledge of God and the Service of God According to the Teaching of the Reformation*. The Gifford Lectures, 1937 and 1938. Translated by J. L. M. Haire and Ian Henderson. London: Hodder & Stoughton, 1938.

————. *Learning Jesus Christ Through the Heidelberg Catechism*. Translated by Shirley C. Guthrie Jr. Grand Rapids, Mich.: Eerdmans, 1964.

Barth, Marcus. *The Broken Wall: A Study of the Epistle to the Ephesians*. Chicago: Judson Press, 1959.

Basil the Great (of Caesarea). *On the Holy Spirit*. Translated by David Anderson. Crestwood, N.Y.: St. Vladimir's Seminary Press, 1997.

Bede, The Venerable. *A History of the English Church and People*. Revised by R. E. Latham. Translated by Leo Sherley-Price. London: Penguin, 1968.

Bellah, Robert N., et al. *Habits of the Heart: Individualism and Commitment in American Life*. Berkeley: University of California Press, 1985.

————. "Individualism and the Crisis of Civic Membership: Ten Years After Habits of the Heart." *The Christian Century* 113, no. 16 (1996).

Bernard of Clairvaux. *Selected Works*. Translated by G. R. Evans. New York: Paulist, 1987.

Bethge, Eberhard. *Dietrich Bonhoeffer: Theologian, Christian, Contemporary*. Translated by Eric Mosbacher et al. Glasgow: William Collins, 1970.

Bettenson, Henry, ed. *Documents of the Christian Church*. London: Oxford University Press, 1959.

Birch, Bruce C., and Larry L. Rasmussen. *Bible and Ethics in the Christian Life*. Minneapolis: Augsburg, 1976.

Bonhoeffer, Dietrich. *Christ the Center*. Translated by John Bowden. Introduction by Edwin H. Robertson. New York: Harper & Row, 1966.

————. *Creation and Fall: A Theological Exposition of Genesis 1-3*. Edited by John W. De Gruchy. Translated by Douglas Stephen Bax. Minneapolis: Fortress, 1997.

————. *Discipleship*. Edited by John D. Godsey and Geffrey B. Kelly. Translated by Reinhard Kraus and Barbara Green. Minneapolis: Augsburg, 2000.

————. *Letters and Papers from Prison*. Edited by Eberhard Bethge. New York: Macmillan, 1953/1971.

————. *Life Together/Prayerbook of the Bible*. Edited by Geffrey B. Kelly. Translated by Daniel W. Bloesch and James H. Burtness. Minneapolis: Fortress, 1996.

————. *Sanctorum Communio: A Theological Study of the Sociology of the Church*. Edited by Clifford J. Green. Translated by Reinhard Krauss and Nancy Lukens. Minneapolis: Fortress, 1998.

Bonino, José Miguez. *Room to Be People*. Philadelphia: Fortress, 1979.

Borg, Marcus. *Meeting Jesus Again for the First Time: The Historical Jesus & the Heart of Contemporary Faith*. San Francisco: HarperSanFrancisco, 1994.

Bretall, Robert, ed. *A Kierkegaard Anthology*. Princeton, N.J.: Princeton University Press, 1946.

Brown, Raymond E. *The Death of the Messiah: From Gethsemane to the Grave*. 2 vols. New York: Doubleday, 1994.

Brown, Robert McAfee. *Unexpected News: Reading the Bible with Third World Eyes*. Philadelphia: Westminster Press, 1984.

Brunner, Emil. *The Christian Doctrine of the Church, Faith, and the Consummation: Dogmatics: Vol. III*. Translated by David Cairns, with T. H. L. Parker. Philadelphia: Westminster Press, 1962.

————. *The Christian Doctrine of Creation and Redemption: Dogmatics: Vol. II*. Translated by Olive Wyon. Philadelphia: Westminster Press, 1952.

————. *The Christian Doctrine of God: Dogmatics: Vol. I*. Translated by Olive Wyon. Philadelphia: Westminster Press, 1950.

————. *I Believe in the Living God*. Translated by John Holden. Philadelphia: Westminster

Press, 1961.

———. *The Mediator: A Study of the Central Doctrine of the Christian Faith*. Translated by Olive Wyon. London: Lutterworth, 1934.

———. *Our Faith*. Translated by John W. Rilling. New York: Scribner's, 1962.

Brunner, Emil, (and Karl Barth). *Natural Theology*. Translated by Peter Fraenkel. London: Centenary Press, 1946. Includes Barth's contrapuntal essay, "No!"

Buechner, Frederick. *Wishful Thinking: A Theological ABC*. New York: Harper & Row, 1973.

Bultmann, Rudolf. *New Testament and Mythology: and Other Basic Writings*. Edited by Schubert M. Ogden. Philadelphia: Fortress, 1984.

Busch, Eberhard. *Karl Barth: His Life from Letters and Autobiographical Texts*. Translated by John Bowden. Philadelphia: Fortress, 1976.

Bushnell, Horace. *The Vicarious Sacrifice*. London: Dickenson, 1880.

Calvin, John. *Calvin: Theological Treatises*. Edited by J. K. S. Reid. Philadelphia: Westminster Press, 1954.

———. *Calvin's New Testament Commentaries: Commentary on II Corinthians*. Edited by David W. Torrance and Thomas F. Torrance. Translated by T. A. Smail. Grand Rapids, Mich.: Eerdmans, 1964.

———. *Calvin's New Testament Commentaries: Galatians, Ephesians, Philippians and Colossians*. Edited by David W. Torrance and Thomas F. Torrance. Translated by T. H. L. Parker. Grand Rapids, Mich.: Eerdmans, 1965.

———. *Calvin's New Testament Commentaries: Hebrews, and I and II Peter*. Edited by David W. Torrance and Thomas F. Torrance. Translated by W. B. Johnston. Grand Rapids, Mich.: Eerdmans, 1963.

———. *Calvin's New Testament Commentaries: The Gospel According to St. John*. Edited by David W. Torrance and Thomas F. Torrance. Translated by T. H. L. Parker. 2 vols. Grand Rapids, Mich.: Eerdmans, 1959.

———. *Institutes of the Christian Religion*. Edited by John T. McNeill. Translated by Ford Lewis Battles. Philadelphia: Westminster Press, 1960.

———. *On God and Political Duty*. Edited by John T. McNeill. New York: Bobbs-Merrill, 1956.

Campbell, John McLeod. *The Nature of the Atonement*. Introduction by James B. Torrance. Grand Rapids, Mich.: Eerdmans, 1996.

Campbell, Will D. *Brother to a Dragonfly*. New York: Seabury, 1977.

Capon, Robert Farrar. *Hunting the Divine Fox*. New York: Seabury, 1974.

Carter, Stephen L. *The Culture of Disbelief: How American Law and Politics Trivialize Religious Devotion*. New York: BasicBooks, 1993.

Chadwick, Henry. *The Early Church*. London: Penguin, 1967.

Chadwick, Owen, ed. *Western Asceticism*. Philadelphia: Westminster Press, 1958.

Chesterton, G. K. *The Everlasting Man*. London: Hodder & Stoughton, 1925.

———. *Orthodoxy*. London: Bodley Head, 1927.

———. *Saint Thomas Aquinas: "The Dumb Ox."* London: Sheed & Ward, 1933.

Christie-Murray, David. *A History of Heresy*. Oxford: Oxford University Press, 1976.

Chrysostom, John. *Homilies on the Gospel of St. John and the Epistle to the Hebrews*. Edited by Philip Schaff. Nicene and Post-Nicene Fathers 14. Grand Rapids, Mich.: Eerdmans, 1983.

Constitution of the Presbyterian Church (U.S.A.): Part I: Book of Confessions. Louisville, Ky.: The Office of the General Assembly, 1996.

Cooke, Bernard. *Ministry to Word and Sacraments: History and Theology*. Philadelphia: Fortress, 1976.

Cross, F. L. and E. A. Livingstone, eds. *The Oxford Dictionary of the Christian Church*. 3rd ed. Oxford: Oxford University Press, 1997.

Crossan, John Dominic. *The Historical Jesus: The Life of a Mediterranean Jewish Peasant*. San Francisco: HarperSanFrancisco, 1991.

———. *Jesus: A Revolutionary Biography*. San Francisco: HarperSanFrancisco, 1994.

Dale, R. W. *The Atonement*. 19th ed. London: Congregational Union, 1898.

Deddo, Gary W., and Catherine A. Deddo, eds. *George MacDonald: A Devotional Guide to His Writings*. Edinburgh: St. Andrew Press, 1996.

Denney, James. *The Christian Doctrine of Reconciliation*. The Cunningham Lectures of 1917. London: Hodder & Stoughton, 1917.

———. *The Death of Christ: Its Place and Interpretation in the New Testament*. 6th ed. London: Hodder & Stoughton, 1907.

Dillistone, F. W. *The Christian Understanding of Atonement*. London: SCM Press, 1968.

———. *The Holy Spirit in the Life of Today*. London: Canterbury, 1946.

Dodd, C. H. *The Apostolic Preaching and Its Development*. London: Hodder & Stoughton, 1936.

Edwards, Jonathan. *Freedom of the Will*. Edited by Paul Ramsey. New Haven, Conn.: Yale University Press, 1957.

———. *Original Sin*. Edited by Clyde A. Holbrook. New Haven, Conn.: Yale University Press, 1970.

Ehrman, Bart D. *Jesus, Apocalyptic Prophet of the New Millennium*. New York: Oxford University Press, 1999.

Eisenman, Robert. *James the Brother of Jesus*. London: Penguin, 1997.

Fairweather, Eugene R., ed. *A Scholastic Miscellany*. Philadelphia: Westminster Press, 1956.

ant, Clyde E., Jr., and William M. Pinson Jr., eds. *Twenty Centuries of Great Preaching*. 13 vols. Waco, Tex.: Word, 1971.

Fatula, Mary Ann. *The Triune God of Christian Faith*. Collegeville, Minn.: Liturgical, 1990.

Ferguson, Ronald. *George MacLeod: Founder of the Iona Community*. London: Collins, 1990.

Fiddes, Paul S. *Past Event and Present Salvation: The Christian Idea of Atonement*. Louisville, Ky.: Westminster John Knox, 1989.

Forell, George Wolfgang. *The Protestant Faith*. Philadelphia: Fortress, 1960.

Forsyth, Peter Taylor. *The Cruciality of the Cross*. London: Independent, 1909.

———. *The Person and Place of Jesus Christ*. London: Independent, 1909.

———. *The Work of Christ*. London: Independent, 1910.

Gardiner, Patrick. *Kierkegaard*. Oxford: Oxford University Press, 1988.

Gilson, Etienne. *The Christian Philosophy of St. Thomas Aquinas*. Translated by L. K. Shook. New York: Random House, 1956.

Green, Michael. *Baptism: Its Purpose, Practice and Power*. Downers Grove, Ill.: InterVarsity Press, 1987.

———. *I Believe in the Holy Spirit*. Grand Rapids, Mich.: Eerdmans, 1975.

Grensted, L. W. *A Short History of the Doctrine of the Atonement*. Manchester, U.K.: Manchester University Press, 1920.

Grenz, Stanley J., David Gruetzki and Cherith Fee Nording, eds. *The Pocket Dictionary of Theological Terms*. Downers Grove, Ill.: InterVarsity Press, 1999.

Gundry, Robert H. *A Survey of the New Testament*. Grand Rapids, Mich.: Zondervan, 1970.

Gunton, Colin E. *The Actuality of the Atonement*. Edinburgh: T & T Clark, 1988.

———. *Enlightenment & Alienation: An Essay Towards a Trinitarian Theology*. Basingstoke, U.K.: Marshall Morgan & Scott, 1985.

———. "The One, the Three and the Many: An Inaugural Lecture in the Chair of Christian Doctrine." London: King's College, May 14, 1985.

———. *Theology Through the Theologians*. Edinburgh: T & T Clark, 1996.

———. *The Triune Creator: A Historical and Systematic Study*. Grand Rapids, Mich.: Eerdmans, 1998.

Guthrie, Shirley, Jr. *Christian Doctrine*. Rev. ed. Louisville, Ky.: Westminster John Knox, 1994.
———. *Christian Doctrine: Teachings of the Christian Church*. Richmond, Va.: Covenant Life Curriculum, 1968.
———. *Diversity in Faith—Unity in Christ: Orthodoxy, Liberalism, Pietism and Beyond*. Philadelphia: Westminster Press, 1986.
Gutiérrez, Gustavo. *A Theology of Liberation: History, Politics and Salvation*. Translated by Sister Caridad Inda and John Eagleson. Maryknoll, N.Y.: Orbis, 1973.
Halverson, Marvin and Arthur A. Cohen, eds. *A Handbook of Christian Theology*. New York: Collins, 1979.
Hardy, Robert R., ed. *Christology of the Later Fathers*. Philadelphia: Westminster Press, 1954.
Harnack, Adolf von. *What is Christianity?* Translated by Thomas Bailey Saunders. New York: Harper & Row, Torchbook edition, 1957.
Hart, Trevor. "Humankind in Christ and Christ in Humankind: Salvation as Participation in Our Substitute in the Theology of John Calvin." *Scottish Journal of Theology* 42, no. 1 (1989).
Hauerwas, Stanley. *In Good Company: The Church as Polis*. Notre Dame, Ind.: University of Notre Dame Press, 1995.
Herbert, George. *The Country Parson: The Temple*. Edited by John N. Wall Jr. New York: Paulist, 1981.
Heron, Alasdair. *A Century of Protestant Theology*. Cambridge: Lutterworth, 1980.
Heschel, Abraham. *Between God and Man: An Interpretation of Judaism*. Edited by Fritz A. Rothschild. New York: Free Press, 1959.
Hodgson, Peter C. and Robert H. King, eds. *Christian Theology: An Introduction to Its Traditions and Tasks*. 2nd ed. Philadelphia: Fortress, 1985.
Hopkins, Gerard Manley. *Poems and Prose*. Edited by G. H. Gardner. London: Penguin, 1953.
Howe, Reuel L. *The Miracle of Dialogue*. New York: Seabury, 1963.
Hultgren, Arland J. and Steven A. Haggmark, eds. *The Earliest Christian Heretics: Readings from Their Opponents*. Minneapolis: Fortress, 1996.
Irenaeus. *Against Heresies*. Edited by Alexander Roberts and James Donaldson. The Ante-Nicene Fathers 1. Grand Rapids, Mich.: Eerdmans, 1981.
James, William. *The Varieties of Religious Experience: A Study in Human Nature*. The Gifford Lectures, 1901-1902. New York: The Modern Library Edition, 1994.
Jinkins, Michael. "The 'Being of Beings': Jonathan Edwards' Understanding of God as Reflected in His Final Treatises." *Scottish Journal of Theology* 46, no. 2 (1993).
———. *The Church Faces Death: Ecclesiology in a Post-Modern Context*. New York: Oxford University Press, 1999.
———. *A Comparative Study in the Theology of Atonement in Jonathan Edwards and John McLeod Campbell: Atonement and the Character of God*. San Francisco: Mellen Research University Press, 1993.
———. "The Devil's Theology: Theological Reflection on James Hogg's *The Private Memoirs and Confessions of a Justified Sinner* (1824)." *EQ: The Evangelical Quarterly* 62, no. 2 (1990).
———. "The God Who Worships: When the God We Worship Becomes the Worshiping God." *Reformed Liturgy & Music* 32, no. 2 (1998).
———. *In the House of the Lord: Inhabiting the Psalms of Lament*. Collegeville, Minn.: Liturgical, 1998.
———. "What's the Use of Divinity: An Apologia for the Study of Theology in the University." *The Times Higher Education Supplement*. June 2, 1989.
———, ed. *Love Is of the Essence: An Introduction to the Theology of John McLeod Campbell*. Edinburgh: St. Andrew Press, 1993.
Johnson, Elizabeth A. *She Who Is: The Mystery of God in Feminist Theological Discourse*. New York: Crossroad, 1994.

Johnson, Luke Timothy. *The Real Jesus: The Misguided Quest for the Historical Jesus and the Truth of the Traditional Gospels*. San Francisco: HarperSanFrancisco, 1996.

Jordan, Clarence. *The Substance of Faith*. Edited by Dallas Lee. New York: Association Press, 1972.

Julian of Norwich. *Revelations of Divine Love*. Translated by Clifton Wolters. London: Penguin, 1966.

Jüngel, Eberhard. *God as the Mystery of the World: On the Foundation of the Theology of the Crucified One in the Dispute Between Theism and Atheism*. Translated by Darrell L. Guder. Grand Rapids, Mich.: Eerdmans, 1983.

————. *Karl Barth: A Theological Legacy*. Translated by Garrett E. Paul. Philadelphia: Westminster Press, 1986.

Kelly, Anthony. *The Trinity of Love: A Theology of the Christian God*. Wilmington, Del.: Michael Glazier, 1989.

Kelly, J. N. D. *Early Christian Doctrines*. 5th ed. London: A & C. Black, 1977.

Kempis, Thomas à. *The Imitation of Christ*. Translated by Leo Sherley-Price. London: Penguin, 1952.

Kierkegaard, Søren. *Concluding Unscientific Postscript*. Translated by David Swenson. Introduction and notes by Walter Lowrie. Princeton, N.J.: Princeton University Press, 1941.

————. *Philosophical Fragments/Johannes Climacus*. Edited and translated by Howard V. Hong and Edna H. Hong. Princeton, N.J.: Princeton University Press, 1987.

————. *Training in Christianity*. Translated by Walter Lowrie. Princeton, N.J.: Princeton University Press, 1941.

Küng, Hans. *On Being a Christian*. Translated by Edward Quinn. New York: Doubleday, 1976.

LaCugna, Catherine Mowry. *God For Us: The Trinity & Christian Life*. San Francisco: HarperSanFrancisco, 1991.

Ladd, George Eldon. *I Believe in the Resurrection of Jesus Christ*. Grand Rapids, Mich.: Eerdmans, 1975.

Lee, Sang Hyun and Allen C. Guelzo. *Edwards in Our Time: Jonathan Edwards and the Shaping of American Religion*. Grand Rapids, Mich.: Eerdmans, 1999.

LeFevre, Perry D., ed. *The Prayers of Kierkegaard*. Chicago: University of Chicago Press, 1963.

Leith, John H. *The Church: A Believing Fellowship*. Atlanta: John Knox Press, 1981.

————. *The Reformed Imperative: What the Church Has to Say that No One Else Can Say*. Philadelphia: Westminster Press, 1988.

————, ed. *Creeds of the Churches: A Reader in Christian Doctrine from the Bible to the Present*. 3rd ed. Atlanta: John Knox Press, 1982.

————, ed. *John Calvin: The Christian Life*. New York: Harper & Row, 1984.

Lewis, C. S. *Fern-seed and Elephants*. London: Collins, 1975.

————. *A Grief Observed*. New York: Seabury, 1961.

————. *Letters of C. S. Lewis*. Edited by W. H. Lewis. New York: Harcourt Brace Jovanovich, 1966.

————. *The Lion, the Witch, and the Wardrobe*. London: Macmillan, 1950.

————. *Mere Christianity*. New York: Macmillan, 1952.

Lightfoot, J. B., ed. *The Apostolic Fathers: Clement, Ignatius and Polycarp*. Rev. Peabody: Hendrickson, 1989.

Lindberg, Carter. *The European Reformation*. Oxford: Basil Blackwell, 1996.

Livingston, James C. *Modern Christian Thought: From the Enlightenment to Vatican II*. New York: Macmillan, 1971.

Locke, John. *On Politics and Education*. New York: Walter J. Black, 1947.

Luther, Martin. *Commentary on Galatians*. Grand Rapids, Mich.: Baker, reprint, 1970.

————. *Small Catechism*. St. Louis: Concordia, 1943.

————. *Table Talk*. Edited by Thomas S. Kepler. Grand Rapids, Mich.: Baker, 1952.

MacDonald, George. *Creation in Christ*. Edited by Rolland Hein. Wheaton, Ill.: Harold Shaw, 1976.

Mackintosh, H. R. *The Christian Experience of Forgiveness*. London: Nisbet, 1927.

MacLeod, George F. *Only One Way Left*. Glasgow: The Iona Community, 1956.

Marney, Carlyle. *Priests to Each Other*. Valley Forge, Penn.: Judson Press, 1974.

————. *The Recovery of the Person: A Christian Humanism*. New York: Abingdon, 1963.

Marty, Martin E. and Dean G. Peerman, eds. *A Handbook of Christian Theologians*. New York: Collins, World, 1965.

McCord, James I. and T. H. L. Parker, eds. *Service in Christ. Essays Presented to Karl Barth on his 80th Birthday*. Grand Rapids, Mich.: Eerdmans, 1966.

McGrath, Alister E. *Christian Theology: An Introduction*. Oxford: Blackwell, 1994.

————. *The Intellectual Origins of the European Reformation*. Oxford: Basil Blackwell, 1987.

McIntyre, John. *The Shape of Soteriology*. Edinburgh: T & T Clark, 1992.

McKim, Donald K., ed. *The Encyclopedia of the Reformed Faith*. Louisville, Ky.: Westminster John Knox, 1992.

————. *Theological Turning Points: Major Issues in Christian Thought*. Atlanta: John Knox Press, 1988.

Meredith, Anthony. *The Cappadocians*. Crestwood, N.Y.: St. Vladimir's Seminary Press, 1995.

Migliore, Daniel L. *Faith Seeking Understanding: An Introduction to Christian Theology*. Grand Rapids, Mich.: Eerdmans, 1991.

Miller, Allen O. et al., eds., *The Heidelberg Catechism with Commentary*. New York: Pilgrim, 1979.

Mills, Mary E. *Images of God in the Old Testament*. Collegeville, Minn.: Michael Glazier/Liturgical, 1998.

Moberly, R. C. *Atonement and Personality*. London: John Murray, 1911.

Moltmann, Jürgen. *The Crucified God*. Translated by R. A. Wilson and John Bowden. New York: Harper & Row, 1974.

————. *God in Creation: The Gifford Lectures (1984-1985): An Ecological Doctrine of Creation*. London: SCM Press, 1985.

————. *A Passion for Life: A Messianic Lifestyle*. Philadelphia: Fortress, 1977.

————. *The Trinity and the Kingdom of God*. Translated by Margaret Kohl. London: SCM Press, 1981.

Nelson, C. Ellis. "Childish Religion." Audio recording of the Robert F. Jones Lectures. Austin, Tex.: Austin Presbyterian Theological Seminary, January 2000.

————. "Toward Accountable Selfhood." *Modern Masters of Religious Education*. Edited by Marlene Mayr. Birmingham, Ala.: Religious Education Press, 1983.

Newbigin, Lesslie. *Foolishness to the Greeks: The Gospel and Western Culture*. London: SPCK, 1986.

————. *The Gospel in a Pluralist Society*. Grand Rapids, Mich.: Eerdmans, 1989.

————. *Sin and Salvation*. London: SCM Press, 1956.

Niebuhr, Reinhold. *Does Civilization Need Religion? A Study in the Social Resources and Limitations of Religion in Modern Life*. New York: Macmillan, 1928.

————. *The Nature and Destiny of Man: A Christian Interpretation*. The Gifford Lectures. 2 vols. New York: Charles Scribner's Sons, 1941.

Nouwen, Henri J. M. *Behold the Beauty of the Lord: Praying With Icons*. Notre Dame, Ind.: Ave Maria Press, 1987.

Noyes, Morgan Phelps, ed. *Prayers for Services: A Manual for Leaders of Worship*. New York: Charles Scribner's Sons, 1934.

O'Connor, Flannery. *Wise Blood*. New York: Noonday, 1977.

Pagels, Elaine. *The Gnostic Gospels*. New York: Random House, 1979.

Parker, T. H. L. *John Calvin*. Tring: Lion, 1975.

Pascal, Blaise. *Pensées*. Translated by A. J. Krailsheimer. London: Penguin, 1966.

Perkins, William. *The Works of William Perkins*. Edited by Ian Breward. Appleford, U.K.: Sutton Courtenay, 1970.

Peterson, Eugene H. *Reversed Thunder: The Revelation of John and the Praying Imagination*. San Francisco: Harper & Row, 1988.

Polkinghorne, John. *Science and Theology: An Introduction*. London: SPCK, 1998.

Prestige, G. L. *Fathers and Heretics: Six Studies in Dogmatic Faith*. The Bampton Lectures for 1940. London: SPCK, 1940.

Rahner, Karl. *Meditations on the Sacraments*. New York: Seabury, 1977.

———. *Theological Investigations: Volume IV*. London: Darton, Longman & Todd, 1966, 1974.

———. *A Rahner Reader*. Edited by Gerald A. McCool. New York: Crossroad, 1987.

Rashdall, Hastings. *The Idea of Atonement in Christian Theology*. London: Macmillan, 1919.

Rhoads, David. *The Challenge of Diversity: The Witness of Paul and the Gospel*. Minneapolis: Fortress, 1996.

Richardson, Alan. *Creeds in the Making: A Short Introduction to the History of Christian Doctrine*. London: SCM Press, 1935.

———. *A Theological Word Book of the Bible*. New York: Macmillan, 1950.

Richardson, Alan and John Bowden, eds. *The Westminster Dictionary of Christian Theology*. Philadelphia: Westminster Press, 1983.

Ritschl, Albrecht. *The Christian Doctrine of Justification and Reconciliation*. Edited by H. R. Mackintosh and A. B. Macaulay. 3 vols. Edinburgh: T & T Clark, 1900.

Ritschl, Dietrich. *Concerning Christ: Thinking of Our Past, Present and Future with Him*. Richmond, Tex.: Well Spring Center, 1980.

Rivkin, Ellis. *The Hidden Revolution: The Pharisee's Search for the Kingdom Within*. Nashville: Abingdon, 1978.

———. *What Crucified Jesus?* Nashville: Abingdon, 1984.

Rogers, Jack. *Presbyterian Creeds: A Guide to the Book of Confessions*. Philadelphia: Westminster Press, 1985.

Rolston, Holmes, III. *John Calvin Versus the Westminster Confession*. Richmond: John Knox Press, 1972.

Rupp, E. G. and Benjamin Drewery, eds. *Martin Luther: Documents of Modern History*. London: Edward Arnold, 1978.

Saldarini, Anthony J. *Matthew's Christian-Jewish Community*. Chicago: University of Chicago Press, 1994.

Sanders, E. P. *The Historical Figure of Jesus*. London: Penguin, 1993.

Schaff, Philip, ed. *The Creeds of Christendom, with a History and Critical Notes*. 3 vols. Grand Rapids, Mich.: Baker, 1983.

Schleiermacher, Friedrich. *The Christian Faith*. Translated by J. S. Stewart. Edited by H. R. Mackintosh. Edinburgh: T & T Clark, 1928.

———. *On Religion: Speeches to its Cultured Despisers*. Translated by John Oman. New York: Harper & Row, 1958.

Schwartz, Hans. *Christology*. Grand Rapids, Mich.: Eerdmans, 1998.

Schweitzer, Albert. *The Quest of the Historical Jesus: A Critical Study of Its Progress from Reimarus to Wrede*. Translated by W. Montgomery. London: Adam & Charles Black, 1910.

Sherwin, Byron. *Abraham Joshua Heschel*. Atlanta: John Knox Press, 1979.

Sittler, Joseph. *Gravity and Grace: Reflections and Provocations*. Edited by Linda-Marie Delloff. Minneapolis: Augsburg, 1986.

Smail, Thomas. *The Forgotten Father*. London: Hodder & Stoughton, 1980.

Tillich, Paul. *Dynamics of Faith*. New York: Harper, 1956.

———. *The Eternal Now*. New York: Charles Scribner's Sons, 1963.

———. *Systematic Theology. Vol. II. Existence and the Christ.* The Gifford Lectures. Chicago: University of Chicago Press, 1957.

Torrance, Alan J. *Persons In Communion: Trinitarian Description and Human Participation.* Edinburgh: T & T Clark, 1996.

Torrance, James B. "The Contribution of McLeod Campbell to Scottish Theology." *Scottish Journal of Theology* 26, no. 3 (1973).

———. "Covenant or Contract: A Study of the Theological Background of Worship in Seventeenth-Century Scotland." *Scottish Journal of Theology* 23, no. 1 (1970).

———. "The Ministry of Reconciliation Today: The Realism of Grace." Edited by Christian D. Kettler and Todd H. Speidel. *Incarnational Ministry: The Presence of Christ in Church, Society, and Family.* Colorado Springs: Helmers & Howard, 1990.

———. "The Place of Jesus Christ in Worship." Edited by Ray S. Anderson. *Theological Foundations for Ministry.* Edinburgh: T & T Clark, 1979.

———. *Worship, Community and the Triune God of Grace: The Didsbury Lectures.* Carlyle, U.K.: Paternoster, 1996.

Torrance, James B. and Roland C. Walls. *John Duns Scotus.* Edinburgh: Handsel, 1992.

Torrance, Thomas F. *The Christian Doctrine of God, One Being Three Persons.* Edinburgh: T & T Clark, 1996.

———. *Karl Barth: Biblical and Evangelical Theologian.* Edinburgh: T & T Clark, 1990.

———. *The Mediation of Christ.* Colorado Springs, Colo.: Helmers & Howard, new edition, 1992.

———. *The School of Faith.* London: James Clarke, 1959.

———. *Theological Dialogue Between Orthodox and Reformed Church: Volume 2.* Edinburgh: Scottish Academic Press, 1993.

———. *Theological Science.* Oxford: Oxford University Press, 1969.

———. *Theology in Reconciliation.* London: Geoffrey Chapman, 1975.

———. *Transformation and Convergence in the Frame of Knowledge.* Grand Rapids, Mich.: Eerdmans, 1984.

———. *The Trinitarian Faith.* Edinburgh: T & T Clark, 1988.

———. *Trinitarian Perspectives: Toward Doctrinal Agreement.* Edinburgh: T & T Clark, 1994.

———, ed. *Theological Dialogue Between Orthodox and Reformed Churches.* Edinburgh: Scottish Academic Press, 1985.

Trueblood, Elton. *The Company of the Committed.* New York: Harper, 1961.

Vanhoozer, Kevin J., ed. *The Trinity in a Pluralistic Age: Theological Essays on Culture and Religion.* Grand Rapids, Mich.: Eerdmans, 1997.

Wainwright, Geoffrey. *Doxology: The Praise of God in Worship, Doctrine, and Life: A Systematic Theology.* New York: Oxford University Press, 1980.

Webster, John. "Theological Theology: An Inaugural Lectured delivered before the University of Oxford on 27 October 1997." Oxford: Clarendon, 1998.

Weinandy, Thomas G. *The Father's Spirit of Sonship: Reconceiving the Trinity.* Edinburgh: T & T Clark, 1995.

Westermann, Claus. *Creation.* Translated by John J. Scullion. Philadelphia: Fortress, 1974.

———. *What Does the Old Testament Say About God?* Edited by Friedemann W. Golka. Atlanta: John Knox Press, 1979.

Wills, Gary. *Saint Augustine.* New York: Penguin, 1999.

Wilmore, Gayraud S. *Last Things First.* Philadelphia: Westminster Press, 1982.

Winslow, Ola Elizabeth. *Jonathan Edwards: 1703-1758.* New York: Collier, 1961.

Witherington, Ben. *The Jesus Quest: The Third Search for the Jew of Nazareth.* Downers Grove, Ill.: InterVarsity Press, 1995.

Wright, N. T. *Jesus and the Victory of God.* Minneapolis: Fortress, 1996.

———. *The Original Jesus: The Life and Vision of a Revolutionary.* Grand Rapids, Mich.: Eerdmans, 1996.

Zenger, Erich. *A God of Vengeance? Understanding the Psalms of Divine Wrath.* Translated by
    Linda M. Maloney. Louisville, Ky.: Westminster John Knox, 1996.
Zizioulas, John D. *Being as Communion: Studies in Personhood and Church.* Crestwood,
    N.Y.: St. Vladimir's Seminary Press, 1985.

Index of Names

Abelard, Peter, 143-45
Akiba ben Joseph, 175
Allison, Dale, 101
Althaus, Paul, 128-29
Anselm of Canterbury, 36,
48, 137, 142-43, 146, 153
Antiochenes, the, 114-15,
122, 123
Apollinarius, 114, 122, 123
Aquinas, Thomas, 54-55,
59, 67, 75, 81-82, 124,
137, 142-43, 250
Aristotle, 156
Arius, 33, 36, 112-14, 122
Athanasius of Alexandria,
33-36, 75, 91, 112-14, 122,
130, 136, 138-40, 146,
149, 178-79, 198
Augustine of Canterbury,
94
Augustine of Hippo, 34, 48,
67, 75, 91-92, 94, 118,
128, 135-36, 142, 170-71,
191-92, 218-19, 241
Aulén, Gustaf, 138, 145,
148, 254
Baillie, Donald E., 138
Baillie, John, 256-57
Bainton, Roland H., 126-28
Balthasar, Hans Urs von,
45, 78-79, 83, 133-34, 220,
233, 237, 257-58
Bamford, Christopher, 257
Barth, Karl, 17, 30, 36, 43-
44, 50, 55, 61, 63, 75, 82,
86, 90, 94, 105-7, 121,
129-30, 135, 137, 138,
145, 165-66, 170-72, 183,
190-91, 197, 107, 213,
222-23, 228, 232-33, 246,
251-52, 258-60

Barth, Marcus, 167-68
Basil the Great of Caesarea,
53, 88, 114, 124-25, 129,
146, 197-98
Bede the Venerable, 42, 94
Bellah, Robert N., et al., 55,
221
Benedict of Nursia, 29, 237
Berlin, Isaiah, 76
Bernard of Clairvaux, 92,
143, 171, 192
Bethge, Eberhard, 58
Birch, Bruce C., 72
Bland, Bobby, 93
Boethius, 157-58
Bonaparte, Napoleon, 182
Bonhoeffer, Dietrich, 17,
52-54, 58-59, 104, 122,
160, 166, 172, 227, 233,
242-44
Bonino, José Miguez, 231
Borg, Marcus J., 102
Bray, Gerald, 34,
Brown, Raymond E., 104
Brown, Robert McAfee, 59,
64-65, 121
Brunner, Emil, 47, 84, 138,
145, 170, 191-92, 250-51
Buechner, Frederick, 192,
236
Bullinger, Heinrich, 210-12
Bultmann, Rudolf, 103-6
Busch, Eberhard, 43, 170,
258
Bushnell, Horace, 138
Cairns, David, 170
Calvin, John, 17, 21, 31, 47-
48, 55-56, 59, 75, 82, 86-
87, 129-33, 137, 144-47,
149, 170, 184, 204-6, 214,
217, 220, 229, 240, 259
Campbell, J. Y., 75
Campbell, John McLeod,
56, 59, 69-72, 130, 138,
143, 146, 149-50, 244
Campbell, Will D., 233
Capon, Robert Farrar, 51-52

Cappadocian Fathers, 53,
82, 91, 198-99
Carter, Stephen L., 55
Chadwick, Henry, 34, 110,
116
Chesterton, G. K., 45, 59,
72, 76, 89-90, 159-60, 172-
73, 233
Christie-Murray, David, 110
Chrysostom, John, 86
Churchill, Winston, 182
Cooke, Bernard, 75
Cotton, James, 93
Cowper, William, 53
Cross, F. L., 81, 170
Crossan, John Dominic, 102
Cyril of Alexandria, 116-17
Dale, R. W., 138
Darwin, Charles, 77-78
Davis, Miles, 26
Deddo, Cathy, 255
Deddo, Gary, 22-24, 255
Denney, James, 138
Descartes, René, 158
Dillistone, F. W., 137, 143,
148, 190-91
Diodore of Tarsus, 114
Dodd, C. H., 103
Drewery, Benjamin, 128
Duns, Scotus, 48
Edwards, Jonathan, 70, 138,
143, 178-79, 243
Ehrman, Bart D., 101
Eisenman, Robert, 104, 110
Emerson, Ralph Waldo, 76
Eutyches, 115, 122, 123
Fatula, Mary Ann, 135
Fiddes, Paul S., 137, 141
Forell, George W., 177
Forsyth, Peter Taylor, 56,
59, 133, 138
Fuller, R. H., 216
Gardiner, Patrick, 161
Green, Michael, 162, 209
Gregory of Nazianzus, 53,
113-14, 199
Gregory of Nyssa, 53, 113,

Index of Subjects

anthropology (doctrine of
  humanity), 154-82
dualistic conception of,
  114
antinomianism, 238-39
Antiochene school of Christology, 114-15, 122, 123
apologetics, 110-11
Apostles' Creed, 16, 60-63,
  77-78, 90, 98, 107, 125,
  135, 180, 203, 235, 247
Arianism, 112-14, 198
Assyrian Christians (Nesto-
  rians), 115
atonement, 113-15, 118,
  124-53
  prospective aspect of (J.
    M. Campbell), 150-52
  retrospective aspect of (J.
    M. Campbell), 149-52
  theories (or models) of,
    139-48
authority, 66-74
baptism, 60, 103, 162, 164,
  168, 196, 212, 239, 241-
  42
Bible/Scripture
  hearing, through the
    power of the Spirit, 205
  read christologically, 22-
    24, 87
  Word of God, 64-74, 228
Brief Statement of Faith,
  Presbyterian Church
  (U.S.A.), 95-96, 232
Calvin's catechism, 90, 223
capitalism (economic
  reduction of humanity),
  157-58
Chalcedonian definition/

symbol of Chalcedon,
  116-17, 123, 193
Christian, definition of, 96-
  98, 107
Christology (doctrine of
  Christ), 22-24, 106-23
  from above and below,
    106-7
  Christ as interpretive lens,
    23-24, 53-54, 87
  divine-human nature of
    Christ, 23-24
  name of, as theological
    starting point, 44-45
Christus Victor model of
  atonement, 148
church
  ancient catholic, 124-25
  body of Christ, 172, 217-
    20, 223-24, 229-30, 239,
    259-60
  called out, 216-17
  catholic (universal), 211-
    13, 215-16
  "Church of Jesus Christ
    without Christ cruci-
    fied" (O'Connor), 243
  community/communities
    of faith, 15-20, 67-74, 98,
    104, 106-7, 177, 204-6,
    212-32, 238-42, 245-47
  congregations, 225-30
  diakonia (service), 227-
    28, 229-30
  doctrine of (ecclesiol-
    ogy), 210-34
  ecclesia, 216
  "Extra ecclesiam nulla
    salus," 214-15
  koinonia (fellowship),
    226-27, 229-30
  kuriakon, 217
  leiturgia (worship), 228-
    30, 259-60
  Locke's definition of, 223
  membership in, 217-20,
    224-25

mission of, 212, 216-17,
  230-32
one and holy, 213
Pentecost, 215
pluralism in, 223-25
priesthood of all believ-
  ers, 226-27
tradition and community,
  65-74
unity of, 223-25
voluntary religious soci-
  ety, 222-25, 243
as womb, 225-27
Confession of 1967, Presbyterian Church (U.S.A.),
  95
conversion, 105-6
and rebirth, 144
Council of Chalcedon, 115-
  16, 122
Council of Constantinople,
  114-15
creation, 77-93
creeds and confessions,
  purpose of, 52
crisis, theology of, 105-6
cross (and crucifixion) of
  Jesus Christ, 56-57, 85-
  86, 101, 103-5, 127-29,
  132, 134, 138, 140-48,
  153, 188, 212, 227, 228
in relation to resurrec-
  tion, 255-56
"dark night of the soul"
  (John of the Cross), 22
death, 256-60
deism, 90, 120
discipleship, 15, 242-47
Docetic Gnosticism, 108-
  10, 122
Ebionitism, 108-10, 122
eschatology, 100-102, 248-
  60
definition of, 249
evangelical faith, 106, 122
evangelism, 238, 245-47
evil, 84-86, 140-42